Introduction

Navidad de los Suenos by Kristin Billerbeck sweeps you into California's historical land of ranchos and sword fights as Isabella Arguello is being forced to marry a despicable man. Her only source of hope is prayer and the counsel of an old circuit-riding preacher. But when Pastor Juan Carlos Vega comes in the place of the old man, it is love at first sight. Isabella would follow the handsome preacher anywhere, but Juan Carlos reminds her of the commandment to honor one's father and he leaves. What is a sad girl to do?

Dreams by Peggy Darty introduces you to Caroline Cushman, the first resident of Pine Ridge, Alabama, to attend college. Her simple country manners stand out among the students of Davis University, attracting the attention of Ryan Blankenship and the scorn of Amelia Gardner. Caroline's only dream is to return to Pine Ridge with an education for teaching, but Ryan has dreams that will stir the Christmas punch.

Eyes of the Heart by Rosey Dow welcomes you to experience a 1925 New England Christmas. Jim Clarke is visiting the Simmons family over the Christmas holiday with his girlfriend Honey. When a sprained ankle keeps him from joining a skating party, he discovers the charm of Honey's blind sister Julie. But will Honey's thoughtlessness and jealousy destroy an opportunity for true love?

Paper Roses by JoAnn A. Grote puts you in the midst of financial collapse during the Panic of 1893 along with the Larson family. They must turn their large home into a boardinghouse, and Thomas McNally is the first boarder to inquire for a room. He teaches a Sunday school class for newsboys, and Vernetta Larson is drawn into helping him with the newsboys and flower girls. It makes her feel useful, but it also puts her recently broken heart in danger of being captured again.

FIRESIDE CHRISTMAS

Four new inspirational
love stories
from days gone by

Kristin Billerbeck

Peggy Darty

Rosey Dow

JoAnn A. Grote

BARBOUR
PUBLISHING, INC.
Uhrichsville, Ohio

ISBN 1-57748-595-5

Published by Barbour Publishing, Inc., P.O. Box 719, Uhrichsville, Ohio 44683 http://www.barbourbooks.com

Member of the
Evangelical Christian
Publishers Association

Printed in the United States of America.

FIRESIDE CHRISTMAS

Navidad de los Sueños

Kristin Billerbeck

one

Rancho de Arguello,
The California Territory, 1844

Isabella giggled as she hung the last of the drying peppers in the scorching summer heat. She danced a fandango to celebrate the finishing gesture. Her older sister shook her head at the precocious young beauty. Isabella had been named for her striking looks. She was blessed with lustrous, silken black hair and full, warm brown eyes that complemented her sun-drenched skin. Her loveliness was renowned throughout the territory, but her grown-up appearance hid a tender and naive young heart.

As Isabella's parents watched their vivacious daughter from their sprawling, adobe home, they discussed her future in serious tones.

"You see, my dear? She is far too young for marriage. She still giggles like a child," Señora Arguello argued.

"She is seventeen. The rancheros have been lining up for marriage since she was ten years old. A beauty like Isabella can only benefit from marriage; remaining here will simply lead to trouble." Señor Jose Arguello shook his head. "She will mature in her wifely role. It is time, Ramona. It is probably past time. The priest will come at Christmas and she will be married. Why wait another year? We can certainly use the cattle her marriage will bring."

"Yes, Señor." Ramona Arguello relented uneasily. "But whom shall she marry? She has had so many offers, yet I've never seen a man who caused her heart to stir." Señora dropped her head sadly, her faded black hair falling forward around her worn complexion.

"Don't talk to me of such fancy of heart stirrings. I am the patriarch of the rancho, and as such, I will choose for my daughter the man whom I see fit. Just as your father did," Señor Arguello added firmly.

Señora Arguello remained undeterred. "But, I loved you, Jose," she pleaded with her husband. "Isabella is not in love."

"She will have better than love. I am offering her to Antonio Fremont for a thousand cattle," Señor Arguello revealed.

His wife inhaled deeply, her hand slapping her chest in surprise. "A thousand cattle! Oh, Jose, no. Not even for a thousand cattle. He is nearly thirty years older and he's already buried two wives! Surely you can find her someone more suitable."

"Are you questioning my judgment?" Señor Arguello charged, his eyes growing thin.

"Of course not, Señor. I–I just. . ." Señora Arguello bowed to the determination of her husband. "I will make arrangements for her dress and the celebration." She walked despondently from the room and the conversation.

Señor Arguello turned to the nearby window. "Isabella!" he snapped impatiently.

Isabella stopped her lighthearted play and grew solemn. "Yes, Papa?" But it wasn't long before her high spirits reappeared. "Papa, look at the peppers. Are they not beautiful this year? I can't remember when they had more color," she pressed excitely.

Her father's demeanor appeared to soften momentarily before his scowl returned. "Your mama needs to see you immediately."

Isabella lifted her full, ruffled skirt and dashed into the dim house to her parent's private room. The occasions when Isabella entered the quarters were rare, so she knew her mother had something important to tell her. Isabella found her mother sitting with her head bowed. She caught her mother surreptitiously wiping her eyes before looking up at Isabella.

"Mama, are you feeling okay? Papa says you must see me. Did you see the peppers are all hung?" the young woman chattered persistently. The golden brown of Isabella's bare shoulders glistened under the midday candlelight used against the darkness within the white-washed adobe walls. Señora Arguello straightened her back and ceased weeping.

"Yes, my darling. Your father and I have decided it is time for a rancho and a family of your own. Your father has made arrangements with Antonio Fremont. You are to be married this Navidad, when the priest comes to visit and celebrate the birth of our Savior. Your papa will make sure Pastor Sola is here as well."

Isabella fell to her knees, nearly fainting at the

news. She felt dizzy and sickened, yet she knew to argue her case was pointless. Arrangements had been made, and to question her father's authority, especially after he had given his word to Señor Fremont, could only lead to disaster.

She remembered the bedraggled, old character who came to the annual cattle counts. She pictured with clarity his oversized belly and the hungry eyes that scrutinized her as if to devour her very soul. She shuddered at the image of marriage to such a man. She was very nearly ill by simply being in the same room with him and his foul smell of drink. Now she would be forced to share a home with the surly ranchero.

"Isabella?" her mother questioned. "Did you hear me?"

"Yes, Mama," was all Isabella could manage to say.

"Señor Fremont is a fine man. He is the wealthiest Califorñio in the territory. You will have dresses of fine Spanish lace for everyday wear. You can plan fiestas and rodeos that last for weeks on end. There are no limits with such a man. You will be the envy of every señorita on the rancho," Señora Arguello said enthusiastically, but her downcast eyes gave her true feelings away.

Isabella knew her mother didn't approve of Antonio Fremont. It was obvious by the tears she'd shed and the desperate attempts to convince Isabella that her new life wouldn't be so desolate.

Isabella closed her eyes in agony. She felt physically weak that she would be leaving the only home she'd ever known to live with a ranchero older than her father. Such was the way of life on the ranchos. Women lived in complete submission first to their father's authority and then to their husband's. She let out a deep sigh. "Yes, Mama, Spanish lace."

"You will own more cattle than any woman in the territory," her mother added brightly.

"The Bible says better a dry morsel, and quietness therewith, than an house full of sacrifices with strife," Isabella quoted.

"It is your duty to make sure your home is without strife, Isabella," her mother reprimanded.

"Of course, Mama. I'm sorry. May I be excused, please?"

Señora Arguello nodded, and Isabella curtsied in deference, then ran to the patio and fell to her knees in desperate prayer. *Oh Lord, why of all men must I marry him? Lord, You have ordained each and every day of my life. Please find a different path for me. Please. I beg You, Lord. Anyone but him, anyone!*

"Isabella?" Victoria, her older sister, blocked the last of the sun from Isabella's view. Tears welled up in Victoria's eyes. "I'm so sorry." Her words let loose a wave of tears and the sisters instinctively embraced.

"Oh Victoria, how can they do this to me? Does Papa care nothing for me?" Isabella cried.

"He cares greatly for you, Isabella," Victoria responded softly. "He has betrothed you to the richest man in all of California. As far as Papa's concerned, that is the best. The other rancheros have been trying to betroth their daughters to him for some time now. Papa would only allow you to marry a true Califorñio. Born and bred on God's land."

"Why did you get to choose your husband, Victoria?" Isabella protested, tears streaming freely.

"Because I am not beautiful, Isabella," Victoria answered gently and plainly, wiping her sister's tears away.

Isabella's eyes widened. "Of course you are. Who told you such nonsense?"

"My sweet sister." Victoria caressed her again before pulling away and looking directly into Isabella's deep, brown eyes. "You see only what you want in those you love. I appreciate that you find me beautiful, and I know in your virtuous way you believe it with all your heart. But the commotion you cause at the annual rodeo shows the difference between you and me. Father has been planning your marriage for a long time, Isabella. I'm sure he knows what he's doing."

Isabella shook her head violently and stood up, her dress whirling wildly. "No, not you." She pointed a long, slender finger at her only sibling. "I can take the lying from Mama because she must support Papa, but I know you can't possibly approve of my marrying that—that squalid, old man!"

Victoria remained silent at the accusation, its truth apparent.

two

Fall descended upon the tranquil valley of Rancho de Arguello. With the new season, the golden hills transformed to a lush green, providing a natural background for the great oaks that dotted the landscape. The cattle roamed freely, enjoying the fresh grass and freedom from the arid heat of summer.

Isabella's exuberant personality had all but disappeared along with the summer's hot season, and fall did not bring its return. She went about her daily activities with a melancholy she had never before exhibited. She walked instead of danced, spoke instead of sang, and wept instead of laughed.

"She has not been the same since I told her," Señora Arguello observed to her husband, lifting the curtain to watch her daughter outside.

"The old Isabella will return when she realizes what I have done for her. She is simply maturing," Señor Arguello answered.

"She is wilting," Isabella's mother replied. "She's not devious enough to act in such a manner on purpose. Isabella would never hurt one of us intentionally."

"Is that an accusation, Señora Arguello? Are you

insinuating that I have hurt my daughter?" The señor's voice was harsh, but his sad eyes told of his own questioning heart.

"Of course not, Señor." Señora Arguello held up her palms, adamantly denying the allegation. "I only meant—"

"I hope so. Preacher Sola will be here tomorrow," Señor Arguello interrupted. "He will talk some sense into her. He's always had such an easy way with Isabella, with her keen interest in spiritual matters. They seem to understand one another." He paused, staring off into the distance. "Yes, it will all be better when Preacher Sola arrives."

"I hope so. Preacher Sola is such a kind, godly man. The first Protestant I ever met," Señora Arguello mused. "I was beside myself when Isabella disappeared that morning. Only three years old and out somewhere on the rancho by herself." The woman's lips trembled at the memory. "She faced certain death out there all alone. I praise God every day for that circuit-riding preacher and his odd ways. Without him, our daughter would not be getting married this Christmas."

"Even so," Señor Arguello hastily added, "he comes here as my guest, not to take part in the ceremony. No Califorñio marriage would be blessed without the Catholic priest from the mission performing the ceremony."

"Of course, dear."

Just then, the pounding of horses' hooves sounded against the road leading to the adobe house, and Isabella sprang to life, dropping her sewing on the patio and running headlong toward the horsemen.

"Preacher Sola!" she squealed excitedly. "Preacher Sola!" She lost her sandal along the way but kept running regardless. Soon, she was within the circle of men, their Bibles readily apparent on each leather horse pack. She stood beneath the churchmen, but with the noon autumn sun glaring down into her eyes, she couldn't find her beloved Señor Sola.

She shaded her eyes with a graceful, slim hand and searched again. Before her eyes could scan all the men, they were stopped cold by the finest man she had ever seen. He looked to be Spanish, with his unruly, dark brown hair and deeply set eyes that seemed darker than coal. His facial features were aristocratic, giving the impression of noble birth, perhaps Spanish gentility. His shoulders were broad, and his legs extended well down the horse's sides. Isabella could not take her eyes from his. The stranger seemed to hold her with an intense, unseen force. At last, he spoke.

"You must be Isabella," he said softly with a respect usually not extended to women on the rancho. She was so awestruck by his courtesy that she could only nod in reply, her mouth falling open.

"Isabella, Preacher Sola has told me so much about you." The stranger jumped down from his horse, and Isabella stood frozen under his warm gaze. She felt so small beneath his towering frame, and she was awestruck by his shaven jawline. She had never before seen a mature man without facial hair, except for the Indians. The straight lines of his features were mesmerizing.

When Isabella remained silent, he spoke again.

"Señor Sola says you are his special girl. I must say, I was expecting a girl of about three by his descriptions. He still sees you as a child, Isabella. Preacher Sola was heartbroken that he could not be here for your wedding ceremony. He sent me in his absence, to let you know his heart would be here."

Isabella woke from her dreamlike state, and she frantically looked among the men once again. "Preacher Sola is not here?" she repeated fearfully.

"No, Señorita. Señor Sola's health is failing, and he was unable to make the trip. I am the new preacher on this riding circuit. My name is Juan Carlos Vega." He bowed before her and gently kissed her hand. She felt her knees weaken and pondered the strange new sensation this man caused within her stomach.

The other churchmen led Juan Carlos's horse away, leaving him alone with Isabella on the plain.

"I'm sorry you're disappointed, Isabella. We would not allow Señor Sola to join us. He would have come anyway if he hadn't been assured of your happiness surrounding your impending marriage."

Isabella tossed her head from side to side, her long dark hair reflecting the afternoon sun. She couldn't believe what she was hearing. All her hopes rested upon Preacher Sola. She needed him. This handsome stranger would never convince her father to break his vow. She finally had words. "I don't know who you are, but I need Preacher Sola. It is vital that he come. I have so many questions about the Bible and my upcoming marriage. He must be here to interpret. No one on the rancho reads."

"I read, Señorita," he replied calmly. "I would be happy to translate for you. Did you have a particular passage in mind or an area troubling you?" He whispered to imply the strictest confidence.

Isabella was transfixed by the magnificence of the stranger's face. She heard nothing of his words. His eyes were gentle and trustworthy, and his expression, genuine and concerned. Her troubles evaporated, and suddenly she had the strangest thought. She didn't want to discuss Antonio Fremont or her disastrous marriage. She wanted to reach up and softly kiss Juan Carlos Vega. She felt the heat rise in her cheeks.

Juan Carlos walked with her to the patio and sat down, taking her hand. "I understand your disappointment that Pastor Sola is not here, but what I don't understand is the sadness in your eyes. Your tears are not from a young woman in love, are they?"

She shook her head. Something about Juan made her trust him instinctively. Perhaps it was that he was her only hope against her father's promise, but she poured out her heart. "Antonio Fremont, my betrothed. He is a vile man, but Papa thinks because of his wealth he is the best choice for me. He has already had two wives. Am I not worthy enough to be a first wife? Because he owns the most cattle, must he own me too?" She threw her hand to her heart. "Oh, I know I sound ungrateful, but you have not met this man. I need to know what the Bible says about honoring your father and your mother and when that honor may be broken. For I know what the Bible says about a wife's submission, and I am not ready to take such a vow with Antonio Fremont."

"I think you know what the Bible says, my child. You just don't want to listen to it," his low voice answered tenderly. " 'Honor thy father and thy mother.' Not just when you want to, but always. I must believe your father wants and is doing what's best for you. Pastor Sola speaks so highly of your father."

She shook her head again. "No, there's another verse. The one about being equally yoked, like the oxen that pull the cowskins. How can I be equally yoked to such a man, who does not have the fear of God within him?"

"You raise a very good point, but I think your father has spoken. From what I understand, a ranchero is not generally given to changing his mind, especially when it means relenting to a señorita."

Isabella fell to her knees at the feet of the handsome preacher. "Oh please, Señor Vega, I beg you. Please find the Scripture I refer to and talk with Papa. If you do not do this, what will I do? I have been endlessly praying to my heavenly Father. I would rather die than marry Señor Fremont."

"I will do what I can, Isabella." The use of her Christian name by his deep voice stirred her heart. She looked at him, and their eyes locked. Not the eyes of a preacher, but the eyes of a man. A man with emotions and sympathy for her plight, and perhaps something else. He rose quickly and left her on her knees in the bright afternoon light. Isabella watched him walk away, wondering at her breathlessness.

three

Isabella tossed her dress carelessly into her bota, her traveling bag made from cowhide. Her sister watched the commotion in disbelief. "Isabella, where can you possibly go? Father will only find out where you are and be angrier than ever. Not to mention your reputation will be ruined and no one will marry you," Victoria added. "Why don't you come stay with Raul and me in the outer adobe for a while? It will get your mind off your marriage until the fiesta."

"No, Victoria. I will not marry that man. I must go. There is no other way. Señor Vega is not willing to fight for me. And Papa will not respect the word of a Protestant other than Pastor Sola. Pastor Sola shall not come this Navidad. I'd rather work the fields like an Indian or tend to the tanning vats than marry Antonio Fremont. Look me in the eye and tell me you wouldn't run too." A moment passed. "You can't do it, can you?"

"Where will you possibly go? I will worry."

"I will run to the mission church. Perhaps I can enter the convent."

"They will not accept such a woman as you. You are of noble Califorñio birth, not a Spaniard or Mexican as

21

the nuns are," Victoria argued. "Isabella, you have never even been off the rancho, you have no idea what awaits you out there. The smugglers, the whalers, the sailors, it is simply not safe!"

"God will guard me, and He cares not of my nationality if I want to serve Him. Good-bye, dear sister. I love you. Do not tell them of my plans, only that I will find work and be safe." Isabella kissed her sister and ran into the darkness of the night with only the full moon to guide her steps.

Isabella walked for over an hour, and the chill of the night began to nip at her core. She pulled her shawl tighter and braced against the cold breeze that carried the coldness of the far-off ocean fog. It would take her nearly two days to reach the edge of her father's land, but she trudged on, knowing her journey was necessary. She must get to the neighboring rancho and the mission that operated upon it.

She had packed dried beef and planned to drink from the small creek she followed. As the night became darker, Isabella found herself wishing she had taken a horse. It would not have been missed until morning, but it would have made her tracks much easier to follow.

She heard a twig snap, and she automatically stopped in her tracks. Looking around her, she could see nothing in the darkness. She stepped as quietly as possible and hid beneath an oak tree, hoping the animal or wayward soul would pass without noticing her. Frozen in her fear for hours on end, Isabella eventually fell asleep under the great tree.

She woke to morning's first light and wiped her

eyes, closing them tightly at first to shield them from the bright morning sun. Its heat felt so good, but the dew on the golden grasses reminded her of her chill. Her whole body ached from walking. Isabella was used to being catered to, not undergoing strenuous exercise, and she wondered if she were truly up to the task of working for a living. Suddenly, her newfound independence didn't seem as hopeful an idea as it had the night before in the warmth of the adobe.

Her stomach grumbled, and she grimaced at the thought of dried beef rather than fresh eggs prepared by the servants. She ate the beef heartily, though with a scowl on her face at its salty taste. She continued to walk while she ate, knowing she'd lost too much time by falling asleep. Isabella was so engrossed in her own thoughts that it was a great surprise when she heard men murmuring nearby.

She stopped chewing and looked around her, hoping she would just find a wayward cow and that the speech she'd heard was as much a part of her imagination as the twig snapping had been the night before. After a moment, she knew her ears were not deceiving her. She ran to hide behind the closest tree, but in the open grassy flatlands that proved impossible, and she was seen immediately in a whirl of black.

One of the men yelled, "It's a woman, over there!"

She heard the loud gallop of horses closing in on her and knew her dash was pointless. Papa would be so angry, she thought, *if* he ever found out what happened to her. She stood in the field, closed her eyes, and murmured a small prayer, bracing herself for whatever lay ahead.

Suddenly, Isabella was swept upon a horse and into the hands of a man. She felt like a child in the large man's arm, and fear gripped her, her heart beating so loudly she couldn't hear another sound, not even the horse's hooves hitting the ground. She trembled. Looking down at the rushing ground alongside her, she closed her eyes tightly again, unwilling to believe what was happening. She let out a deep breath and opened her eyes, seeing only the black leather gloves that held the reins and her waist in a firm grip. *Oh, what have I done? Papa, I'm so sorry.*

She swallowed hard at the sight of a long, silver blade at her side. In one swift movement, invisible to her eyes, the sword was lifted high above them and they were forging ahead under the glistening blade. She watched its sun-filled reflection until it blinded her, forcing her to shield her eyes with her free hand. They galloped toward the group of horsemen, but the assembly seemed to be running from them, not leading them.

Recognition seized her, and she jerked her head around and saw the noble face of Juan Carlos Vega, smiling knowingly down upon her. He kicked the horse with a yell, spurring them closer to the band of horsemen. Isabella turned her face into his chest and held tightly to his black jacket, never more joyous to see anyone in her life. Suddenly the riders split up and tore in two different directions while a designated rider turned to face them. Isabella prayed at the sight of the stranger forging ever closer, fear mounting once again. When he was within several feet of them, the man stopped the horse and jumped from his mount, pulling out his own saber in invitation to Juan Carlos. The man was short and stocky, with full muttonchops and a scraggly beard. He held death in his eyes, and Isabella feared for Juan Carlos and the trouble she had led them both into.

Her rescuer took her hands from his coat and roughly handed her the reins with his free hand. He bolted from the horse easily, leaving her to handle the trotting horse herself. Isabella thanked God that she was an excellent horsewoman and steered the horse away from where it might be spooked, wishing she could just keep running and get home to safety. When she was a fair distance away, she heard the clanking of metal and turned to see Juan Carlos in a dangerous dance of sword fighting.

"Oh Father, please protect him," she whispered.

Juan Carlos kept his eyes on his opponent and circled the man. Suddenly the swordsman lunged at Juan, and the fighting began again. Isabella had watched many sword fights during the annual rodeo when vaqueros showed off their many cowboy skills, but never before had she witnessed a true duel. Juan's technique seemed beyond compare to that which she had witnessed, perhaps because the others were staged. She wanted to turn away, but her interest was too keen, her mind too anxious, the outcome too important.

Juan Carlos moved the sword like a dancer, thoroughly in touch with his partner, blocking each jab his opponent made with a graceful, muscular arm. Juan Carlos seemed to know where the man would strike and almost casually deflected any attempts on his life. The sound of steel against steel rang into Isabella's ears, and she shuddered at the constant noise, praying it would end soon with Juan Carlos still easily in control.

Fatigue began to overtake the bearded man, but Juan Carlos held the saber high in the air, as though its great weight had no impact on his muscular frame. Suddenly Juan Carlos lunged unexpectedly and swooped the sword away from his opponent. Isabella began to gallop closer, but when the man picked up his sword and came at Juan again, she pulled the reins back. The opponent lifted his sword once again but dropped it from the overwhelming weight, too tired to fight any longer. Juan Carlos stepped on the blade, keeping it firmly upon the ground.

"You are on Arguello property. Are you aware of this?" he asked sternly.

"Just kill me swiftly," the man begged.

"I will not kill you. I am a man of God. You are trespassing with the intent to rustle cattle, no?" he asked.

"Yes," the man admitted.

"Take your pistol and your blade and get off this land. The next man that finds you may not be as forgiving as I." Juan Carlos lifted his foot and allowed the sword to be raised.

The man scrambled to get off the ground and ran to his horse, galloping away as if in fear for his life. Isabella was mystified by this man of God, as he called himself, and turned to Juan Carlos questioningly. His skills with a sword were certainly nothing like those displayed by the men at a rodeo. Juan Carlos held a subtle mastery over his sword, as one who used his talent often. He ran to her, breathless from his battle, and caught his horse by the reins. Placing his sword back into its sheath, he looked at her with the same intense brown eyes that had made her powerless the day before.

"Why did they not use their guns?" Isabella asked innocently.

"The noise would have alerted your father to rustlers. Most likely, they don't ride as well as your father's vaqueros, and they would have all been killed. Are you well, my child?"

"I'm not a child!" she exclaimed as she brushed off her skirt.

"A figure of speech. No need to be offended," he said as he tightened the reins on the horse. His eyes never met her own, but she could see he held back his smile.

"Where did you learn to fight like that? Certainly Pastor Sola did not teach you that." She watched him suspiciously.

He laughed, his brown eyes seeming to delight in her question. "You are a perceptive one, no?" He mounted his horse, and suddenly she felt his warmth against her back. Her fiery spirit left her as she basked in the protection of his arms. "Let's get you home," her rescuer declared. "You might still make breakfast."

"I'm not going home!" she said defiantly. "I will take care of myself." She remembered her plight once again and knew Juan Carlos's arms would not protect her back at the adobe from her papa's wrath. She squirmed to get loose of his embrace.

"You will take care of yourself," he said incredulously. "And how will you ward off the next group of rustlers that comes your way? There's no way to hide in this flatland until you reach the hills." She felt his arm leave her as he pointed toward the horizon.

"You just let me worry about that." She tried once again to jump from the horse, but his strong grasp of her waist made escape impossible. Her struggle was in vain against his bigger size, and she sighed miserably. She knew she should have been grateful for his timely heroics, but she held only contempt when he led the horse back to Rancho de Arguello.

"I will not let you run to danger," he said evenly. "Pastor Sola would never forgive me."

"You don't understand," Isabella protested. "You're sending me into danger. The way home is the path to destruction! By God's own Word, 'Enter ye at the strait gate: for wide is the gate, and broad is the way, that leadeth to destruction.' You see? It would be too easy for me to marry such a man and live in wealth. God has chosen another way for me. It must be true. I want to serve Him, but how can I do so when I'm married to Antonio Fremont?"

To her surprise, he stopped the horse and dismounted, helping her gently from the saddle. He tethered the horse near the creek and sat on a flat rock at the water's edge, lifting his arm for her to join him. Men gave little attention to what women had to say in Isabella's experience. Yet Juan Carlos heard her, and by stopping the horse he was actually acknowledging her in a way she'd never known.

four

The creek ran peacefully behind them, its gentle trickle allowing Isabella to become lost in Juan Carlos's deep brown eyes. Her thoughts were broken by his deep voice.

"Pastor Sola said you knew your Scripture well. He was starting to teach you to read last time?" Juan Carlos asked. Pastor Sola was the only other man who had ever spoken to Isabella without giving her an order. She felt herself instantly drawn to Juan's interest.

"I know my letters, but I still struggle with the words." Her voice trailed off in discouragement. "Papa says there's no need to read, especially for a lady. So I practice in secret." She shrugged.

"Isabella," he said softly. "Isabella, it is a very dangerous world out there. Your papa is right to give you away in marriage. This way he knows you will be safe." He cupped his hand around her face, and she felt herself starting to cry. "You are trying to choose your own path, when God has already directed your circumstances through your papa's ordination. Marrying Señor Fremont will keep you safe. Life in California off the rancho is a very different place. A violent place." He didn't look at her for a reply.

Isabella shook her head. "No, Juan Carlos. You have no idea what you're asking of me. Please find the Scripture that will release me. If Papa fears the wrath of God, perhaps I will be free. Pastor Sola would not have just given me away to a heathen like Antonio Fremont. Why should I suffer because you have come instead of him?"

"Isabella, you must honor your papa's word. It is one of the Ten Commandments."

"Am I bound by the law when I live under the cross?" Isabella squared her shoulders.

A look of wonder crossed Juan Carlos's face, and slowly a smile presented itself. "You know your Scriptures *quite* well, Isabella. Better than any woman I've met on the circuit. It is a rare quality indeed."

"I will learn more as I get better at reading. Help me, Juan Carlos. Take me to the convent."

Juan shook his head. "God will bring you other blessings, if your marriage isn't to be one of them." The bubbling creek echoed behind them, and Isabella thought how beautiful her papa's land was. She would be so sorry to leave it, but she would indeed leave it. The horse turned, and Isabella was blinded once again by the molded, elaborate, silver handle of Juan Carlos's sword.

"Where did you get that sword?" she inquired, transfixed by its elegant design.

"My father gave it to me. He was a Spaniard. Mexico issued him land near Mission Carmel for his work in the territory. He died before he ever got to settle there." Juan Carlos looked so strong, it felt odd to hear him talk in such a melancholy tone.

"I'm sorry. How old were you when he died?"

"Sixteen, just a year younger than you are now." His brown eyes looked to the brook.

"You made it without getting married." She lifted her chin confidently. "Why shouldn't I give my life to God and avoid marriage altogether?"

"Isabella." He shook his head, a sly smile lifting the corner of his straight mouth. "It is different, and you know it. I am a man, and I haven't always been a man of God. I once lived by the sword instead of the Word. And if you leave the safety of your father's way for you, you will live by the sword too. Living in darkness with God is far better than life without Him. You must trust me on this. A beautiful woman like you is not safe alone in the territory. You need a husband." His tone left little room for argument.

Nothing he'd said registered except that he thought her beautiful. She had been told such nonsense since she was a child, but never had it meant anything to her until uttered by the dashing, sword-fighting Juan Carlos Vega. She looked at him with renewed interest. Perhaps she did need a husband after all. A believing husband her father just might approve of. A Spanish nobleman was nothing next to the birthrights of a Californio, but perhaps Pastor Sola's blessing might convince her papa otherwise. Isabella's mind reeled with the possibilities.

Suddenly a high-pitched squealing came toward them. Juan Carlos's eyes popped open wide, and he flew to his feet. "Get on the horse now!" he shouted, and Isabella did as she was told without hesitation. Before she could turn around to see the intruder on their quiet moment, Juan Carlos was behind her, giving the horse a start. They pulled into a full gallop within seconds and left the wild boar that chased them in the dust.

The aggressive boar had accomplished one thing. Isabella was headed toward home without further delay. The rancho came into view, and she couldn't believe she'd walked all that way and was mere minutes from her adobe. "No wonder you laughed at me," she said quietly. "I was such a short way from home that I never would have made it to the mission church." She ached that Juan Carlos knew just how foolish she'd been, ached at knowing her valiant escape effort had been so pathetic.

"No one is laughing at you, Señorita." She thought she felt Juan Carlos close his arms a little tighter around her, but it was probably wishful thinking. Her girlish ways would only be an amusement to such a fine man of noble birth. A man who listened to her thoughts. It seemed a dream to have the character of her beloved Pastor Sola dwell inside a man who looked like Juan Carlos Vega. Of course, it was no more than the dream. She was engaged to be married to a Californio. *As it should be,* she thought sadly.

"Isabella!" Her father's stern voice called out to her from the adobe. Her entire family came running toward the horse, and she wished she might crawl under a rock. "Isabella, in your room immediately. Your mother will be along shortly."

She looked to Juan Carlos and noticed he tried to ignore the reprimand, but it was ludicrous to think he'd missed it. She was but a child to him. Any thoughts to the contrary were in vain.

She sat in her darkened room, opening the curtain slightly when her sister came in to soothe her. "Isabella, I am glad you did not get far. I would have been sick with worry. Juan Carlos is a good man. He offered to go searching for you early this morning. He whispered something to Papa and so he was allowed to go alone."

"He is a fine man, Victoria. He is a true hero. He rescued me from a band of cattle rustlers, then he had a sword fight like a Spanish conquistador, then he pulled me out of harm's way from an angry boar."

Victoria giggled, "Oh Isabella, your imagination. It is good to have you home." Victoria patted her arm condescendingly. "Mama will be here soon. I must see to the servants and dinner."

Just then Senora Arguello came into the room, and Victoria left them alone. "Isabella." The señora stroked her daughter's cheek and pulled her into a warm embrace. "I'm sorry Señor Fremont is not who you would have picked, but you must never betray your father again, do you understand?" Señora Arguello pulled away. "He will lose authority with the Indians and vaqueros, and that could be dangerous for us all. There's no telling what might have happened to you out there alone," her mother added ominously, and Isabella kept her adventures quiet this time. "Now I'll arrange for you to bathe. Antonio is coming tonight for dinner. I've laid out your best lace gown."

33

"Mama, why must I marry a wealthy man? Cannot a poor man who loves the Lord take care of me?"

"Isabella, this is far too hard for us women to understand, but your papa says the Americans are coming and our wealth is more important than ever to maintain the territory. The Mexicans want control of this land, the Spaniards want control, and now the Americans as well. The Californios have worked hard to remain under Mexican rule while still being independent. Papa says it is only because of our wealth that we maintain that rule. Your marrying Antonio Fremont helps us all, you understand that?"

Señora Arguello gave her daughter a loving smile, and Isabella simply nodded in agreement.

"It is a hard thing for a ranchero to have no sons, but a blessing indeed to have such a daughter that would bring in so many cattle," Isabella's mother continued.

Isabella ached at the notion that the value of her life could be measured with cattle. They were such big, stupid animals. Who cared how many cows she was worth? Pastor Sola didn't. And perhaps Juan Carlos Vega didn't either.

Later that day Isabella dressed in her finest, but she didn't feel like dancing or celebrating, not with the knowledge that Señor Fremont would be arriving for dinner. As the sun began to descend, she walked along the patio, taking in the beautiful orange and pink sunset that lit the clear winter sky.

"It's kind of dark to be out alone, isn't it, little one?" Juan Carlos appeared from the shadows, his Bible in his hand.

He seemed to come from a dream, and Isabella did not want to let him out of her sight. His handsome, chiseled features held her. She walked toward him, as though drawn by his eyes. Without another word, Juan Carlos swept her into his arms and led her in a contradanza, a dignified dance from Spain.

"My mama taught me this dance." He closed his eyes momentarily. He hummed an accompaniment, and Isabella giggled with enjoyment, relishing every sensation he sent her body soaring into. *This is how a woman should feel about the man she marries,* she thought dreamily.

Too swiftly his joyful humming ceased, and Isabella opened her wide, brown eyes. "We are finished?" she asked, disappointed.

His tone was fatherly, reserved. "Isabella, I want you to be kind to Señor Fremont tonight. It is very important to your father. . .and to me," he added.

Isabella could only nod. Being nice to Señor Fremont was the last thing on her mind. She wanted to become lost in an elegant dance again, to forget she was marrying another. Life had been so simple until she was asked to grow up so suddenly.

"Make your papa proud. Do what he asks of you. Let us go in now." He took her arm, looking straight ahead, avoiding her admiring eyes.

"Wait." She stepped in front of him and looked at him fiercely, trying to ascertain whether the feelings between them were only hers. She caught his deep-set brown eyes. Instantly she knew: Juan Carlos did not think her a child after all. The recognition set her stomach aflutter, and for the first time since her engagement, she felt hope.

"Let us go," he said again by way of excuse.

"No," she pleaded. Juan Carlos was about to kiss her. She may have been naive about many things, but this she was sure about. He gazed at her a moment longer but remained stoic and immobile. She finally reached up and kissed him timidly, softly. His eyes closed, and he returned her kiss sweetly before breaking from her embrace, holding her at the shoulders.

"Isabella, you are a betrothed woman and that kiss is for your husband and no other," he said firmly, a stern look replacing the smiling brown eyes.

She nodded. "Very well then. I suppose you must marry me now." She crossed her arms.

"Isabella, even if I were in a position to marry you, which I am not, your father would never allow it. I am a Spaniard, not a Califorñio, and if you knew of my past, you would understand how impossible such an idea is. You are to marry Antonio Fremont, though it pains me to say it. It is what's best. Any ideas to the contrary are mere folly."

"Because you were born a Spanish nobleman, you were baptized a Catholic, so my papa should not object to you, is that not true?" she challenged.

"Isabella, your family awaits. Honor your father and your mother."

She watched him walk purposefully into the adobe, his broad shoulders straight with resolution. His defiance only made her more certain that she would never marry Antonio Fremont, for she loved the preacher, Juan Carlos Vega.

five

J uan Carlos sat at the edge of the great table opposite the man who would marry Isabella. Everything
she had told him about Señor Fremont reverberated
in his ears with vivid clarity. Although Señor Arguello
did not serve hard drink, the coarse ranchero had
brought his own and was drunk by the main course of
the meal. The foul words he flung easily disgusted Juan
Carlos, and the vulgar way he eyed Isabella made Juan
Carlos want to take to the sword once again.

Juan Carlos knew Señor Arguello loved his daughter, and he saw in the older man's eyes fear. Fear that his
daughter would suffer for his mistake.

With clenched teeth, Juan Carlos forced himself to
keep his eyes from Isabella. In her exquisite, Spanish
cream lace gown, her beauty was legendary; but if others
saw what Juan Carlos felt, the preacher would have no
credibility with Isabella's father. Juan Carlos planned to
appeal to the ranchero for Isabella's freedom, and any
feelings of his own would definitely harm his chances for
success.

No matter how many cattle Isabella was worth, her
papa had to see that Señor Fremont was an abhorrent

choice for a husband. Getting a ranchero to admit his wrong and change his word, however, was not going to be easy. In the California Territory, a man's reputation was as important as the number of cattle he owned.

"Isabella, come sit on my lap, my dear." Señor Fremont pulled away from the table, screeching his chair against the planked floor, and reached around his abundant belly to pat his round legs. His speech was slurred from drink, and he looked as though he was having a difficult time holding his head up.

Juan Carlos waited for Señor Arguello to protect his daughter, but the father remained silent. No admonition escaped his mouth. Isabella was obviously frozen with fear, and she remained seated, seeming to ignore the plea from her intended, offering him more water instead.

When Señor Arguello motioned for Isabella to move over to their guest, Juan Carlos stood up angrily. "I must protest. Isabella is not married yet, and therefore, in the eyes of God, this is sinful. Would you ask Isabella to sin before the very preacher who saved her life as a child? As I sit here in Pastor Sola's absence, I ask that you not do so in front of me." Juan Carlos looked at Señor Fremont, and the man threw out an arm in disgust.

"Sit down, Isabella. The preacher is right," Señor Arguello commanded, a look of discomfort crossing his brow. Isabella sighed with relief and mouthed "thank you" to Juan Carlos.

After the meal, Antonio Fremont bedded down for the night, too intoxicated to stay awake any longer. Isabella quickly scurried into her room, anxious to get away.

"Señor, may I have a word with you." Juan Carlos pulled Señor Arguello aside, anxious to share the Scripture that would release Isabella from such a disastrous marriage. They walked into the crisp night air and sat under the stars. "The Bible says a man is to love his wife as Christ loves the church. A man like Antonio Fremont is not capable of such a love. He does not walk in the way of our Lord—that much is obvious."

The night was dark and the torches were snuffed out for the evening, so Juan Carlos could not see a reaction and prayed silently his words would be taken well.

"Why do you talk to me of love?" Señor Arguello replied. "I love my daughter enough to give her to the wealthiest Califorñio in the territory. Any father would be proud to call Antonio Fremont his son. A thousand cattle she is worth."

"She is worth far more than that. The Bible says that a virtuous wife is worth far above rubies."

"I will be the wealthiest Califorñio when Isabella is married. You cannot put a price on that!" Señor Arguello stated proudly, lifting his chin.

"You have put a price on it: Isabella." Immediately, Juan Carlos regretted his words.

"Pastor Sola would never come into my adobe with such insolence. What gives you the right to question me? You, a Spaniard," Señor Arguello said before he spit in contempt. "Worse yet, a Spaniard without a birthright, who travels the territory with nothing to call his own except a Bible. Isabella is a woman and she'll do what she's told."

"You are acting in greed, not Christian love, and it

is my duty as a man of God to tell you so. You have the right to do as you see fit, but I must preach the Word as God has given it. Just as Nathaniel once did to David."

"And what would your Book tell me to do, preacher? Give my daughter to a man of God without a single steer to call his own?" Señor Arguello asked accusingly. "Just because you are handsome, you think yourself a worthy husband for my daughter? You. . .a Spaniard. You all think yourselves superior to us! Well, I'll have none of that. Isabella will marry a Califorñio as she was born to do."

Juan Carlos tried to hide his shock. He had mentioned nothing of his feelings, yet Señor Arguello knew what his thoughts were. Isabella's father must have recognized his jealousy during the evening meal. Either that or Señor Arguello had seen so many men fall victim to Isabella's innocent charms, he just assumed Juan Carlos was not immune. And he was not.

Juan Carlos took a deep breath. He had nothing to lose now. "If you did give Isabella to me, I would care for her like no other man, certainly unlike Antonio Fremont."

"I've seen your sword, Juan Carlos. I know you've lived by the knife—it's obvious by the condition of your blade. You haven't always been a man of God. Why should I believe you're one now and not just some poor man making cow eyes at my daughter to gain my herds?"

"Pastor Sola, for one thing. Do you think he would send someone who might harm his precious Isabella? He thinks of her as the daughter he never had. I can't give you an assurance that you would believe. I can only ask you to look at my heart and judge my actions. I will tell you that if I had a mind to take Isabella for my own, we'd be gone without a trace. But as I've said, I've given up that life. And I'm trusting you will come to see that I am now a man of God. I say these words in honor and respect, Señor. I would never seek to harm Isabella or her family." With those words, Juan Carlos turned on his heel and left Isabella's father alone in the night air.

❄

"He threatened me. The man of God threatened me!" Jose Arguello paced the floor of his room. "He comes into my adobe and questions my authority. He will be off this property tomorrow. No Spaniard is going to threaten my daughter's future of wealth." He pointed to the wooden floor. "He had the audacity to suggest I give her to him, a common beggar." Isabella's father let out a short laugh.

"Jose, maybe you're overreacting," Señora Arguello said hesitantly. "He does have a point—Señor Fremont committed several of the seven deadly sins just while sitting at the dinner table. He blatantly dismisses the commandments of our Lord, and he is so old, Señor. Juan Carlos is just telling you his observations. You needn't kill the messenger."

"You see, now you are questioning me. This Juan Carlos has done enough damage. I want him off the rancho tomorrow, and I'll have every vaquero behind him to insure he goes."

"But Juan, think of Isabella. She is beside herself without Pastor Sola here. Wouldn't it be wise to have the

41

young preacher here at least until the priest arrives?"

"She will adjust," Jose said sharply.

❄

Isabella listened at the door of her parent's bedroom. All hope within her died. If Antonio Fremont's heathen behavior hadn't convinced her father, nothing would. She had to run again, but this time she wouldn't go alone. She would go with Preacher Juan Carlos Vega, with or without his assistance.

She tiptoed up the hallway and knocked quietly on Juan Carlos's door. He had a candle lit, and his Bible lay open on his cot. He opened his mouth, but Isabella cut him off in a whisper. "I must speak with you. Meet me at the stable."

She hurried outside and ran across the expanse to the horses' stalls. She found an empty one and huddled down in the hay to wait. It wasn't long before Juan Carlos called her name.

"I'm here," she said quietly, and he came toward her with a candle, which he blew out when he came closer. She couldn't even make out his form in the pitch black of night, but she could feel his warmth and hear his labored breathing from running the distance to the structure.

"Juan Carlos, my papa is unrelenting. I will have to marry Antonio Fremont if I stay." Her mouth felt so dry from nervousness. All her life everything had been taken care of for her, but now she felt she must act on her own or suffer the consequences. She drew in a deep breath for courage. "Tomorrow my papa will see to it that you are thrown off Rancho de Arguello, and I beg you to take me with you. I will do anything," she said breathlessly. "I would even—"

"Shh," he said. "Pray Isabella. Believe in the Lord your God and not in me. Call on Him. I am but a man and a weak one at that. The Lord has sent me to do His work, and already I find I am tempted beyond measure by your beauty. Isabella, I wish I could protect you, but I cannot. You must ask God. If I helped you, it would be as a man, not as a preacher, and I cannot go against your father's word because it would break my vow to God."

"I don't care how you help me. Just help me," she pleaded.

He found her face with his hands and held her ever so gently, kissing her softly on the forehead. She knew his kiss meant good-bye, and she grew more anxious than ever.

"Would you leave me to this fate? To have Antonio Fremont take me as his wife?" she asked desperately, hoping for a reaction.

"Antonio Fremont is not in the wrong, Isabella, I am. Is Antonio Fremont standing here kissing another man's fiancée in the dark of the night? Is he telling her with words and actions how he loves her when he knows she belongs to another?"

"I will never belong to another," she whispered through her tears.

"You already do, Isabella." He reached down and smoothed her cheek and walked out into the night.

Isabella felt more desolate than ever and chased him frantically, grasping his shoulder. "I know you were a smuggler. You could have me off Papa's property without a trace. We could leave tonight. Why won't you help me?"

"Where did you hear this?" he demanded.

"I heard the rustlers fighting over who would battle you. They knew of you. . .feared you. You were apparently quite renowned," she said accusingly.

"Isabella, I left that life behind when I joined God's army. Let this go and marry Antonio Fremont. I will not help you escape." He said with finality, "You are better off in the life you've known. God will provide." His voice trailed off, and he resolutely turned his back and was gone.

six

The next morning the fiesta celebration of Isabella's engagement began bright and early with a hearty breakfast of steak and eggs. Although the California winter chill was brisk, the warm sun allowed for the meal out on the patio. Juan Carlos sat across from Isabella but refused to look at her. He said the prayer over the morning meal and quietly ate his breakfast.

At the close of the meal, Senor Arguello stood up to speak. "I'm sorry to announce that Señor Vega will not be staying for the wedding celebration. The preacher is very busy this time of year and has other commitments." He turned to Juan Carlos. "Preacher Vega, I have prepared a cart of cowhides for you to take to Preacher Sola in payment for your trip. Please give him our best and let him know how much we've missed him."

With the announcement, Juan Carlos nodded, rose, and said his excuses. Isabella felt like a caged animal and stood abruptly. "I will see that the servants have sent the proper provisions."

Isabella raced to grab her packed bota, then quietly

snuck it into the cowhide cart. She pretended to go to speak with the stable chief but instead ducked into the oxcart and hid under the dried leather skins. She felt the cart lifted as it was hitched to a team of horses rather than oxen to speed their travel. About an hour later, she heard Juan Carlos's gentle voice, and her heart quickened.

"Señora, I am sorry I must leave on such a harsh note. Please give Señor my best and relay my sincerest apologies if I have offended him. May I see Isabella before I leave? I'd like to tell her good-bye."

For a moment Isabella felt guilty about deceiving those she loved. How she would miss her mama and papa and especially her sister. But one thought of Antonio Fremont, and she knew what she had to do.

She heard her mother's quiet voice. "You would be more than welcome to say good-bye to Isabella, but I'm afraid she is off pouting somewhere. No one has seen her since breakfast. No need to worry. She is probably by the creek sulking. This has been a very trying time for her. Marriage is not an easy step. The servants will bring her back, and I will relay your greetings. You have been most kind to us, Señor. I'm sorry you must leave."

"You are most kind, and I will pray, Señora."

"Sí," Isabella heard her mother say sadly.

Isabella soon felt a sharp tug on the wagon, and she tensed, praying she would not be discovered until she was well off her papa's property.

Hours passed, and Isabella grew hot under the cowhides, lifting them often to allow more air to circulate in the cart. She gulped deep breaths of fresh air but finally grew tired of pressing against the heavy hides. As more time passed, Isabella started to feel dizzy, and the darkness under the pelts invaded her head. She felt the horses slowing just before the blackness overwhelmed her.

❊

"Juan Carlos Vega! Back to your old ways, I see. There must be a hundred California banknotes in that cart." Brigadier General Manuel Torena in full Mexican regalia circled Juan Carlos's horse, smiling smugly at the preacher. "I knew your conversion was just a ploy. Once a thief, always a thief!"

Juan Carlos held his chin high, watching his old nemesis cautiously. "I am a man of God, General. These skins are a gift from Señor Jose Arguello for Preacher Sola's ministry."

"No Califorñio would give such a generous gift to a Protestant minister!" The general dismounted and motioned for his horsemen to do the same. "Search the cowskins!" he shouted. "Juan Carlos Vega does not simply smuggle pelts. He's got other provisions in there, I know it. Search!" he repeated with urgency, and the uniformed soldiers scrambled to carry out the order.

The men lifted the leathers, tossing them carelessly on the muddy soil of the road. Soon, one of the men screamed excitedly, "Murderer!" The soldier looked at Juan Carlos accusingly. "He's got a dead woman back here. And what's worse, she's a Califorñio! Look at her gown."

The soldier lifted Isabella's limp body out of the oxcart, and Juan Carlos felt the blood rush from his face.

47

"Isabella!" He jumped from his horse and ran to her. The soldier held a gun to Juan Carlos, but the preacher stared at the man with fire in his eyes. "Call him off, General!" he cried.

Juan Carlos's successful fighting reputation had not diminished, and the general motioned for his man to move.

"Isabella, my sweet. Wake up, my darling," Juan Carlos whispered as he held her seemingly lifeless body. He looked up at the men who had accompanied him on his journey. "Get some water!"

Isabella's raven tresses fell around her pale face. The red lips, once so full, so moist, were now colorless and dry, and her great brown eyes appeared sunken.

One of his horsemen brought a canteen forward, and Juan Carlos sprinkled the liquid into Isabella's mouth while he prayed over her. "Dear heavenly Father, restore her, Lord, restore her." He rocked her gently while the horseman took the canteen and let several drops of water fall into her open mouth. Soon, Isabella's pink tongue licked the drops, and eventually her eyes fluttered opened.

"Juan Carlos, where am I?" she asked. "Are we off Papa's rancho?" Isabella then noticed the soldiers, and she tried to sit up quickly but fell back wearily into Juan Carlos's arms.

"You're near Monterey," he answered softly. "You became dehydrated under the cowskins." He was furious with her for sneaking away. She might have been killed had they not been discovered by the general, but he kept his anger in check. It would not help his case with the general, and more importantly, it would do nothing for the frightened woman he loved. The sight of her filled him with an overwhelming instinct to shield and protect her. He would never let anyone harm her.

The general came beside his horse and removed Juan Carlos's sword. "Confiscate his gun!" he yelled, and the soldiers searched Juan Carlos roughly for a weapon the preacher no longer carried.

A soldier lifted Isabella to her feet while the general tied Juan Carlos's hands together with a vaquero's horse rope. Isabella cried in fear, "What are you doing to Preacher Vega?"

"Your Preacher Vega is smuggler, Juan Carlos Vega. He is no man of God, and now we can add kidnapping a Califorñio to his crimes. You will surely hang this time, Vega!"

"No!" Isabella protested. "I stowed away in the oxcart. The cowskins are a gift from my papa to Preacher Sola. I wanted to get away from my betrothed. I never meant to bring harm upon Preacher Vega!" Isabella struggled to be free from the man who held her, but he only smiled with dry amusement at her effort. "Juan Carlos did not even know I was with them. You must ask my papa! Surely, you will hang, General, if they find you killed an untried man of the cloth. You, not even a Califorñio!" she spat out viciously.

Juan Carlos marveled at her intelligence. Discerning that the general was a Mexican national and not a native Califorñio was one thing, but using that knowledge against him was amazing for an innocent young woman who'd spent her entire life on a sheltered rancho.

She had obviously listened well to her father's prejudices and politics. The Californios, while under Mexican rule, considered themselves above their ancestors' nations. They were in every sense pure Californios. They wanted no part of Mexico or Spain.

The general paused for a moment, trying to decide whether Juan Carlos's fate might also affect his own. "You will spend the night in prison until we verify your story," he said to Juan Carlos. "The señorita will stay with my wife until we have proper guards to return her to her rancho. No false moves, Vega, or the lady may pay the price, *comprende?*"

Juan Carlos clenched his teeth, knowing the general was just cruel enough to harm Isabella and blame him. For now, there was nothing he could do but pray.

❄

Isabella bit back sobs as she watched Juan Carlos walk the remaining distance to Monterey with his hands tied behind his back. Every so often, the general would kick the preacher to speed his pace, and Juan Carlos would grimace in pain. The rest of Juan Carlos's circuit-riding preachers were set free without the cowskins, which the general had confiscated.

The blue sea of Monterey glistened under the foggy sky, and Isabella marveled at the enormous schooner in the beautiful bay. The port was a hubbub of activity—soldiers marched in unison, shoremen worked the docks—but the busy trading post stopped all activity as the general passed by with his prisoner. Much to Isabella's dismay, they paid no mind to Juan Carlos, but they studied her with eager eyes. Isabella caught her breath and bit her lower lip nervously. A woman was obviously a rare sight in Monterey.

She could see in Juan Carlos's eyes that he wished to protect her, and his inability to do so only seemed to frustrate him more. Isabella cringed at the trouble she had brought to the man she supposedly loved. Her self-ish actions had only succeeded in harming those she cared for: Pastor Sola would not get his California bank-notes to support his ministers, her papa would not get the cattle as part of her marriage agreement, and worst of all, Juan Carlos might hang for her sins.

"Isabella, all will be well. Just pray, my love. God's plan will be for the good, no matter what that plan includes, do you understand?" Juan Carlos asked her when they arrived at the general's mansion. It was just like Juan Carlos to think of her when he was in danger.

"They will have to kill me first before they let you hang!" she shouted.

"Isabella." He let his head drop. "God's will be done, my dear. Go back home and marry Antonio Fremont."

"Antonio Fremont? She is betrothed to Señor Fremont?" the general inquired uneasily.

"Si, that's right, the richest ranchero in the territory, and she belongs to him, so it is in your best interest to get her home safely," Juan Carlos warned, and Isabella could see the general's face go ashen.

The general's home was a lovely two-story adobe on the shores of the bay. It was furnished with inlaid tables from China, camphor-wood chests, and embroidered silk bedspreads; but for all its wealth, the home was devoid of any warmth. Isabella felt this lack as soon as she walked into the general's lavish quarters. His wife Martina met them in the foyer.

"This here's Fremont's betrothed," the general told her roughly. "Take care of her or our post will be in serious jeopardy," he shouted, just before he ripped Juan Carlos from Isabella's sight.

"Trust in God!" she heard him yell behind the closed door.

Martina Torena studied Isabella suspiciously. "So, you are Antonio Fremont's choice," she said slowly as she crossed her arms and walked around the young woman. "What brings you to Monterey alone? Surely you are not here for a gown, for no decent ranchero would allow his daughter to roam the streets of Monterey without guards. You are running away, no?"

"No," Isabella lied. "I wanted to go to Preacher Sola, and I knew that Juan Carlos Vega could get me there, so I snuck into the cowskins." Martina's eyes thinned, the woman's disbelief apparent.

"I do not like pretty women in my home. You will tease my husband and ruin my marriage. I do not have a son yet, so I will not stand for your presence here. If the general does not find a way back for you by tomorrow, you will go alone, understood?" Señora Torena's dark eyes seemed to drill right through Isabella.

"Yes, Señora," Isabella replied meekly.

"Very well. The upstairs bedroom at the end of the hall is yours. See that you stay there and out of my husband's sight. Your meals will be brought to you."

Isabella scrambled upstairs, anxious to be free of

this jealous wife. At the rodeo, women talked about her, but Isabella had always been protected from other women's jealous actions by her father's status. Here, she held no such power, and should she say something out of line, Juan Carlos's fate might be worse.

Hours passed for Isabella in her darkened chambers. She prayed, pleading that the Lord would be with Juan Carlos and that he would be freed from the false charges. "Dear Lord, do not let Juan Carlos suffer for my selfishness. I have acted on my own power, not trusting You to work all things together for good—even my papa's plans to marry me to Señor Fremont. I have struggled against only You, Lord, and I beg for Your forgiveness. I will marry Antonio without further delay, and while I have no right to ask You any favors, please spare the life of Juan Carlos. Oh, to have his blood on my hands is more than I can bear." She buried her tear-drenched face in her hands.

Just then the great wooden door opened from the hallway. A young Indian servant came in carrying a tray of fish. She shut the thick door forcefully behind her. "Juan Carlos Vega will come for you tonight. Listen at the door of the balcony." She pointed to a door in the back of the room. "He will not wait long."

"How do you know this?" Isabella asked desperately.

The servant ignored the question, obviously worried over being missed. "The general will visit the cantina tonight. You will only have a short time to escape. I must go," she said fearfully.

"Wait," Isabella pleaded.

"I am a believer. Go with God," the servant answered

soothingly, holding Isabella's hand in her own.

The door swung open violently. "What is going on here?" Señora Torena's cold, evil stare froze Isabella in place. The older woman held a rod in her arms, lightly beating her hand with it.

Isabella squared her shoulders. "Your servant has not shown me proper respect as a Califorñio," she said haughtily, knowing that if the young woman proved to be a friend of Isabella's, she would suffer severe consequences.

"Ha! You impertinent. You are in the home of Brigadier General Torena, a Mexican national by birth, and I myself am a Califorñio. Your native status means nothing in Monterey, and it means nothing to me. Rosa, go!" she shouted to the maid as an afterthought.

The young Indian scurried from the room, anxious to escape the rod. Señora Martina Torena continued to beat the rod in her hand as she glared down on Isabella.

"Do you mean to harm me?" Isabella inquired uneasily.

Martina ignored her question. "Why will you marry Señor Fremont? He is old enough to be your grandpapa. He has children older than you."

"My papa has chosen him for me," she answered honestly, wishing she had submitted to that fact days earlier.

"Antonio does not love you," Señora Torena said viciously. "You are like an imported treasure, beautiful and useless. You are not worthy to marry him."

Isabella tilted her head, trying to understand why a complete stranger would sling such hateful words at her. "How—how do you know if Antonio loves me or not?" she asked nervously. Of course Antonio didn't love her—he didn't even know her. She was but an ornament to him. Why Señora Torena would trouble herself with such details was a mystery.

Señora Torena threw her head back and laughed harshly. Without a word, she turned and strode from the room, slamming the door with a vengeance behind her.

Isabella was left alone with her cold fish platter and her questions.

seven

Isabella's room was pitch black and she was never offered a candle, but she was too nervous to do anything but wait for the expected knock. Although her door was unlocked to the second-story balcony, her captors knew she would never venture out into the rough port city alone. She was far safer in the cold, dark room of her enemy. She prayed all evening that Rosa's words were true, that Juan Carlos would indeed rescue her.

The noise from the drinking establishments began to fill her room—a low rumble at first, then an outlandish roar as the night lengthened. A small knock sounded at her balcony door, and she bolted upright from her chair. She whispered through the door. "Who is it?"

"It is me, Isabella. Open quickly."

Recognizing the voice she had hoped so desperately to hear, Isabella opened the door as quietly as possible. Immediately her room was overwhelmed by the whoops and obnoxious laughter that filled the street. It sounded as though the entire town was immersed in criminal activity. At the sight of Juan Carlos, however, Isabella was tempted to forget all about her submission to her

56

father's marriage plans. Even in the light of the feeble moonlight and city torches, Juan Carlos exuded strength and confidence. His regal profile and smooth, sun-blessed skin made him the ultimate knight in shining armor.

Although she was on the second floor, the low ceilings of the first floor made reaching her balcony a mere step up from his horse for a tall nobleman like Juan Carlos. He didn't wait for her to speak. He simply lifted her easily into his strong arms, arms she had grown so accustomed to in their short acquaintance.

"Hang on to my neck," he whispered as he climbed over the low, spindly wooden banister of the balcony and transferred them onto his faithful horse. With a quiet kick to the horse's sides, they were galloping like the wind into the thick, damp night. They rode past the mariachi bands in the taverns. Soon the lights from the city streets thinned, and he slowed the horse's pace to an easy canter.

In the blackness of the starry night and free from the darkened prison of Monterey, Isabella relaxed against Juan Carlos, letting out her first relaxed breath of the long day. "We are free," she stated simply.

"No, Isabella, you are free. I will go back to Monterey to pay the consequences for my past choices."

"No, Juan Carlos!" She turned to face him. "They will let you hang. Why did you steal me away if you were only going to run back into danger? Surely, this will make things worse for you!"

"I am a preacher. I must obey the law. And I have been arrested," he reminded her.

"But you have made it worse for yourself by taking me away in the night. Why?" She stared angrily into his eyes.

"You are trouble to the general, and I was afraid his wife might harm you," he answered without looking at her. Instead, he steered the horse along the dirt path that led back to the rancho.

"The general's wife. Why should she care about me? Just because I stir her ridiculous jealousy?" Isabella crossed her arms, leaning against Juan Carlos again. She could not fathom why he would take such a chance.

He spoke evenly. "Señora Torena, the general's wife, was in love with Antonio Fremont, your husband-to-be."

Isabella gasped, sitting upright once again.

"He made her no offer of marriage, and she finally married the general after waiting a year for a proposal that never came. Her family disowned her for not marrying a true Califorñio, and I was worried she'd take her vengeance out on you."

Isabella shuddered at the thought of the cold, dark eyes that belonged to the general's wife. Suddenly the woman's chilling stares made sense—the hostility, the jealousy. She turned on the horse to speak directly to Juan Carlos. "I won't let you go back to Monterey. You can live in the stables; the Indians will help you."

Juan Carlos laughed. "Isabella, I am a former smuggler. If I wanted to run, I assure you, no one would ever find me, but I don't want to run. I want to preach the Word of God, and perhaps His will is for me to do that in prison, as Paul did."

"How can you just accept such a fate? Will you not

even try to save yourself?" Isabella was incredulous. She had always thought she lived for God, but Juan Carlos defied her beliefs. He was willing to give up his freedom for his faith—freedom that would have been his if she hadn't struggled so stubbornly for her own.

"It is not my job to save myself, Isabella. It is God's. You have tried to save yourself instead of letting God work His wonders for you. And here you are in the middle of the cold night on a horse with a former thief. You must trust in God, not just when times are good, but when they seem impossible. Only then will you see the true nature of God."

Isabella sighed. "But we could run together. I could go back to Pastor Sola's church and take care of him. Or I could just follow you." She felt like such a simpleton. She was so weak, weak and foolish. Only moments before she had been promising God that she would submit to her papa's wishes, and now she was throwing herself at a man who didn't want her.

"It is folly to covet what I cannot have," Juan Carlos said.

"Then you do have feelings for me?" she asked timidly.

She felt his warm breath alongside her ear and heard him whispering, "The first time I laid eyes on you, you pierced my heart to its very core. The look of joy you held in your sparkling eyes, so quickly replaced by sadness when you realized Pastor Sola was not with us. I will never forget that moment, Isabella. For it was then that I felt I had known you for a lifetime, that you would always be with me in my heart." He gallantly struck his arm over his chest, and she closed her eyes, treasuring his tender words.

"Then how can you ask me to marry another, when you feel as I do?" she questioned.

"You need only look at the trouble you brought upon yourself today, my little one. You are a Californio, I am a Spaniard. You know a life of luxury that I only knew as a child. . .and when I stole for it. God asks us to submit to Him. He asks us to honor our parents. You can only do that by marrying the man your papa has chosen for you. If you love me, you will honor your papa. I will have you home by morning, before the adobe rises, and you will go on with your life."

"You think I can just go on, knowing I have destroyed your chances for an honest life?"

"Isabella, you have nothing to feel guilty about. You made your choices, and I have made mine. I am not being punished for your sins, but for my own. When my father died, I made my choice. I entered a pirate ship of my own volition. I stole cargo from whaling ships, cowskins from rancheros, and jewelry from wealthy travelers."

"Then how did you come to know God if not from your parents?"

"My mother was Catholic and loved God with all her heart. But when she died shortly after my father, the church could not help me. They were too burdened with the needs of the local Indians. I had to go my own way. And I did, until Pastor Sola found me on a ship and told me of Jesus again. I had forgotten," he said softly. "I knew then I would turn my life over to God."

"So Pastor Sola saved both our lives," Isabella said.

"I suppose he did."

She felt herself relax once again, praying for God's mercy.

"Shh." Juan Carlos sat upright, and Isabella turned to watch him look around them. "Someone is following us. We're going to have to make a run for it. Hang on. Yah!"

The horse bolted into a full run, and Isabella suddenly heard the hooves that were indeed behind them. The chase escalated, and Juan Carlos's horse increased his speed. Isabella had never known a horse could go so quickly, and being in the darkness only magnified the effect.

She closed her eyes tightly, almost waiting to strike a tree, but the horse just kept running in the darkness with Juan Carlos guiding them safely. The wind whipped through her hair and she felt frozen to the bone, yet the horse raced on, swiftly and gracefully. They ran for what seemed like an eternity, but eventually Juan Carlos slowed the pace and steered them into a grove of trees, making the darkness even blacker. Suddenly a cabin appeared in the thick stand of trees.

"What is this place?" she whispered breathlessly.

"It's a smuggler's cabin. We'll be safe here until morning." He dismounted from the horse and took her frozen hands in his own. "Don't be afraid, Isabella, they'll never find us here."

Juan Carlos lit a fire in the hearth and read from his Bible by its light. After he had selected several passages, he stood. "I'll be outside just in case there's trouble. Get some sleep, Isabella. Tomorrow's a big day."

eight

The dawn was just breaking in the tranquil valley as Rancho de Arguello came into view. Isabella felt her heart in her throat at the sight of it. She was thankful for the familiarity and the safety it represented but fearful for her future and for that of Juan Carlos. Her papa's anger would not be silent, and this time she would pay a heavy toll for her rebellious actions.

She climbed off the horse, knowing it was the last time she would ever be in the comfort of Juan Carlos's arms, and she stared up at him longingly. "Juan Carlos, I—"

"Isabella, I must go. Your papa will not be kind if he finds me on his property. You are safe, and that's all that matters to me. I love you, Isabella. Pray, sweet one."

He spurred the black steed, and Isabella watched as the man she loved rode into the morning light. She fell to her knees on the grassy knoll near the adobe, sobbing for all she was losing.

"Isabella?" Victoria grabbed her and picked her up from the dirt. "Oh, Isabella, it's all right."

Isabella leaned into her older sister and continued

to cry. "They'll hang him, sister."

"They won't hang him. Papa will see to it," Victoria said to comfort her.

"The general hates him. He will surely hang, and it will be my fault. My foolishness, my selfishness," she wailed. "It will be as though I made the noose myself."

"No, Isabella, no. Papa would never let that happen. Pastor Sola trusted Señor Vega, and Papa will always insure Pastor Sola is taken care of."

"Victoria, leave us." Señor Arguello stood in the winter sun, a severe frown on his worn face.

Isabella looked up to him fearfully. "Papa, I'm sorry."

"Sorry! Isabella, it is a miracle you are alive. Where have you been all night?"

"I've been in Monterey. I snuck into Señor Vega's oxcart under the skins. Señor Vega was arrested by General Torena and taken away. Juan Carlos came for me in the middle of the night and returned me here, then went back to Monterey for his punishment."

Isabella's papa came down beside her and sat on the hard ground. She stared at him awkwardly, unsure of what to think of his uncharacteristic warmth. "Juan Carlos is a Spaniard, you know," he explained gently. "And Spaniards think less of Californios."

"Juan Carlos doesn't. He says we are all equal in Christ, and why would he have placed himself in danger to rescue me?"

"Yes, I admit I was wrong about Señor Vega. Only a decent man would have brought you back to us without alerting the Mexican soldiers. Not only are you safe, but your reputation is intact, thanks to Juan Carlos's restraint. He should be rewarded for his efforts," Señor Arguello said as if to convince himself.

"Papa, I was wrong to leave, to not listen to you. Juan Carlos told me that, and now I must beg something of you, Papa. Though I know I am in no position to ask for favors, I only ask that you would send word to Monterey and see that Juan Carlos's life is spared for his valiant rescue of me."

"Isabella, that is not an easy favor to grant." Señor Arguello stood, and she also got up. "The Mexican guards and the Californios already have a strained relationship. Juan Carlos was a thief before he became a preacher. He stole the hides and tallow that we work so hard for. If he is executed, it will be of his own doing." Señor Arguello looked disappointed.

"But Papa, he has changed," Isabella argued.

"I know he has, or he would have never brought you back to me," her father admitted. "I will do what I can, but your wedding is in one week and the preparations must be made. He is a Spaniard, a former nobleman of some kind. And the Mexicans don't want war, so his life should be spared. I will look into his release, Isabella. I will do what I can."

"I will help Mama immediately, Papa. And I will never disappoint you again, Papa. I'm sorry." She looked at him with sad brown eyes, and for a moment, she thought she saw tears in her rugged papa's eyes. How could she have ever questioned her papa's love? Yes, he held fast to the patriarchal system in place on the ranchos. And yes, his word was law, but there was a gentleness about her father. A warmth she'd never seen in the other rancheros.

He nodded in reply. Then, for the first time in her life, Isabella felt her father hug her, awkwardly at first, then tighter. She stood stiff in his embrace, unsure of how to react, but eventually she fell into his hug. Her throat tightened with emotion.

❋

Isabella helped her mother drape white muslin cloth from the rafters of the patio. Wispy, white material flowed in the afternoon breeze, and her mother placed handmade, faux flowers elegantly around the circumference of the adobe. The entire home was awash with a festive air, and as the Indians prepared the ingredients for the baked goods for the party, Isabella found herself becoming less anxious over her wedding. She faced it with a certain resignation, knowing that if her father was able to spare Juan Carlos from punishment, she could endure a marriage with Señor Fremont. During her prayer times, God had spoken to her, telling her not to be anxious, and strangely, she wasn't.

Visitors began arriving the following day for the week-long festivities, and Isabella was assigned to insuring their comfort until her wedding. Although it was customary for the bride to remain idle, Isabella's papa thought it best for her to keep busy. She watched her papa load up an oxcart full of cowskins and ride toward Monterey. Never before had she had so much respect for her papa. It was unheard of for a ranchero to deliver his own cowskins, but Señor Arguello obviously loved her enough to see to Juan Carlos's release on his own.

The sound of lowing permeated the ranch, and

Isabella looked outside to see a huge herd of cattle being rounded into the grazing lands. Their deep calls shattered all sense of quietness and peace. "That's what I'm worth," she said solemnly. "All those cows."

"Isabella!" her mama chastised.

"I'm sorry, Mama. I didn't mean it disrespectfully. It's just ominous to see my payment coming toward the adobe. I'm grateful for what you and Papa have done for me, really I am," Isabella said truthfully.

"I know you are, darling. You know, most women have to take the cows with them. If it wasn't for your beauty, you'd cost your papa quite a few California banknotes."

"I know. I'm glad Papa will get so many cattle."

"Your papa loves you so, Isabella. When you were gone, he cried like a baby." Isabella's mother held her hand.

"He did?" Isabella was stunned. Her papa was not given to showing emotions, and to know that he had actually shed tears filled her with an unidentifiable feeling.

"Yes, he did. It hurts him so much that you do not like Antonio Fremont, but he fears for your future if you stay here on the rancho. You must have a place of your own. Our land will go to Victoria's husband. Do you see now why your papa has promised you to Señor Fremont? It is not to make him wealthier. It is to insure your future."

"I know that now, Mama. I'm sorry I was so spoiled, so selfish. I will tell Papa immediately when he gets back," Isabella promised.

"He already knows, sweet. He would never say so, but he was hurt deeply when you ran away. He's only doing what's best for you, and sometimes that is painful."

"I know, Mama. Thank you." Isabella reached over and planted a swift kiss on her mother's cheek. "I'll go make sure the guests have everything they need."

nine

Isabella could hear her intended's obnoxious laughter from the other room. Luckily, Califorñio tradition prevented her from seeing him, and she didn't have to worry about being near him until the wedding day. She cringed at the thought of looking at him through the ceremony, but she would not be ungrateful again. And if she had to stare at him lovingly for her parents' sake, she would, no matter how much acting it took.

Isabella waited patiently for her papa's return, creating more fake flowers for the trellis over the patio; but when the darkness began to descend upon the landscape, keeping her hands occupied no longer soothed her mind. Just as the last of the sun slipped past the top of the mountain, Isabella saw her papa approaching. She ran to him, desperate for news and thankful for his safe return.

"Papa, Papa!"

He dismounted and looked at her sadly. "I'm sorry, my dear. There's no word. The general would not give me any information, but Juan Carlos was not at the jail. I asked several witnesses, and they said he had been taken away. Isabella, I'm sorry. No one knew where they took him."

Isabella broke down. "Papa, I love him. You don't think they'll kill him?" she inquired frantically.

"Shh. You must not say such things. Señor Fremont may hear. Juan Carlos is still a Spanish citizen, so most likely they shipped him back to his country, safe and sound. Whatever happens, it is no longer your concern," he said firmly.

But Isabella thought her father seemed preoccupied with something, something he didn't dare share with her. She thought she saw fear in his eyes.

"Papa, thank you for going to Monterey. I'm sorry I haven't been more grateful. I love you, Papa."

Her father was clearly uncomfortable at her emotional outburst. "Go help your mama," he ordered, dismissing her.

"Papa," she continued tentatively. "I trust you." Then she turned on her heels and ran into the house.

Isabella took out the family Bible and stared at it determinedly. She practiced the words she knew, looking for them within the great book. "Jee-sus," she pronounced cautiously. "God. Luv."

The next morning at daybreak, her papa galloped away on his favorite mare. Isabella couldn't imagine where her father might be headed on such an important day as the beginning of her wedding celebration, but she dismissed it, thinking he was probably just checking on the vaqueros' morning rounds.

When he didn't return by the next afternoon, Señora Arguello was calming the gathering of well-wishers, assuring them her husband would return by the evening to give his daughter away in marriage.

Isabella spent her day in prayer, preparing to meet the end of life as she knew it on her familiar rancho. Soon she would be Señora Antonio Fremont and have a rancho of her own. She solemnly prayed to her heavenly Father, still beseeching Him to intervene, but outwardly accepting her fate.

"Mama?" Isabella spoke to her mother. Señora Arguello jumped with alarm. "Mama, where is Papa?"

"He'll be here," she said sternly, wringing her hands nervously.

"Mama, it will be nightfall soon. The guests are beginning to wonder at his disappearance. He should be here to entertain our guests," Isabella said.

"Isabella, is this your rancho?"

"No, Mama, I just—"

"Then don't question your papa again, do you understand? I would think you would have learned by now that your papa knows what he's doing," Isabella's mother snapped uncharacteristically.

"Mama, I'm sorry." Her mother's reaction frightened Isabella.

Señora Arguello put a palm up. "I don't want to hear that again, Isabella. If you are going to be a wife, you are going to have to learn your proper role. This questioning attitude must disappear. Instead of saying I'm sorry all the time, why don't you learn how to keep your mouth in check?"

"Yes, Mama. I'm sor—"

"Go check and see if the Indians are done with the cake," Señora Arguello ordered.

"Yes, Mama, I'll see to it right now." Isabella curtsied

and ran into the house. She knew the cake was fine, so she simply went to her room. Victoria was there, packing Isabella's trunk.

"That's the last of it. Mama made you a fine trousseau, but I'm afraid the gowns are nothing compared to what you will be able to afford as the owner of California's biggest rancho. Papa says you can see the ocean on one side of your rancho and the great hills on the other and that everything in between belongs to Señor Fremont."

"Is that a fact?" Isabella said absently.

"Isabella, if you're still dreaming of that Spanish preacher, it's best to start thinking of your own husband. God will not honor such deceitful behavior," Victoria reprimanded.

"I'm not thinking of Juan Carlos, Victoria. I'm thinking of Papa. Where could he be on my wedding day? When he has become the most important Californio in all the territory, what could be more important than giving his daughter away?"

"I don't know, Isabella, but I'm sure as women, it's none of our concern."

"Victoria, Mama is not here, so you do not need to pretend you're not worried. Papa loves a good fiesta. Something is wrong. We must pray."

"You're right." The two women got down on their knees and held hands.

"Dear Father in heaven, we are so worried about our papa, and we know You know where he is. Please keep him safe. Lord, we just ask that You would bring him back soon and that You watch over him."

"Yes, Father, we pray that whatever Papa is doing, You are with him," Victoria added.

"Amen," they said in unison.

ten

The sun was nearly over the lowest peak when they heard the loud gallop of several horses. Anxiously looking out the small portal, Isabella saw her papa leading several men in Mexican uniform. "Soldiers!" she announced frightfully.

"Where?" Victoria came to the opening and gasped. "What could they want with Papa?"

Isabella drew in a sharp breath. "The woman with them! That's Señora Torena, the woman who was so vile to me in Monterey."

"Isabella, look! Pastor Vega is with them."

"Juan Carlos is here," she whispered numbly, her breath momentarily forgotten. She let it out with a deep sigh. "He's safe, oh thank the dear Lord, he is safe. Let us go!" Isabella said excitedly.

"No! We must wait for Papa. This can only mean trouble, and we have no place in it. Perhaps the soldiers are taking Juan Carlos away." Victoria's words reminded Isabella of Juan Carlos's troubles.

"Perhaps they are here for someone else," she answered hopefully. "Perhaps they are here for the ceremony."

"Isabella, Juan Carlos has been arrested. He will not be set free without a trial of the Mexican officials."

"What would Señora Torena be doing here?" Isabella looked at the darkened eyes that had frightened her so deeply days before, and she shuddered. "It cannot be anything good," Isabella admitted.

"No, it cannot. There must be a hundred soldiers with them."

"Perhaps I will not have to marry Señor Fremont after all," Isabella said brightly.

"What would the general's wife being here have to do with you marrying Señor Fremont? Isabella, I thought you had submitted wholly to this marriage."

Isabella opened her mouth to tell her sister that Señora Torena was once in love with Antonio Fremont, but she slapped it shut when she realized Juan Carlos had told her that information in confidence. It was not meant as idle gossip. "I am committed. I will do whatever Papa asks of me. He promised me he would help Juan Carlos, and it seems he has. I can ask nothing more."

It wasn't long before their mama came in to get them. "Girls, come now! Your father wants you on the patio."

"But, Mama, Señor Fremont will see me before the wedding," Isabella reluctantly reminded her. But her true fear was that Juan Carlos would watch her marry another. How could she look into the eyes of the man she loved and say "I do" to another?

"Your papa says to come," Señora Arguello replied firmly. "Now is not the time to argue tradition."

They walked swiftly to the outdoor patio, throwing on their shawls to protect them from the crisp night air. Isabella caught Juan Carlos's eye, and he smiled warmly at her, giving her more confidence. He didn't look frightened but curious as to why they were assembled. She returned a shy smile, and he winked at her. She felt her heart skip a beat and looked away from the warm, brown eyes she'd thought she'd never see again. _Thank You, God. Now I know he is safe._

Señora Torena's eyes thinned at the sight of Isabella in her wedding gown, and Isabella felt all the fear from Monterey invade her body. She trembled under the icy glances the señora gave her, and she felt herself shiver. Pulling her shawl tightly around her shoulders, she focused on her papa, who cleared his throat.

"Senors and Senoras, I know that you have come here today expecting a wedding, but there will not be one," Señor Arguello announced to astonished eyes and collective gasps. "We will celebrate the Navidad in three days as usual, and I hope that you will all stay with us for the celebration. Father Pico has agreed to stay on with us."

Señor Fremont looked the most surprised of all. "What is the meaning of this? I have paid you a fair dowry, and now you deny me my bride!" He grabbed Isabella harshly, and she felt his fingers dig into her arm.

Señora Torena shouted angrily, "She does not love you, you fool! Let go of her. She is young enough to be your granddaughter! I have come to save you the humiliation of another child bride! You have destroyed my reputation, so there is nothing to stop me from telling you what an old fool you are. Everyone's thinking it, but no one is brave enough to tell you. I have nothing left to lose, Antonio. Nothing!" The vengeance in Señora Torena's voice was nothing like Isabella had ever heard. There must have been a great deal of pain for her to ride out to the rancho just to make such a scene.

"You will let go of my daughter now!" Señor Arguello stepped forward, but the soldiers came instead, rescuing Isabella from Señor Fremont's tight grip. Her papa continued to speak. "Amigos, I have a very sad announcement to make today. One that pains me greatly. It seems one of our own, a Californio, has become a traitor."

Another gasp erupted from the gathering, and Isabella felt herself swoon. She would not marry Señor Fremont today. Did anything else matter?

"Dare you insult a Californio in front of outsiders?" a ranchero yelled, upset over the Mexican army's presence.

"Mexico has domain over this land, whether we like it or not. Mexico granted us our land, and Mexico enforces its boundaries. It is the law whether we like it or not," Señor Arguello reminded them. "Without Mexico's militia, we are powerless to defend our land, do you deny that?"

"Who do you bring charges against?" Juan Carlos asked, shifting the conversation.

"Señor Antonio Fremont!" Señor Arguello pointed at the man he had supposedly given Isabella to, and a scowl of hatred overtook the older ranchero's eyes. Señor Arguello continued his charges. "He has stolen land

76

from us. Without a thought or care should Spain come to retrieve its land from all of us, defeating Mexico's armies."

"Lies!" Señor Fremont pointed an accusing finger at his attacker.

Señor Arguello held up a portfolio of papers. "I hold here the original *disuenos*, the maps drawn by the Mexican government. I think you'll see how our land grants compare with what we hold today." He threw the maps on a table, and the assembly studied the boundaries carefully. Though none of them could read, they knew their land well enough to know the maps gave them substantially more land than they actually held in their possession.

"What is the meaning of this?" a ranchero inquired.

"Señor Fremont and General Torena. They have redrawn the maps. Years ago, when General Torena took possession of the territory as a brigadier general, he wanted a wife of Califorñio birth to insure his future in the post. Señor Fremont traded his intended, Señora Torena, for the original maps. Señor Fremont got the land intended for Señor Juan Carlos Vega's father, as well as some of our own property. In trade, General Torena received thousands of California banknotes a year and a Califorñio bride, Señora Torena. These men stole the grant. They have used their power to confiscate the land. Our land. Juan Carlos, please."

Señor Arguello held his hand out, beckoning the preacher to look at the map. "Your papa's land is here, swallowed up by Señor Fremont and his holdings. I have the deed in my pocket." He patted his heart. "It will be yours once again."

Señor Fremont started to run, but he was stopped easily by the mass of soldiers, who tied up his hands and threw him to the ground.

Señora Torena's evil, haughty grin filled her face. "You should have never underestimated me, Antonio. I might have lived my entire life silent, but when you chose to mock me by marrying this child. . .I found the maps!"

"Where is General Torena?" Señor Fremont asked. "He can verify my story."

"He's gone, Antonio," Señora Torena answered. "He ran to Mexico, and he won't be back to pay the price. You'll pay it alone. I warned him because he treated me well." She let out a long, loud laugh.

Juan Carlos traced his father's land with his finger, confusion reigning on his face.

"Juan Carlos!" Isabella could not help herself. She ran to his side to comfort him. "Juan Carlos, you are free!" She broke into a sob. In the flash of a moment, her marriage to Antonio Fremont was off and Juan Carlos was an officially recognized Californio by the Mexican government.

He rubbed his temples roughly, then looked to the Mexican soldiers. "What does this mean?" he asked the leader.

The soldier took the papers from Señor Arguello and studied them thoroughly before answering. "Señorita is right. You are free." He handed the papers to Juan Carlos, clicked his heels, and led away his men and their prisoner, Señor Antonio Fremont. "We will camp on the rancho until first light."

"*Gracias,* Lieutenant," Señor Arguello answered.

The fiesta band took a cue and began strumming their guitars and playing their horns. All other sounds and the gossip were drowned out by the cheery tunes, though no one felt like dancing or celebrating. Each ranchero was anxious to get a closer look at the map to see where he had been cheated. Juan Carlos seemed numb, and Isabella thought perhaps he was best left alone for a while. She moved away from him slowly, realizing no one thought her action the least bit curious since they were so involved in their own problems. Once she knew she wouldn't be missed, she exited the patio, running for her favorite quiet place.

Juan Carlos watched Isabella flee from the gathering, and he cringed at his callous self-concern when she'd just been humiliated in front of the rancheros. He was just so overwhelmed. He assessed his father's land carefully. It was all there, the fertile coastland property his Spaniard father had been assessed to keep a Spanish presence in the California territory. He'd just been given his life back, but he had no idea what to do with it.

Now that Isabella, his true love, was free, could he marry her? Would her papa allow such a marriage? His property made him an official Californio by Mexico's account, but the Californios were a tightly woven bunch. Would they ever accept him as their own? Certainly there were many men willing to pay for Isabella's hand in marriage. Payment with cattle he didn't own. He needed to pray, but first he needed to find Isabella and comfort her torn heart. She had been on the verge of a huge cliff, ready to jump into a marriage she clearly didn't want, and suddenly her impending marriage ceremony—the reason everyone had gathered—was dropped like a hot branding iron, without a thought to her feelings.

He found her on the back patio in tears. "Isabella?"

She looked up, then away. A lone torch caused the tears on her cheeks to glisten.

"I thought this was what you wanted? To be free from Señor Fremont."

"It is, but I am so overwhelmed. Papa told me nothing of his suspicions until all our family and neighbors were standing there. Just yesterday Papa was telling me Señor Fremont would take care of me, and today, I have no idea what will become of me."

A young ranchero came and announced his presence with a cough. "Ahem. Preacher Vega, would you mind if I spoke with Isabella alone?"

Juan Carlos felt his jaw clench at the sight of a young suitor already. "Yes, I would mind, Señor. The señorita is in need of prayer and counseling, young man. Please, your conversation can wait."

The young ranchero gave him a vicious look before sulking away.

"You see, there are many men who will willingly take Señor Fremont's place." *I am willing to take Señor Fremont's place*, he thought.

Her tears flowed freely. "How can you say such a thing to me? Do you think I kiss men freely? You still think of me as a child when I love you as a woman!" She ran into the adobe and left him alone to contemplate his poorly chosen words. He had tried to ease her pain and instead increased it. How foolish he'd been. Of course he loved her. Why hadn't he just said that?

❋

Isabella sat in her darkened room alone, weeping for her broken pride. She had finally relented to marrying the old, squalid ranchero when her father released her at the most embarrassing opportunity, her wedding celebration. Everyone on the neighboring ranchos now knew she was discarded material. Of course men wanted to marry her anyway, but she had nothing to do with that. It was that cursed beauty they said she possessed, something she had nothing to do with. *It is a curse,* she thought. *Juan Carlos will never own the cattle to marry me, and so I will be offered to the highest bidder once again. Just like the cattle auction at the annual rodeo.*

Although her pride was wounded by being jilted on her wedding day, it was really Juan Carlos's words that hurt the most. He'd been given enough land to acquire cattle, and she had thought he would at least try to ask for her hand. Even if her papa wouldn't give her to him, the young preacher could have at least tried. His apathy told her his true feelings. Any man who truly loved her would have taken a chance to make her his bride. As she sat sobbing, a knock sounded at the door. She took her sleeve and wiped her eyes.

"Yes?" she tried to say as calmly as possible.

"Isabella, it's Victoria." Her sister opened the door, and the light from the candle she held lit her face. "Juan Carlos is on the patio. He wants to speak with you."

"No," she sniffled.

"Isabella, he's leaving tonight. It may be the last

time you see him. After all he's done for you, you owe him a decent good-bye," Victoria reprimanded. "Get your shawl on and get out on the patio, or I shall let him into your room." The expression on Victoria's well-lit face told Isabella her sister was not bluffing. "You keep saying everyone treats you like a child. Well quit acting like one!"

Isabella rose and grabbed her shawl quickly. Just that morning, she had feared for his very life, prayed for his safety, and tonight she was angry because he didn't return her love. What a child she had been! Her sister was right. She dashed to the patio and found Juan Carlos under the bright torchlight.

He looked up, his deep brown eyes showing his sympathy. "I'm sorry, Isabella." He came to her and took her hand. His touch sent a familiar shock through her frame.

"No, it is I who should be sorry. This morning I prayed to God for your safety, and I am so grateful that He has answered my prayer. To ask for more is greedy. God has granted me my wish. You are safe, and I am free of Señor Fremont."

He brushed her long hair behind her shoulder with the back of his hand. "This morning I was a criminal and this evening I am a ranchero. It is too much to comprehend." His jaw tensed. "I just wanted to be a preacher. Yet, He has given me this land, and I don't know why. I do know that I love you, Isabella. You must believe that."

"But you will leave anyway, and you will not take me with you, will you?"

He tipped her chin and pleaded to her with his eyes, but she turned away.

"I must go," he said quietly. "I must find the general. He has disappeared, and I can track him. He's not a simple man. He will not be able to live outside the city and its delights for long."

"No!" she said fearfully. "Let someone else go. You are a Califorñio now. This is not your concern!"

"It is." He forced her gaze to his once again. "The general needs to be in prison for his deeds. I can put him there, and I must. To ignore it is to allow evil to reign."

"No, it's the Mexican army's problem, not yours!" she pleaded.

"I will return, Isabella. Count on it." With those words, he strode away from the adobe.

He would return, Isabella realized, but in all likelihood, she would already be married, sold for the greatest number of cattle.

eleven

C hristmas morning held no joy for Isabella. The house was awash with eucalyptus wreaths and pyracantha berries in celebration, but the day seemed desolate to her. The priest would come from the mission to say Christmas Mass that very evening, and her papa would most likely announce her engagement. But to whom? That remained the question.

Victoria brought in Isabella's gown for the evening's religious ceremony. Her wedding gown had been cleaned and pressed by the Indian servants, leaving no hint to its history. Looking upon the glorious Spanish lace creation, Isabella could only think of Juan Carlos. Where was he? It had been three days, and no word of the general's whereabouts had been sent to the rancheros staying at Rancho de Arguello.

"Isabella, look at your gown. The Indians have sewn a red sash on it. Isn't it the most beautiful thing you've ever laid eyes on?" Victoria asked cheerfully.

"Yes, it's wonderful," Isabella agreed. She stood and picked up the dress. "I have been in prayer for three days for Juan Carlos, but I must trust in the Lord. That is one reason He sent His Son—so that we could be free of this bondage of worry," Isabella proclaimed. "I have trusted in myself alone, and Papa chastised me for it rightly."

"Isabella, you are back!" her sister said in delight, hugging her tightly.

"Let us go string pyracantha berries in the grand room. Mama will love it! The room will sparkle with the bright color." Isabella grabbed her sister's hand, and they dashed out to the patio to collect the berries.

Once outside, Isabella giggled in between renditions of their favorite Spanish hymns. For the first time in months, she felt wrapped in the arms of her Lord, trusting in Him fully. Her papa's stern voice brought her from her reverie.

"Isabella!" he said sharply.

"Yes, Papa?" She stood up straight. This was it. Her papa had probably promised her to another ranchero and had come to give her the name of the man who would become her husband.

"Come here, my child. Victoria, go see if your mother needs anything. Your husband will be off the range soon enough."

"Yes, Papa." She curtsied and ran for the adobe.

"Isabella, you said when you returned from your. . . trip to Monterey that you trusted me. Is that true?" he asked.

"Yes, Papa. You saved Juan Carlos from the gallows, even when you thought you couldn't. And you saved me from marriage to Señor Fremont." She said the name with distaste.

"Isabella, you must find a husband, you know this?"

"Yes, Papa, I know this," she agreed.

"And you will trust my judgment from here on out, correct? No running away, no childish tantrums." He crossed his arms.

"Papa, I—"

"Isabella, when I make a decision for you, I make it because I know things you cannot know. Do you understand that?" he asked sternly.

"Of course, but—"

He pointed at her. "When you ran away, it was only by the grace of God you were kept safe. Juan Carlos was a thief and a smuggler, but he had the good sense to bring you home untouched."

"Juan Carlos is a man of God, Papa!" she answered excitedly. "And he is a ranchero now, a Califorñio by all accounts," she reminded him.

"He was born in Spain. The other rancheros will always see him as a Spaniard."

She knew to argue was pointless. Her father's mind regarding Juan Carlos was clearly made up. "Why did you rescue him if you think him no better than a common thief?"

"He is the one who told me of the true *disuenos*, the maps from Mexico. He obviously didn't know of his own holdings, or he would not have been in prison. When I remembered Señora Torena, I knew she'd be eager to take her revenge upon Antonio Fremont."

"Papa, don't you see? Juan Carlos gave you back your land. He is no longer a smuggler."

Her father's tone was without emotion. "Juan Carlos is a good man, but he has no holdings, Señorita. Now, before we discuss your wedding plans, I must have your word that you will trust me from the beginning this time. No more waiting until the last minute to listen to my plans for you."

"Yes, Papa, I will marry whom you choose without question," she promised.

❅

That evening the celebrants gathered for the annual Christmas service and the priest read from the Scriptures about Christ's birth and the road it offered back to heaven. The words offered Isabella hope and gave her a confidence that she hadn't possessed before her trial of obedience. She bowed low and took communion with heartfelt repentance and overflowing thankfulness.

Afterward, her papa made an announcement. "Friends and neighbors, what a great deal we have to be thankful for this Christmas evening. My daughter has been delivered from a disastrous marriage, and she has obediently offered to marry the man I have chosen for her."

Isabella's heart beat rapidly at her father's proclamation. He was going to announce her fiancé's name to the entire group before she was aware of the name herself. She steeled herself for the name, trying to slow her rapid breathing and prepare for whatever name he announced. She turned all the possibilities over in her head, hoping for the lesser of several evils.

"And tonight, in honor of my daughter's faithful compliance to the future I have selected for her, I ask you all to celebrate in the wedding of my youngest child this very evening."

Isabella dropped to the floor in a heap, and when she

awoke, her mama was fanning her with an imported, fluted fan. "Isabella, get up," she whispered through clenched teeth.

Isabella rose flushed and swallowed the huge lump in her throat. The priest waited at the makeshift altar, and her papa held out his arm to walk her down the short aisle. Her sister came to her side and threw a lace veil over her face, and before she knew it, Isabella was being escorted down the aisle to the strains of the Spanish bridal march. Her weakened legs struggled to make the ten short steps. She had passed out cold before her papa had announced her betrothed and so had no idea who she was marrying.

From the side door of the adobe, she saw Juan Carlos enter, and she blinked several times to make sure she wasn't seeing things. She looked to her father questioningly, and a twinkle touched his eyes. "You see, my dear," he whispered. "You should trust your papa."

Juan Carlos reached for her willingly and led her before the priest, securely wrapping his muscular arm around her waist. His touch sent her soaring with excitement, still unable to fathom if it were real or if she were in a sweet dream. Isabella looked back at her father for confirmation, and he smiled and winked, taking her mother into his own arms.

Isabella faced the man she loved, the man who had made her believe she was more than a whimsical child who delighted in the simple pleasures on the rancho. He had opened her eyes to new sights and adventures, and she relished the idea of a lifetime with such a man. She didn't know where they would live, how they would make a living, or if they would even settle into one place, but neither did she care. She would willingly travel the world to be at the side of a man like Juan Carlos Vega.

The priest began the ceremony, and Juan Carlos smiled down at her, his straight jaw clean-shaven and brushed with the scent of eucalyptus oil. She inhaled deeply to make sure she was awake and felt invigorated by the masculine, woodsy scent.

"Do you, Juan Carlos Vega, nobleman of Spain and recognized Califorñio, take this woman, Isabella Arguello, to be your lawfully wedded wife? To love, honor, and cherish as long as you both shall live?"

"I do," he answered through a smile, his brown eyes mere slivers in their joy.

"Do you, Isabella Arguello, daughter of Califorñio Jose Arguello, take this man, Juan Carlos Vega, to be your lawfully wedded husband? To have and to hold, to honor and obey, as long as you both shall live?"

Isabella couldn't prevent a small giggle from escaping. "I do!" she said happily.

"Then, by the power vested in me by the holy church, I now pronounce you man and wife." The priest finished by announcing to the people witnessing the ceremony, "May I present to you, Señor and Señora Juan Carlos Vega."

The solemn congregation let out a holler, and the mariachi band broke into a bright fandango. The festivities had begun, and the crowds gathered around them to wish them the best.

Isabella was overwhelmed by the well-wishers, and she searched the room desperately for her papa. Seeing him across the room, she looked to her new husband. "Juan Carlos, I must speak with my papa," she whispered. He nodded knowingly, and she dashed through the crowds, smiling at all the congratulatory remarks.

At last she reached her father's side. "Papa, I don't understand. How is it that Juan Carlos should be my husband?"

"He owned the most cattle," her papa said simply.

"But he owns no cattle!" she answered in further confusion.

"This morning he owned no cattle, this evening he is the proud holder of five thousand head of cattle. He will make a fine son-in-law." Her papa grinned. "He is a true Califorñio as a land-grant holder, which insures the future of the territory. And he was baptized Catholic according to church records. He is everything I planned for you."

"Papa, where did Juan Carlos get five thousand cattle?"

"I gave them to him," he said simply.

"Papa, why? You say you could get another thousand cattle for my marriage, but you chose to give up five thousand more for me. I don't understand." She shook her head.

"Someday when you have children of your own, you will. I love you, Isabella. Be a good wife."

"I will," she promised.

He kissed her on the cheek. "Go find your husband. And do not question his authority as you questioned mine."

"Of course not, Papa."

"Go, Isabella, go and live your Navidad de sueños, your Christmas of dreams. I would do anything to give you the gift of your heart, and God has made it possible."

twelve

The fiesta lasted late into the night until at last Isabella had her husband alone on the patio. "Oh, Juan Carlos, I cannot believe you are truly my husband." She looked at the fire's bright reflection in her exquisitely carved gold band. "This ring is a masterpiece. I have never seen real gold before. Where did you get it?"

"In Monterey, after I had the general arrested," he announced proudly. "One day when Pastor Sola and I were on the mission field, we stopped to make soup from wild onions in the fields. When I pulled an onion from the earth, that gold nugget on your finger was attached to the roots. I had it made into a ring as soon as your papa said yes to my proposal a few days ago."

"My papa said yes a few days ago?" She looked at him incredulously.

"I knew months ago," he whispered, kissing her softly behind her ear. "When I saw you, I knew some how, some way, God would make you mine. I felt it the first moment our eyes locked. Your papa was determined to get those maps and make our wish come true. And he knew just how to do it. It is true what they say of a woman scorned." He brushed her lips gently with a kiss. "Let us go."

"Go? Where would we go? It's the middle of the night," she asked, not caring if he took her to Spain itself.

"I have prepared a honeymoon suite worthy of my bride." He bowed before her.

His talk of travel sparked her curiosity. "Will you continue to preach?" she asked, suddenly realizing that she had no idea what the future held.

"Of course I will," he said, kissing her cheek.

"Will you be a ranchero?"

"I suppose if I own five thousand cattle, I will be," he said, tracing her lips with his finger.

"Juan Carlos, you are not answering me."

"Yes, I am. You just want to know more than is necessary. Do you believe I will take care of you?"

"Always."

"Do you believe I will make sure you are fed, clothed, and given shelter each and every night?"

"Absolutely."

"Then what more do you need to know?"

"Nothing," she admitted.

"Good, let us go." He helped her upon his horse, and he wrapped his Spanish cape around them both, surrounding her with his warmth.

"Where are we going?"

"Tsk, tsk. Will you never learn?" He held back his smile, but she could hear it in his voice.

Once again, the horse was in full gallop with only the moon and stars to light their path. She closed her eyes and allowed the wind to whip against her face, its cold sting fruitless against her rejoicing, warm heart. She snuggled closer to Juan Carlos, not caring where he led her or even if their ride would end. How could their destination possibly have any effect on her mood? She had been granted her fondest wish on Christ's birthday.

The horse seemed to know its route and slowed to a quiet, gentle pace under a blanket of starlight. Isabella kept silently thanking God, praising Him for the gift and miracle of Juan Carlos Vega, her husband.

It seemed mere seconds before they arrived at the smuggler's cabin where they had spent the night after escaping Monterey—he on the outside of the cabin, and she on the inside. Juan Carlos once again helped her from the horse.

"My lady." He gallantly held out his arm and invited her to open the door.

Once she did, she gasped in surprise. "Oh, Juan Carlos!" she exclaimed, bringing her hand to her mouth. In place of the cold, sparse, dirty redwood cabin she'd visited earlier was an immaculate cozy honeymoon cottage. An elegant, carved bed from Spain dominated the little room, and candles were set everywhere. A roaring fire was lit in the fireplace. Eucalyptus petals were strewn on the bed and floor, giving an inviting, earthy scent.

"How did you do all this? Who started the fire? What—?"

He put a finger to her lips. "Shh. I can't tell you all my secrets." He took her by the hand. "Now I have one more gift for you to wish you a *Feliz Navidad.*"

She shook her head violently. "No, Juan Carlos. I think my heart may burst if I receive something else. God has been so good. My papa has given me in marriage to the only man I will ever love and the cattle to start our own rancho, and best of all, I am Señora Juan Carlos Vega." She threw her hand to her heart and giggled.

He laughed at her and placed a kiss on her forehead. "These pearls were my mama's. I became a thief before parting with these, and while I'm not proud of my sins, I am glad their beauty will hang on the long, beautiful neck of my beloved Isabella."

She fingered the string of pearls gingerly. "Oh Juan, I have never seen anything so beautiful. They shimmer!"

"Like your eyes, my darling. You deserve nothing less, but before you think you will live the same life of luxury you are accustomed to, you must know of my plans for the Rancho de Carmel and the cattle your papa has entrusted us with."

"We will not live there?" she asked in shock.

"God has called me to preach. We shall leave the management of the rancho to Pastor Sola, and while we are young enough, we will travel the California Territory and tell of God's miracles."

"Together?" she asked. She had never heard of a woman on the preaching circuit.

"I would have it no other way. The money from the cattle will allow us to travel freely, and Pastor Sola can retire comfortably at the rancho. I will teach you to read, and we can travel until we have children," he said softly.

Isabella felt a blush rise in her cheeks. She nodded in agreement. "It's perfect." As Juan Carlos stopped her words with a kiss, Isabella felt a warmth she had never known. Although she had lived on the rancho her entire life, it was on this night in an abandoned smuggler's cabin that she knew she was truly home. And though her future might be uncertain, she knew she would always be in God's hands, where she belonged.

Kristin Billerbeck

Kristin Billerbeck was born and raised in Redwood City, California, to a father who loved history and who dragged the family around to all the historic sites. Now Kristin shares her father's love for history and drags her kids along to the same sites. She makes her home in the Silicon Valley with her real-life hero: Bryed, an engineering director for a high-tech firm. They have three sons under four, so writing time is limited, but stolen moments are greatly appreciated. In addition to writing, she enjoys painting, reading, and conversing with her on-line writing groups. She has three published novels in the **Heartsong Presents** series.

DREAMS

Peggy Darty

one

August 15, 1894
Pine Ridge, Alabama

Caroline Cushman sat on the board seat of the one-mule wagon as her grandmother gripped the worn reins and guided Ol' Bill down the red clay road.

"Granny, how many times do you reckon you've driven this road?" Caroline smiled tenderly at her grandmother.

"Oh, child, I can't count that high. Spent my life here at Pine Ridge and only left a few times. Never could wait to get back."

Caroline sighed. "I know I'm going to be homesick. But I want to make you proud."

"I'm already proud of you, Caroline!"

Caroline was a slim, five feet, six inches with hair as dark as a raven's wing, pulled back from her oval face in a neat bun and secured with the black satin bow she had made the night before. Her deep blue eyes were large and wide-set, fringed with dark lashes. The round nose and mouth contrasted to her square chin, a determined chin—just like her father's, Granny often boasted. Her cheeks were smooth hollows, her cheekbones soft ridges. Her complexion, normally a smooth ivory, was still tanned from the summer sun, for she had worked many long hours out in the vegetable garden beside her grandmother. Selling vegetables was their main source of income, and Caroline had planted, hoed, gathered vegetables, and sold or canned them with Granny for most of her life.

Suddenly, all their years together blended into one sweet memory as Caroline glanced again at her grandmother. A tower of strength resided in the seventy-year-old body, and although her hair was white and her tanned face deeply lined, there was still a joy for life that gleamed in her bright blue eyes and quick smile.

Caroline reached across to touch her grandmother's hand. "Thanks for all you've done for me," she said, her throat tight.

"I think we're about even," Belle said, squinting down the road. "You've been a blessing from God after so much tragedy. First my beloved Clarence, then your parents. . . ." She broke off for only a second, then continued bravely. "I'd 'ave shriveled up and died with them if I hadn't the gift of you to raise."

Caroline's blue eyes swept the Alabama hills, and for one anxious moment, she wondered if she could bear to leave the only home she had ever known. Well, there *had* been another home, but she was too young to remember it. As a child she often had nightmares of flames and smoke; she would wake up screaming. Then Granny would be at her bed, hugging her, assuring

Caroline she was safe.

The wagon rattled on, making the last turn into Pine Ridge. The Nashville-Birmingham train ran along the tracks opposite the storefronts once a day at twelve o'clock. If a red flag hung from the pole beside the platform, the train stopped to pick up a passenger or some cargo going into Birmingham. If there was no flag, the train never slowed down.

Her eyes flew to the pole. The red flag was flying. "I'm glad Mr. Willingham didn't forget to put up the flag."

"He wouldn't dare!"

The front door of the general store opened and Frank Willingham lumbered out, hands thrust in the pockets of his overalls.

"Morning, Belle. Caroline." He angled down the front steps to wait as Ol' Bill trudged into the vacant spot at the hitching rail. Then he reached into the wagon and removed Caroline's suitcase. "Young lady, you're the only person from the ridge ever to go off to college."

"To Davis University," Granny spoke the words proudly. "The good Lord blessed my child with a real sharp mind," Belle stated, braking the wagon and hopping down as spryly as a teenager.

Caroline lifted the long skirt of her blue cotton dress and planted her black ankle boots firmly on the ground. The boots had been a gift from the Women's Missionary Society, and everything else she owned had been sewn by her and her grandmother during many a long night at the treadle sewing machine.

"Train's on time," Frank said, crossing the street with her little suitcase as Granny and Caroline hurried after him.

In the distance, the chug-chug of the approaching train filled the summer day, and both Caroline and her grandmother looked north until they spotted the train, like a giant cockroach, lurching toward them.

Suddenly, a feeling of panic clutched at Caroline's stomach. Could she really do this? Could she really go off to a world of strangers?

She whirled to her grandmother and met a glow of pride in the blue eyes that looked Caroline up and down. "You look mighty pretty, Caroline. Just don't go forgetting any of the morals you've been taught."

Caroline shook her head, close to tears. "I won't. I couldn't."

Her arms flew around her grandmother, who was shorter by several inches and weighed no more than a hundred pounds. The scent of lilac engulfed Caroline, and she knew that whenever she thought of Granny, she would always recall the pleasant sachet she wore. Despite her efforts, Caroline couldn't hold back the tears.

"Now don't do that or I'll start blubberin'," Granny scolded, turning pale. "We already talked about this. You're gonna write and it ain't that long till Christmas."

Caroline sniffed. "I know."

The train's whistle and then a screech of brakes ended their conversation. Caroline turned, squaring her shoulders, as a little man rushed down the train steps and reached for her suitcase and ticket.

"Good-bye, Mr. Willingham," she called.

"Good-bye, Caroline. You do your granny proud, now. You hear?"

She nodded, blinking. "I'll do my best."

"All aboard," the little man said, interrupting their emotional good-byes.

Belle's arms flew around her in a tight hug, then with an even mightier strength pushed Caroline forward. "Go now."

Taking a deep breath, Caroline lifted her skirt and climbed the steps to enter the train. She located a seat near the window and looked out at Mr. Willingham and Granny. Caroline waved again, trying to memorize every feature of the little woman she loved so much.

Then the train was speeding off and tiny Pine Ridge gave way to rolling green hills. She pressed her head against the seat and closed her eyes, praying for courage and guidance in the coming days. Comfortable and warm, Caroline soon forgot everything as her eyelids grew heavy after a sleepless night.

Sometime later the conductor's voice jolted her awake.

"Bir-ming-ham," he announced, walking down the aisle.

She sat up, staring wide-eyed through the window. The train was puffing into the station and her eyes flew over the waiting crowd. In her last letter from Davis University, she had been informed that a Miss Agnes Miller, Dean of Students, would meet her train. She smoothed her hair in place, straightened her dress, and summoned her courage.

When she stepped tentatively onto the platform

and scanned the sea of strangers, she spotted a small, handmade sign that bore her name. A blond woman in a gray taffeta dress and matching hat held the sign. She had a slim face with sharp features and clear hazel eyes, now sweeping Caroline as she approached.

"I'm Caroline Cushman," she said, smiling at the woman who was slightly shorter but at least ten pounds heavier than she.

"I'm Agnes Miller, Dean of Students. Welcome to Birmingham." Her gloved hands lowered the sign. "William," she said over her shoulder to a tall man emerging from the crowd. "You'll need to pick up Miss Cushman's trunks." She turned to Caroline. "How many do you have?"

Caroline swallowed. "Just one suitcase." She described her cardboard suitcase to the man, certain he would have no trouble spotting it among the trunks.

"This way," Dean Miller said, lifting her skirt and walking ahead of Caroline. "You're going to like Davis."

"I'm real excited." Caroline trailed after her to an elegant carriage.

William had caught up with them, her suitcase swinging lightly from his hand. He opened the carriage door and withdrew a small rail that enclosed three steps.

As Dean Miller proceeded Caroline into the carriage, a lace-edged petticoat peeped from beneath her flowing skirts. Caroline followed, knowing there would be no dainty rustle of her skirts as she settled into the butter-soft seat.

"Thank you for coming to pick me up," Caroline said, smoothing out the folds of her skirt. In the process, her fingers brushed a fold of the taffeta skirt Dean Miller wore. She had never felt anything so soft and fine in a garment, and she wished she could touch it again.

"My pleasure," Dean Miller replied, peering out the window as William climbed into the driver's seat. "Was the train ride comfortable?"

"Yes, ma'am, it was."

Caroline stole another glance at the elegant woman beside her. Her face was rather plain beneath the jaunty little hat. Caroline guessed her to be at least middle-aged, and although she was much younger than Granny, her eyes lacked the sparkle that danced in her grandmother's eyes.

Silence fell, and Caroline looked out the window. She didn't know how to talk to a woman like this, so instead she concentrated on the fine-looking shops along the boulevard. *Riding in a fine carriage pulled by sleek black horses was quite different from bumping over country roads in a wagon,* she thought to herself. In less than an hour, she had dropped out of one world into another, one so starkly different that it had taken her breath away. There were fancy buggies and carriages everywhere, and the women wore dresses with yards and yards of fabric, giving them the look of floating rather than walking. Their hats, all sizes and shapes, matched their dresses. Men departed the shops in black suits and hats, looking distinguished and quite busy and in a hurry to get wherever they were going.

"We were quite impressed with your entrance score," Dean Miller spoke up.

"Thank you," Caroline replied. "I studied real hard,

but then I have what Granny calls a passion for books. I never get tired of reading." She wondered what Dean Miller was thinking as her eyes lingered on Caroline's face. She felt nervous and uncomfortable and turned back to the window as an escape.

❄

Dean Miller was thinking about the beautiful girl beside her and wondering how she would fit in with the students at Davis. Caroline Cushman would say exactly what she thought. She had dealt with all sorts of girls, but she knew from having studied this student's background that this girl would have a lot to learn in the social graces. Still, she had made one of the highest entrance scores in the history of Davis. Upon receiving Caroline's records from Oak Grove, the community school near Pine Ridge, she had been astonished at what she read. This bright student had made straight A's from first through eighth grade, in the one-room schoolhouse. Then, upon entering high school, she had traveled with a neighbor in a wagon to Oak Grove, five miles each way, to finish school. During all those years, she had missed only three days of school, and she had graduated at sixteen. She was barely seventeen now, and yet she seemed older and wiser than most of the girls at Davis.

Dean Miller stole a quick glance at her pitiful little dress. Davis maintained a reputation of high standards both academically and socially. She had a feeling this beautiful young woman with the alert blue eyes would have no trouble making her grades, but she was concerned about how the other students would react to her clothes and her country twang.

The carriage turned into the campus driveway, sweeping past manicured lawns where boys and girls strolled, laughing and talking. She tried to see the campus through Caroline Cushman's eyes, and in doing so, suddenly felt younger.

"Dean Miller," Caroline whirled on the seat, "this is the most beautiful place I've ever seen in my life! What kind of bushes are those?" she pointed.

"We have several types of *shrubs* here, Caroline. I'm not sure just what those are."

"They're so *pretty*," Caroline replied. "Do they stay green like that all year?"

Dean Miller frowned. Did they? "Yes, I believe so. Actually, I don't notice them that much. You're very observant, aren't you?" She looked at Caroline, noting the way her eyes glowed as she stared at her new world. Suddenly, Dean Miller felt sorry for this young woman, who was so. . .fresh, so untainted by the sophistication of city life.

❊

Caroline felt the woman's hazel eyes boring through her face. She bit her lip and turned back to look out the window. She was talking too much; Granny had warned her about that.

Shrubs, she thought, *I must remember to call them shrubs.* She was still curious, however, about their beauty. "I reckon it makes the place more cheerful to have green things growing in the dead of winter, doesn't it?" She bit her lip, wondering why she couldn't just shut up.

Dean Miller nodded and her gray hat slipped lower

on her forehead. She reached up to adjust her hat pin. "Yes, it does."

The carriage rocked gently to a halt and Dean Miller lifted her gloved hand to point at yet another brick building. "This is Brunswick Hall, the dormitory where you'll be staying."

"It's beautiful," Caroline sighed, admiring the way the ivy made a dainty crisscross pattern up the side of the dark red brick wall.

The man named William had jumped down from his seat and was opening the door of the carriage. Caroline studied the way Dean Miller gave him her hand and gracefully descended the fancy little steps. Caroline followed, trying to hold her skirt the way Dean Miller did.

Once her feet touched ground, her eyes flew around, absorbing every inch of her new setting. She felt as though she had just stepped into the pages of one of the classics. Her eyes drank in the surroundings, admiring the stately buildings and the rows of *shrubs* and the brick walls surrounding everything.

She turned to the right, studying another handsome brick building. Through a large window, she could see a boy and girl sitting at a table.

"That's the library," Dean Miller explained. "I imagine you'll be spending plenty of time there."

"Oh yes," Caroline nodded. "I can't wait!"

❄

Ryan Blankenship sat in the library with Amelia Gardner, trying not to look bored as she chattered on about the garden party her family was hosting. His eyes strayed to the window and halted suddenly on a young woman getting out of the school carriage. He could see that she was a new student for the driver was unloading her suitcase.

She was dressed a bit differently; was that what had caught his eye? She turned her face and looked toward the window and he caught his breath. What an exquisite face! He sat upright in his chair, feeling the boredom lift. Who was she? Where had she come from? And the eyes, wide-set and bright blue, were looking everything over carefully. She seemed to have a keen interest in everything around her. He couldn't help wondering if a conversation with her would be more enlightening than this one he was struggling through with Amelia.

It occurred to him that Amelia had finally stopped talking. He glanced at her.

". . .What did you think about it?" She tilted her blond head and batted her eyelashes.

Ryan blinked and wondered what she had asked. "I'm sorry. What did you say?"

"What did you think about the Wilfords' party?"

He shrugged. "It was fine."

"Oh. Well. . . ," she rambled on, unaware that she no longer held his interest.

It was amazing how girls thought he cared about social events and fashion. He wanted to socialize with them, but he would enjoy discussing something else, like politics or world news or nature. He really enjoyed discussing anything pertaining to nature. And, of course, medicine, which was his field of study. He couldn't expect girls to be interested in that, however.

He sneaked a glance back to the window, and as

usual, Amelia hardly noticed. He spotted the new girl, who was turning toward the front steps of Brunswick. Her clothes were obviously plain, but she had a nice figure and excellent posture. He watched her disappear into the building, disappointed that she was gone.

❋

Dean Miller pointed out the parlor with its gleaming furniture, thick drapes, and nice carpet. She then led the way down the hall and Caroline glanced right to left, absorbing the gleaming wooden floor, the creamy walls, the *electricity*. At the ridge, not one single family had electricity.

Dean Miller greeted two girls in the hall who gave her a wide smile, then turned surprised faces to Caroline, particularly her dress. She and Granny had worked long into the night for weeks, trying to copy the dresses they had seen in the mail order catalogs. And she had felt so good about her clothes; but now she realized that while they had copied the style of dresses, they could not duplicate the fine fabric. Even by scrimping and saving, the best they could purchase was quality cotton. She had never owned silk or taffeta or any of the fine fabrics she saw floating past her.

"You're in number eleven, halfway down." Dean Miller pointed, hurrying ahead.

"Oh, hello! You must be Emily Ellison," Dean Miller was saying as she swept into a large room where a girl with brown hair and green eyes turned from the dresser and faced them.

Emily was an inch taller than Caroline and at least five pounds heavier. She was wearing a taffeta dress that was the palest shade of gold, like fading sunlight in late November.

"Yes, ma'am. I'm from Atlanta," the girl replied in a smooth, rich voice.

"Nice to meet you. I'm Dean Miller and this is Caroline Cushman."

"Hello," Emily said, staring at Caroline.

"Hello, Emily," she responded and smiled. She wished her stomach wouldn't hurt and that she wasn't so nervous and self-conscious.

"Caroline is on *scholarship*, Emily," Dean Miller continued smoothly. "She'll be a good roommate."

"A scholarship?" Emily's green eyes suddenly lit up.

"Yes, now I'll leave you two to get acquainted."

"I'm glad you're smart," Emily said, still looking Caroline over. "I barely sneaked by on my entrance exams. And to be perfectly honest, I'm not fond of studying."

"I'll be glad to help you if I can. I really like to study," Caroline replied.

"You do? Not me. I wouldn't even be here if my parents hadn't forced me to come."

"Forced you?" Caroline placed her cardboard suitcase in the empty closet as soon as she spotted the handsome trunk near Emily's bed.

Emily shrugged. "Let's just say they gave me no choice. Does it matter which bed you take?"

Caroline glanced at the twin bed by the window where Emily's clothes were haphazardly dumped. "This one's fine," she said, turning to the bed by the door. She saw the bare mattress and wondered if she was required to bring bed covers. She thought she had memorized every word in her letters from Davis.

"What's wrong?" Emily asked, watching her.

"I didn't bring. . . ," her voice trailed away as she stared at the bed and felt the blood rush to her cheeks.

Emily tossed a set of sheets and matching pillowcase onto the bare mattress. "Mother must have bought me a dozen."

Caroline reached down and trailed her fingers over the creamy linen. "Oh, I couldn't. . .I mean. . ."

"Don't worry about it," Emily replied indifferently.

Caroline hesitated, wondering how to respond. "That's very nice of you," she answered slowly. "Maybe I can do something for you."

"Maybe. You found your closet." Emily inclined her head toward the one Caroline had chosen. "They're much too small. I can't get half my clothes in there."

Caroline peered in. She could get her clothes in with space left over.

"At least we're near the central bath," Emily continued. "It's only a few doors down. Father was disappointed that there aren't more bathrooms, but then he owns a hotel and is accustomed to having plenty of baths." She studied Caroline. "What does your father do?"

Caroline's back stiffened, though she kept her smile in place. "He's dead."

"Oh, I'm sorry."

"Thank you." Caroline looked from the mahogany twin beds and nightstands to the small matching dressers. "I think we'll like it here, don't you?"

Emily slumped on her bed. "No, I'll be miserable. I

left a boyfriend over in Atlanta, and already I miss him so much I could just die." Tears filled her eyes. "They think Tommy isn't good enough for me. He has a good job, but he didn't go to college." She studied her emerald ring and sighed. "What my parents won't accept is that I'm not smart enough to make it at Davis."

"Oh, I'm sure—"

"No, I struggle with school." She looked at Caroline. "Do you have a boyfriend?"

"No," Caroline replied. She was burning with dreams and ambition and she hadn't time to think of boys. Besides, who would she have chosen for a boyfriend? The only boy she'd ever liked was Billy Joe Whitaker, who had gotten himself killed in a horse race.

"Well, at least you didn't have to leave anyone. Where is your home, anyway?"

"Pine Ridge. It's a little place over in Blount County, an hour by train. Well, I guess I'd better get unpacked."

With Emily's eyes following her every move, Caroline stood up and went to the closet to open her suitcase. She shook out the five good dresses she had brought and hung them in the closet. Then she took her box of toiletries to the dresser drawer, along with her undergarments. When she glanced at Emily, she noticed her green eyes were huge, as though she didn't believe what she was seeing.

Caroline imagined that Emily was probably amazed at how little her new roommate owned. Well, it couldn't be helped. She was Caroline Cushman from Pine Ridge. She wasn't going to put on airs or pretend to be something different. Still, Caroline knew that life here was not going to be easy.

She returned to her suitcase and withdrew her Bible. The black leather cover was worn from years of use, but she treasured it, and as long as she could hold it, she didn't feel quite so frightened or alone. She laid it on the nightstand and smiled across at Emily. "Are you a Christian?" she asked.

Again, the girl's brows rose in twin peaks. "I guess so."

Caroline averted her eyes, wondering how you could guess about something so important. Unlike Emily, she wasn't worried about her studies; she was worried about adjusting to these people and their lifestyle. Until she did, she had to remember to think before she spoke. And that would be the hardest thing of all.

two

I n the coming days, Caroline became totally absorbed in her classes. She had chosen English as her major, and her mind was fertile soil begging for seeds of wisdom. Books and their interpreters were gifts, challenging and exhilarating her, explaining the restlessness of adolescence, the boredom. Davis was the answer to her prayers. There was one problem, however; she knew she looked and sounded different from her classmates.

She tried to limit her conversations until she learned to pronounce her words more clearly. When called upon to answer a question, her answer was always correct, no matter how challenging the question. An occasional snicker reached her, but those around her soon conceded that even though she didn't talk or dress like they did, she was smarter.

She was a model student, poised on the edge of her seat, her blue eyes keen with interest, her pen quickly filling her tablet. She devoured every word her instructors spoke, even lingered after class to ask questions. At night, she haunted the library.

On the second week in October, Emily reluctantly

joined her at the library. "I have to find a dumb old reference book," she complained. "Have you noticed how musty this place smells?"

"Old books," Caroline replied. She didn't mind a musty book; she respected its age. Her eyes swept the tall ceilings and rows of books that brought a surge of excitement to her. She loved exploring the priceless treasures at her fingertips. "What are you looking for?" she asked helpfully.

Emily related her assignment and Caroline located the specific reference area. "Just decide what you want. Give me your satchel, and I'll find a table."

Caroline entered the adjoining room, where students sat at desks, absorbed in books. She hardly noticed anyone in her haste to get to the nearest table to deposit her load. She took a seat and opened her English book. Suddenly someone bumped her chair. She jumped, and the book tumbled from her hand to the floor.

"Oh, I'm sorry."

She turned and looked at the dark head beside her, kneeling to retrieve the English book.

"Here you are," he said, placing the book on her desk.

"Thanks," she replied as he straightened and faced her.

She had noticed him in English class. He was very handsome and he dressed well. Looking up at him, she realized he was five ten or eleven, with a nice physique. Friendly brown eyes were set in an oval face with a high brow, slim nose, and strong chin.

"I'm Ryan Blankenship," he said. "I'm in your English class." He slipped into the adjoining chair.

"I'm Caroline Cushman."

"You look awfully busy," he said, glancing at all the books.

"I am." She felt nervous just looking at him, so she fidgeted with a book.

"Have you finished the theme Mrs. Stockton assigned us?"

She glanced at him, smiled, then looked back at her book. "No. I don't know what to write about."

"She mentioned a special vacation," he said.

"I've never been on a vacation."

"I think Mrs. Stockton was just making suggestions when she mentioned a vacation. I believe the important thing is to write about something we care about. What about the area you come from?"

Her gaze inched back to him. "I do care about Pine Ridge. When I graduate from Davis, I plan to go back there and teach school and write." She bit her lip, wishing she hadn't told him the part about *writing*. Why was she talking so freely to this stranger? Still, her eyes lingered on his face; she sensed a kindness there, and he had a nice, friendly smile. He acted as though he really cared about what she was saying.

"Tell me about Pine Ridge."

"Pine Ridge is over in Blount County. It's only an hour by train, but it seems like another world compared to here."

"How is that?"

"Pine Ridge is a quaint little community where

119

only a few people have running water and nobody has electricity. In fact, most folks there have never even been to Birmingham. And yet. . . ," her voice trailed. She didn't want to offend him.

"And yet what?" He leaned closer, his dark eyes wide, as though he really wanted to know what she had to say.

"Well, the community is like one big family. Everyone helps everyone else. If someone's house burns down, we all pitch in and help rebuild. We have quilting bees and shivarees—"

"Shivarees?" he repeated curiously.

"It's an all-night get-together for newlyweds where we bring gifts and food, and Clarence Johnson plays the fiddle and Uncle Mack and Aunt Jenny clog and the Robertson kids play the spoons."

"Play the spoons?" he repeated, smiling at her. It was a kind smile, she decided; he wasn't making fun.

"Sure? Haven't you ever heard of playing the spoons?"

He shook his head, but he was still smiling. She liked the way his brown eyes crinkled when he smiled. In fact, she liked almost everything about him. He was nicer to her than nearly anyone she had met at Davis.

"Tell me more about Pine Ridge," he said, propping his elbow on the table and staring deeply into her eyes. "It's obviously a special place for you. Why?"

She hesitated, trying to form her words in her mind before speaking. As she glanced back at him, she decided to lower her defenses a bit. "Promise you won't laugh?"

His dark eyes widened. "Of course I won't laugh! Why would you even ask?"

Caroline shook her head. "I don't know." She glanced nervously around the crowded library where everyone seemed to be buried in their books, paying no attention to her. She looked back at the gentle boy beside her and swallowed. "Sometimes people snicker when I say things."

He blinked, looked away for a moment, then back again. "I promise you," he said emphatically, "I will never laugh at anything you say."

She took a deep breath and began. "It's the little things in life that have meaning for me: seeing a baby chick break out of its shell, watching the ducks follow their mothers across the lake in a perfect line, catchin' fireflies on Saturday night and holding them in the palm of your hand to study their magic, feelin' the night silence surround me. . ." She stopped. She was forgetting to pronounce her *ing*s.

"There's the subject for your English theme, Caroline. What you just said to me was very special."

She tilted her head and looked at him. "Why was it special?"

"Because it's real. So many people I know fill their lives with things that are superficial. You're talking about the beauties of nature and how a person can enjoy them. I think that's wonderful."

"You think so?"

"Sure!"

Footsteps approached and Emily stood before them, wide-eyed.

"Hi, I'm Ryan Blankenship." He stood and smiled.

Emily stumbled through her name, then stared at Caroline.

"Did you find your book?" Caroline asked.

"I found one I can check out. Do you want to stay longer?"

"No." Caroline stood, gathering her books.

"I'll see you in English class tomorrow," Ryan said. "Good luck with your theme."

"Thanks. You too."

She walked quickly out of the library with Emily's eyes on her. Once they were outside, Emily spoke.

"Caroline, do you know who he is?"

"Ryan Blankenship. He's in my English class. Why? Don't you like him?"

Emily rolled her eyes. "Of course I like him. There isn't a girl on this campus who doesn't like him. What were you discussing?"

"We were talking about our English themes," Caroline said, looking up at the moonlight filtering down through the oaks.

"And what did you say?"

They had passed under a big oak, and Emily's face was shaded in darkness, but Caroline heard the concern in her tone. "Don't worry, Emily," Caroline said with a sigh. "I didn't say ain't."

"Ouch. Aren't you being a bit sensitive?"

Caroline sighed. "Maybe. I'm different from the students here, and I know it," she added quietly as they stepped back into the lights of Brunswick Hall.

Emily touched her hand. "I didn't mean to offend

you, Caroline. You're the kindest person I've ever met."

"Thanks." She smiled at Emily as they entered the dorm and walked to their room.

❊

Ryan had inspired Caroline to begin her theme. She sat at her desk, writing furiously, pouring onto a blank sheet of paper her lifelong knowledge of Pine Ridge.

"Caroline," Emily wailed, "how can you keep at it for hours?" She was lounging on her bed, her dress wrinkled, her books scattered.

Caroline shrugged. "I don't know. Mrs. Stockton may not like my theme; it probably won't be as good as the others."

"Will you stop that?" Emily cried. "Don't you know how bright you are? If not for you, I'd have failed both tests this week." Her eyes dropped to Caroline's dress. "I've been thinking." She got up and went to her closet. "I have some dresses I'll never wear. I want you to have them in return for helping me."

"Emily, you don't have to do that! I've helped you because I wanted to, because it's the Christian thing to do."

"Then let me do the Christian thing and give you something in return." She opened her closet door. "Mother chose these dresses for me, and I don't care for bright colors. I'm more comfortable in soft, muted shades." She pulled out three dresses of vivid green, purple, and blue. "These should fit you because I was thinner when she bought them. I started eating more out of frustration. They might be a bit too long." She frowned, glancing back at Caroline's dress.

"Oh, I can hem them," Caroline blurted, then bit her lip. "If you really feel it's the Christian thing to do."

"I do." Emily handed the dresses to Caroline and smiled. "You know, Caroline, you'll probably have lots of pretty dresses someday. You're pretty enough to snag a rich man and smart enough to keep him." She grinned. "I saw the way Ryan Blankenship was looking at you tonight."

She thought about her conversation with Ryan. He was kind and intelligent and seemed to enjoy talking with her, as she did with him. But. . .she knew he lived in a different world. She didn't belong there, nor did she want to.

"No," she shook her head, pushing Ryan from her thoughts, "I'm not interested in a rich man, as you put it. I'm going back to Pine Ridge to teach and write. It's my dream."

Emily shook her head in despair. "I just don't understand you."

❊

Later, after Emily had closed her books and gone to bed, Caroline threaded a needle and studied the beautiful dresses Emily had given her. Her heart danced with joy as she tenderly touched the soft green taffeta she planned to wear tomorrow. Mrs. Stockton had said she would ask a few students to read their themes aloud. Caroline sighed. She knew she wouldn't sound right, but she had been praying about that too. Maybe God would answer her prayers about talking, the way He had answered her prayers about clothes.

She had big dreams, but sometimes those dreams

brought her heartache. The snickers and stares had been difficult, but she prayed folks would adjust to her, just as she must adjust to them.

Ryan Blankenship sneaked back into her thoughts and her heart lifted. Emily thought he liked her, but Caroline doubted that. She sensed he was the kind of person who was nice to everyone. She was grateful he had encouraged her to write about Pine Ridge. She missed home something fierce, but she would be going back for Christmas; still, that seemed a long time away.

Suddenly a wave of longing for Pine Ridge rolled over her. She swallowed hard and tried to concentrate on what she was doing; but a tear slipped down her cheek as she painstakingly hemmed the dress that Emily had given her.

three

Caroline hurried into English class, hugging her books against her chest. She loved the way the green taffeta swirled about her ankles; she felt good about herself today. The theme she'd spent half the night composing was folded carefully inside her English book, and even though she had dressed well, she still hoped Mrs. Stockton wouldn't call on her.

She sank into the middle chair of the first row. It was the best seat in the classroom, although most students seemed to prefer seats in other rows behind her.

A slim blond passed, staring at her. She had seen this girl at the dormitory and tried to be friendly, but the girl turned her head. *Probably homesick,* she thought, glancing at Mrs. Stockton. She was an attractive, middle-aged woman who wore bright floral dresses and smiled with her eyes, unlike Dean Miller.

"We're going to read our themes aloud today," she said, taking her seat. "We'll start with you, William." Her eyes lit on a boy in the back row.

The tall, lanky boy ambled to the front of the room, unfolded his paper, and mumbled about Eli Whitney, the inventor. The subject was interesting, but

Caroline thought he could have done better. Mrs. Stockton thanked him for reading. He grinned and ambled back to his seat.

"Amelia, would you like to read your theme?"

The blond girl who had snubbed Caroline strolled up to the front of the room. She wore a beautiful blue silk dress with lace on the collar and cuffs and a wide ruffle around the hem. Caroline admired her dress and the nice cameo at her throat, and she listened with interest as Amelia read about a family vacation in New York. Her voice was filled with confidence, and her grammar was excellent, but her theme had no beginning, middle, or end. She just rambled. Caroline looked down at her book, embarrassed for her.

When Amelia had returned to her seat, Mrs. Stockton's eyes moved slowly to Caroline. Caroline dropped her eyes, praying she wouldn't call on her.

"Caroline, let's hear your theme," Mrs. Stockton said in a gentle voice.

Caroline's eyes shot to Mrs. Stockton in horror. Didn't she know that sometimes the students laughed at her? She bit her lip, trying to think of a reason not to read.

Nervously, she uncrossed her ankles and her new green taffeta rustled. Maybe this was why God gave her the dress. She got up and walked to the front, facing two dozen curious faces.

Ryan smiled at her, encouraging her. She took a deep breath and looked down at her meticulous handwriting. She had revealed the absolute truth about herself and her home, and now she wondered if that were a mistake. The paper was beginning to rattle in her fingers. Someone snickered.

God, help me, she silently prayed. And then, a new strength seemed to flow through her. She realized it didn't really matter what these people thought; what mattered was that she was reading about the most special place in the world. And she knew that Mrs. Stockton and Ryan Blankenship weren't going to laugh.

"My name is Caroline Cushman," she began shakily, "and I come from Pine Ridge. Pine Ridge is a small community and to me it is a very special corner of the world, fashioned by God's hands and nestled deep in the forest. In the winter, when the lake freezes over, we make skates and sleds out of farm machinery. Everyone goes ice-skating, from the children to the old people. In the winter, we have all-night singings and taffy pullings and hoedowns and quilting parties."

She paused to draw a breath.

"At Pine Ridge we make our own musical instruments and on Saturday nights we have parties. Grandpa Sam, who's not really anybody's grandpa, is good with the Jew's harp. Willie Mayberry is a natural on his drums, and Pearline Jones is pretty good with her guitar. Our music brings a smile to the saddest face and warms the hearts of those who have lost loved ones. When little Angela Jones was dying, her mother bundled her up and brought her to our Christmas party. Everyone made special gifts for her, things she never had because her family is poor. Angela played the part of the Christmas angel, and on that snowy Christmas eve, God decided it was time to take His angel home. Everyone had gathered around her to sing 'Silent Night'; when the carol ended, we looked and little Angela had gone to be with the Lord."

She paused, swallowed hard, and continued.

"There is a special kind of love at Pine Ridge, a love for God and our fellow man. I miss the people of Pine Ridge, but I also miss the special things of nature that were a fascination to me when I was growing up." She glanced up from her paper, meeting Ryan's glowing brown eyes.

She looked back at the paper and read the verbal picture of baby chicks breaking out of their shells, ducks on the lake, and the beauty of a winter morning when ice sculpted the trees and icicles glittered like diamonds. She read the sentences quickly, never looking up again.

Without risking a glance, she hurried to her seat and busied herself folding her paper. Mrs. Stockton's voice broke the silence around her.

"That was excellent, Caroline. We enjoyed it very much. Thank you for sharing Pine Ridge with us."

When Mrs. Stockton dismissed class for the day, she asked Caroline to remain. Caroline's heart thundered in her chest. What was she going to say to her? She was so nervous she could hardly thank Ryan when he stopped to compliment her theme. From the corner of her eye, she saw Amelia. This time Amelia was glaring at her.

Then, when everyone had left, Mrs. Stockton looked across at Caroline and smiled.

"I was very touched by your theme," she said warmly. "I wonder if you're really aware of what a unique place you come from or of your knack for telling about it. The students were fascinated and I think other people would be."

Caroline's eyes widened. "You mean I should write more about Pine Ridge?"

"I do. I don't often say this to students, but I think you have a good chance of getting published."

"Getting published?" Caroline asked, wondering if it were possible to achieve one of her dreams this soon.

"Yes. I have a friend who is an editor for a journal that features the best writing of college students. As the year progresses, and you learn more about writing, I think we might want to send her something."

Caroline was dizzied by the prospect. For once, she was at a loss for words. She wanted to throw herself in Mrs. Stockton's arms and give her a big hug, but she knew folks in the city were more formal. So, instead, she looked at Mrs. Stockton with all the gratitude that was overflowing her heart.

"Thank you," she said, trying hard not to cry.

❄

"Don't forget we're having that get-together in the parlor," Caroline reminded Emily when she returned to her room and found Emily sulking on her bed.

"I don't want to go," Emily complained.

"Why not?"

"I don't see any fun in standing around with the girls in the dorm, sipping punch and pretending to like one another."

Caroline laughed. "Maybe we do like each other."

Emily said nothing as she looked Caroline over.

"Come on, let's go. You just might enjoy yourself," she coaxed.

With Emily halfheartedly joining her, they walked down the hall and entered the parlor. An enormous chandelier poured soft light over the marble-topped tables, the Duncan Phyfe sofas and matching chairs, and thick gold drapes.

Caroline's stomach tightened as they crossed the gleaming floors and stepped onto the lush Oriental carpet. A group of girls stood at the serving table, with Amelia in the center. Caroline had decided to compliment Amelia's theme, and perhaps she could make friends with her—or at least figure out why she acted so unfriendly.

"Hi, Caroline," a small voice spoke up from behind her.

"Oh, hi, Claire." Caroline smiled.

Claire was tiny and frail, looking even more so because she was partially crippled on her right side. On Tuesday, Caroline had seen Claire struggling with a load of books and helped carry them to her room. Like Caroline, Claire often seemed to be alone.

"Here." Emily joined them, handing Caroline a dainty crystal cup filled with punch.

"Thanks. Emily, do you know Claire?"

Just as Caroline was introducing Claire to Emily, someone jostled against her back. The punch she had been holding against her chest, sloshed onto her green bodice, leaving an ugly red stain in the center. Horrified, she turned to see what was happening behind her, and Amelia stood glaring at her.

"You bumped into me," Amelia cried.

Caroline awkwardly took a step back from her and as she did, the girl moved as well. The sound of cloth ripping cut across the quiet room as everyone stared.

"Now look what you've done." Amelia played to her audience. "You've torn my dress!"

Caroline's eyes shot to the floor, and she saw an edge of pale blue ruffle lying on the carpet.

"I. . .I'm sorry," Caroline stammered.

"What's wrong?" Dean Miller had rushed over.

"She bumped right into me," Amelia cried, glaring at Caroline. "And now my dress is ruined."

"I'd say Caroline's dress is in worse shape than yours, Amelia," Emily spoke up, moving closer to Caroline.

"Well, it's her own fault," Amelia lashed back. "Some people just don't know how to conduct themselves in social situations." She flung the words at Caroline, then daintily lifted her skirt with its trailing ruffle and swept out of the room. Her circle of friends followed, tossing one last disgusted glance in Caroline's direction.

Humiliation scalded Caroline's cheeks as she looked at Dean Miller. "I'm so sorry," she said shakily.

"Dean Miller," Emily spoke up, "Amelia bumped into Caroline. If anyone was to blame it was Amelia."

Dean Miller lifted a dainty shoulder of her black silk dress. "Either way, do try to be careful, Caroline," she said with a little smile before she turned and strolled back to chat with the housemother.

"Here, let me take that cup," Claire offered, reaching for Caroline's empty cup and placing it on the nearest table.

"Let's go!" Emily rasped in her ear.

"I'm leaving too," Claire said, looking sadly at the group who watched them.

As soon as they reached the hall, Emily huffed an angry sigh. "I'm getting more disgusted with this dorm every day. They're just a bunch of snobs."

"Do you really think Amelia bumped Caroline on purpose?" Claire asked in her weak little voice.

"Of course she did," Emily said as they entered the room. Emily closed the door and faced Claire and Caroline. "Amelia has a crush on Ryan Blankenship, and I don't know why the girls here can't see through her little act."

"Act?" Caroline repeated. "What do you mean?"

"I hear Amelia is really hurt that he's quit courting her. If he ever was. Surely you can see that he's completely taken with you, Caroline. He speaks to you every chance he gets and stares at you as though you're a goddess—"

"Oh, I don't think—" Caroline interrupted.

"No, you don't think so because you're too modest, but it's true. I see the way he looks at you, and I know that look, believe me." She sank onto the bed and tears filled her eyes for a moment. "I miss Tommy so much I could just die."

Claire looked from Emily back to Caroline, her little face bleak. "I'm so sorry about everything."

Caroline shook her head. "It doesn't matter."

But it did, and she felt heartsick when her eyes dropped to the ugly red smear on her bodice. It was the most flattering dress she owned, and if what Emily had said about Amelia was true, she had picked the right dress to ruin.

"Why don't you take the dress off and let me have it?" Claire suggested. "My father owns a shop here that specializes in cleaning garments. Maybe he can get that stain out."

"I hate to put your father to any trouble."

"My father will be glad to help anyone who has helped me. And you have," she said, touching her hand gently.

Grateful for those words, Caroline changed into one of her old dresses, glancing intermittently at Emily, who had stretched out on the bed, her face to the wall.

After Claire left, Caroline thought of how Emily had defended her. She wanted to tell her she appreciated it, but she didn't seem to be in the mood for conversation.

She cleared her throat. "Emily, why don't you write a letter to Tommy? Maybe that would make you feel better."

"I won't feel better until I see him again," she wailed.

Caroline's eyes drifted to her Bible on the night-stand. She sat down on her bed and picked it up, trying to think of a chapter to read to calm her nerves. Was it true what Emily had said? That Ryan really liked her? Was that why Amelia had behaved as she did?

Caroline glanced across at Emily. "Do you think Ryan likes Amelia?"

Emily rolled over and looked at Caroline. "No, of course not. And Amelia is humiliated because she's made a fool of herself over him."

"I guess that would be humiliating," Caroline said.

"Feeling an ache in your heart is much worse than getting a stain on your best dress. The dress someone very nice gave me." She smiled sadly.

"Well, Amelia has a heartache *and* a torn dress, which was her fault, by the way."

Caroline frowned. "How? I stepped on her dress."

"That dress was so long it spilled over her feet. She was standing so close that if you took a step, it would be on her dress. And didn't you notice the way she suddenly backed up?"

Caroline frowned. "It was my fault."

Emily shook her head. "I still say Amelia is a little schemer, particularly when she dislikes someone."

"And she dislikes me," Caroline said with a sigh, looking down at her Bible. She remembered a verse Granny had taught her. *Love your enemies, do good to those who despise you. . . .*

Did Amelia really despise her? And if so, what could be done to change that?

She had been a seamstress all of her life; Granny had taught her well. In her mind's eye, she saw again the bit of torn fabric. It could easily be reattached to the skirt at the edge of the ruffle. She could do it by hand. Probably tonight.

She glanced at Emily, who had taken up her pen and stationery, still ignoring her books. It would do no good for Caroline to remind her she needed to study; she knew that. If she chose to write a letter to Tommy—and Caroline had no doubt he was the inspiration for the letter—then that was Emily's business.

She got up from the bed. There was no point in

telling Emily her intentions. Emily would only argue with her.

"I'll be back in a few minutes," Caroline said, but Emily scarcely heard her.

In the hall, Caroline tried to remember where Amelia's room was. When they had met in the hall, Amelia had snubbed her, then turned and entered a room. Which room?

Caroline wandered down the hall, noting the numbers on the left side. It had been a door on the left. Halfway down, one door was ajar and she could hear voices coming from inside.

She stopped at the open door. Inside, two girls lounged on their beds while another leaned against a dresser.

"She comes from some—" All three had spotted Caroline and were staring wide-eyed at her.

Caroline focused her attention on Amelia, wearing a beautiful pink lounging gown as she propped against her pillows, munching chocolate candy.

"Excuse me," she called from the open door.

No one spoke. They just stared at her.

"I came to apologize to you, Amelia. I'm sorry about your dress, and I would like to mend it for you."

Amelia glanced from Caroline to the other girls. Then her lips curled and her blue eyes shot sparks. "No, thanks. I don't think you would know how to mend a fine garment."

Caroline had never met anyone so cruel, but rather than be embarrassed now, she was proud of herself for not stooping to Amelia's level.

"I know how to forgive," she said slowly, making her point, "and I know how to be polite." She lifted her chin and turned from the door.

"Isn't she pathetic?" Amelia's voice rang out. But no one answered.

four

The next day Caroline took a different route to class. During the past week, Ryan had begun waiting for her near the science building. From there, they walked to English class, but not today, not anymore, she had decided. Furthermore, Mary Elizabeth, whose room was next door to her, had informed Caroline that she often saw Ryan and Amelia together. At that, Caroline decided Mary Elizabeth knew more about Amelia and Ryan than Emily, and she must not interfere.

As she traveled the rear path, she glanced toward the front walkway and saw Ryan through the trees. He was standing with his back to her as he looked down the walk toward the approaching girls. She bit her lip, feeling guilty. She had to do this, she told herself, walking faster, forcing her eyes straight ahead.

"I missed you somehow," Ryan said, pausing at her desk when he entered the room.

She glanced briefly at him and felt her heart wrench. "Sorry," she said, busily opening her book and searching for a pen.

"Me too," he added, then turned and walked away.

She avoided Amelia, but she could feel her eyes upon her at times. As soon as Mrs. Stockton dismissed class, Caroline grabbed her books and was out the door. If Ryan wondered what was wrong with her, perhaps Amelia could explain.

❄

Ryan spent the next week trying to figure out what he had done to offend Caroline. At first, he thought she was only preoccupied with her studies, but now he was certain she was avoiding him. He wanted to ask her why, but he never got the chance. She was always gone before he could catch up with her.

He sat in the library, staring through the window to Brunswick Hall. Why couldn't he get her out of his mind? She was like a breath of fresh air in his stifled world. Sometimes, after his eyes were dazed from studying, he would think about her and the way she had read her theme on Pine Ridge. To him, she was the most beautiful girl on campus, for there was something radiant and pure flowing from her soul. He longed to get to know her better; he even had a crazy desire to go to Pine Ridge and see that way of life firsthand. But she continued to ignore him, day after day. He stayed busy with schoolwork, poring over his books long into the night, determined to make his family proud as he followed the family profession of medicine.

"Why didn't you come to the Addison party?" The voice pulled him back to reality as he shifted against the library table and focused on Amelia. She had slipped into the chair opposite him. He noticed that she was a pretty girl, but she just didn't appeal to him.

"I've been busy with schoolwork. And besides," he added more truthfully, "I'm tired of parties." He was flattered that she liked him, and he could tell that she did; but they had nothing in common, other than family background. They had none of the same interests, and he suspected Amelia did not take her studies seriously, which bothered him even more.

"Oh. Well, I never see you anywhere," she said, starting to pout.

"I never go anywhere," he said, sounding more abrupt than he intended.

Silence lengthened between them as her eyes dropped to his open book. "I'll let you get back to studying since you seem to enjoy it so much."

A wry grin tilted his lips as he took the verbal jab with no offense. "See you," he said, turning back to his anatomy book.

❋

The days grew shorter with the approach of November. The sun rays softened as autumn's cooling breezes settled over the campus. The oaks, maples, and hickories turned to brilliant hues, but Caroline thought that city trees didn't compare to those out in the country, where there was more room for the branches to spread wide. Still, she appreciated the color and shape and texture, and she was always stopping to pick up an exceptionally pretty leaf to press between the pages of her book. She collected so many they often fell from her books, and most instructors, upon finding another stray leaf on the floor, knew the source.

During the second week of November, she had

stopped to capture one last dying leaf when she heard a familiar voice over her shoulder.

"This one is prettier."

She was kneeling on the grass, reaching for the leaf, when she heard his voice. She turned and looked up. Ryan was holding a huge maple leaf, the most beautiful shade of scarlet she had ever seen.

She gasped. "I thought all the pretty leaves had died. Where did you get that one?"

"In the backyard of my parents' home." He helped her to her feet and handed the leaf to her. "I know you collect leaves, so I brought this one back for you."

Her eyes met his, and her wall of reserve toppled. "That was awfully nice of you," she said, dropping her gaze to the leaf. It hurt to look into his friendly brown eyes and recall how many times she had avoided and even ignored him.

"There's a catch," he said, as she reached for it.

Her hand paused in midair, as her blue eyes widened questioningly.

"You have to have lunch with me."

"Oh," she said, dropping her hand.

He tilted his head and stared down at her with shocked eyes. "Is it that painful?"

She laughed softly, seeing the humor. "Of course not. It's just that. . .I'm awfully busy these days."

"I'm sure you are," he nodded patiently, "but I assume you do take time out to eat." His eyes swept down the dark taffeta dress she had worn at least once each week. "Still, you look as though you eat like a sparrow."

She laughed again and allowed herself to look

141

directly into his eyes. Their gazes locked as she stared into his and thought of warm chocolate. "I don't know why I do that," she said, blinking and looking away.

"Do what?"

"Compare colors to favorite things." She shook her head. "I'm battin' the breeze," she bit her lip, trying to shut off more country talk.

"Are you comparing this leaf to a place in Pine Ridge?" he asked, trying to catch up with her thoughts.

Her blue eyes danced as she looked at him. She wasn't about to tell him what she was really thinking. She took the leaf from his hand and placed it in her book. "Thanks."

He didn't seem to mind that she hadn't answered him, and they fell into step along the walkway leading back to the dorm.

"You didn't answer my question about lunch. Tomorrow. Or any day next week. We'll go someplace different."

She took a deep breath, staring at the brick walls of Brunswick Hall. It would be rude to say no, for she couldn't make excuses for every day of the week. Besides, Amelia was still just as rude as ever, so Caroline had begun to wonder if avoiding Ryan really made a difference, after all.

"Tomorrow?" she asked shyly.

Tomorrow was Saturday and she would welcome a chance for a nice lunch, especially with Ryan. Her scholarship covered meals in the dining hall, but she was beginning to get tired of looking at the same walls every day.

"Great." A wide smile stretched over even white teeth as he looked down at her. "How about a picnic lunch?"

She stopped walking and turned suddenly. "A picnic? I've been wantin' to go on a picnic, but nobody. . ." Her voice trailed as she glanced toward the dorm then back again. "Where would we go?"

"There's a park not far from here. . .and a lake," he added. "Maybe we'll see some ducks."

She smiled at him. "You remembered what I said in my theme about ducks."

"I remember every word of your theme." They had reached the steps of the dorm and were gazing into each other's eyes, oblivious to everything else.

"Hi, Caroline," Claire called with a smile.

"Hi, Claire. Do you know Ryan Blankenship?" Of course she knew of him, everyone did, but she wanted Ryan to meet Claire. Ever since Claire had returned her dress with most of the stain gone, she had been indebted to her. Claire had even given her a locket on a long chain, measuring it carefully so that the locket covered the small stain on her bodice.

"Hello, Claire," Ryan was saying. "I'm glad to meet you."

"Nice to meet you." Claire blushed, smiled quickly at Caroline, then slipped away.

It always touched Caroline to see how Claire carried herself with great dignity, despite her crippled side.

"She's nice," he said as his eyes followed Claire briefly before he turned back to Caroline. "I'll call for you here at noon tomorrow. Will that be okay?"

She nodded, hugging her books. "I'll be looking for-ward to it. And thanks for the leaf," she added, smiling at him.

❄

When Ryan called for her the next day, Caroline wore the green taffeta dress with her locket and a black knit shawl that arrived in the mail for her the day before. She knew Granny had spent weeks knitting it, and as she wrapped the shawl around her, it was as though Granny's loving arms enveloped her as well.

Ryan was dressed in casual slacks and a long-sleeved white shirt. As she signed out of the dormitory, he opened the front door and she spotted a sleek buggy and black horse waiting at the curb.

She held her tongue, having begun to practice that art now, as they walked to the buggy and Ryan talked about the weather. It was a beautiful fall day with just enough crispness in the air to bring a glow to one's cheeks and spark a sense of adventure.

When Ryan assisted her into the seat of the buggy, she spotted the picnic basket on the floor.

"Mmm. Something smells good," she said, smiling at Ryan as he got into the buggy.

"Aretha fried chicken." He stopped suddenly, as though he had revealed an important secret.

"What's wrong?" she asked.

"Nothing." He lifted the reins and clucked to the horse.

"Who is Aretha?" she asked, suspecting he was em-barrassed over having a cook.

Ryan hesitated. "Aretha helps Mother in the kitchen."

Caroline nodded. "Then I'll look forward to the chicken."

She had heard that his family was wealthy, and now the carriage and his reference to "help" confirmed it. She turned and looked out across the campus as the horse trotted smoothly up the street. Ryan couldn't help being born into wealth, just as she couldn't help being born at Pine Ridge, which she considered a blessing.

Her thoughts turned quickly to the scenery around them. Beyond the campus the boulevard was lined with all kinds of shops—a dry goods store, a meat market, another clothing store—with nice buggies and carriages parked in front of them.

"Are you liking Davis?" Ryan asked.

She turned and looked at him. "Yes. By the way, I've been wondering about your field of study." She had wondered *a lot*, in fact, and had intended to ask before their campus walks got interrupted.

"I'm in premedical studies. I want to be a doctor."

"That's wonderful. What made you choose that profession?"

He hesitated as he steered the horse down a side street. "My father is a doctor, and my uncle, as well."

"Here in Birmingham?" she asked.

"Yes. They have a private practice downtown. Here we are."

Caroline turned and looked out at the park. "This is beautiful. Do you come here often?"

"As often as I can," he said, getting out of the buggy and coming around to her side. "When school starts to wear on my nerves, I come here and walk around the lake."

"I reckon it makes you feel better."

"It does." He handed her down and then reached for the picnic basket. "I've thought of inviting you, but you haven't been too friendly lately," he said, pressing her hand into the crook of his arm, with the picnic basket swinging from his other arm.

She turned her face away from him and looked at the lake. "Do you think we'll see any ducks?" she asked.

He chuckled. "You know how to dodge subjects, don't you? Yes," he looked at the lake, "we may see a duck or two."

They located a small wooden table beside the lake and opened the picnic basket. Spreading a cloth over the planks of the table, Ryan lifted out containers of chicken, potato salad, and chocolate cake.

"Ryan, this is so thoughtful," she said, smoothing her skirt as she settled onto the narrow bench. "I really appreciate it."

"I know you do." He smiled across at her as he sat down. "That's why I wanted to bring you here."

She looked out across the lake as it rippled in the slight breeze. An occasional leaf floated there, reminding her of the maple leaf he had given her. Smelling the food, absorbing the lovely autumn day, and feeling the glow of his attention, Caroline thought her heart would burst with joy.

"Aren't you going to eat?" he asked, indicating the plate he had prepared for her.

She hesitated. "Could we say a prayer first?"

He looked startled for a second, then his eyes twinkled. "My mother would love you, Caroline."

Would she? Caroline wondered. *Is she like you, or is she more like Dean Miller?*

But she merely smiled and lowered her head and offered a brief prayer of thanks.

"You're a Christian?"

She nodded.

"So am I. Maybe we could go to church sometime."

"I'd like that."

"When are you leaving for Thanksgiving holidays?"

"I won't be going home," she said, trying not to feel homesick.

"Why not?" he asked, surprised.

She sighed. "I'm waiting until Christmas."

He was silent for a moment, munching his chicken. "Why don't you have Thanksgiving dinner with my family and me?" he asked suddenly.

The question took her completely by surprise. She touched the napkin to her lips, thinking about an answer. "It's nice of you to ask, but I already promised to spend Thanksgiving with some of the other girls in the dorm who aren't going home."

"All of Thanksgiving? Can't you join us for one meal?"

She shook her head, hoping he wouldn't press her. She just wasn't ready to go to his home and meet his family. Her memory darted back to the spilled punch and the nightmare of her one social event, and she lowered her eyes to the food.

"If you won't come Thanksgiving, let me put in a

reservation with you now for the Christmas holidays."

She looked up, wondering what he meant.

"We have an annual Christmas party the first week in December at my house. I think it'll be around the fifth this year. That's about the time everyone is leaving to go home." He frowned. "You won't leave before then, will you?"

"No." She looked out across the lake, thinking. "When I first came to Davis, Christmas holidays seemed to be years away. The time is going pretty fast, though."

He was watching her thoughtfully. "Caroline, how would you feel about my driving you home for Christmas? I'd get the carriage and our driver so you wouldn't be cold."

She smiled at him, keeping her thoughts to herself. She could imagine the responses in Pine Ridge if she returned in a fancy carriage. "I appreciate your offer, but I've already purchased the ticket. I got a round trip when I came here." And then her return to Birmingham would have to be scraped together over the holidays.

"Too bad. But I do want to see Pine Ridge sometime. I've been fascinated ever since you read your theme."

She studied him for a moment. "You'd probably find it boring compared to Birmingham."

"No, I've been here all of my life, and frankly I'm tired of Birmingham. I'll probably practice medicine somewhere else, even though my father and uncle want me to remain here."

"If you don't stay here, where would you go?"

"I haven't decided. I have another uncle in Montgomery who wants me there."

"You have a lot to decide, don't you? I'm relieved that I don't. It's always been my dream to get a good education and then return home to share what I've learned."

"That's a nice dream," he said quietly.

She held his gaze for a second and then looked away. Her heart was bumping around in her chest, irritating her, and now fresh doubts were creeping into her mind. She enjoyed being with him; in fact, she liked him too much. She had her dreams and he had his, and they certainly could never mix.

"Want to take a walk?" he asked lightly, as if sensing her mood.

She nodded and returned the empty containers to the picnic basket. Then they spent the next hour strolling around the lake, enjoying the view, saying little.

"It's nice to be with someone who doesn't have to talk all the time," he said after one of their silences.

She laughed softly. "Granny says I talk too much."

"You have your times of being quiet and thinking, and I like that about you."

"Thank you," she said. He looked deeply into her eyes and the nervousness that had disappeared during their walk came lurching back. "It's time for me to go back to the dorm," she said.

"So soon?" he asked, obviously disappointed.

"Yes." She didn't bother to explain why, and he didn't ask. They returned to the picnic table and he lifted the basket.

"Thanks for coming," he said, offering her his arm again as they headed for the buggy.

"This is the best time I've had since I've been at Davis," she admitted.

It had been a perfect fall day with a beautiful view and delicious food and the company of the nicest man she had ever known. It was a golden memory to keep and treasure.

five

Thanksgiving holidays dragged for Caroline. She helped Emily pack and listened to Emily's plans for the holidays. When Emily's parents came for her, they were a nice, older couple who seemed to dote on their only child.

"Emily has written us about how kind you've been to her," Mrs. Ellison said, looking at Caroline with the same green eyes of her daughter.

"Oh, she's the one who's been kind," Caroline said. "I'm going to miss her."

The girls had hugged as Emily left with her parents, and after Emily, the others began to leave. Caroline waved good-bye to all the girls, then walked alone to her room, hearing the hollow echo of her shoes in the quiet hallway.

Sadness engulfed her then, and she missed Pine Ridge so much she could hardly stand it. Since coming to Davis, she had written to Granny twice a week, painting vivid pictures of her life here. While Granny could read, her handwriting was poor, so letters from Pine Ridge were scarce and usually written by Miss Wallace, the visiting schoolmarm.

Since their picnic, Caroline had spoken with Ryan only twice. They had taken a long walk around the campus and discussed how busy they were, studying for exams. Ryan had neglected his health and come down with a severe cold, which resulted in his missing several days of school. He had told her he was planning to relax over the holidays, enjoy his mother's pampering, and tease his little sister.

※

"Caroline, are you eating with us?" Jenny Winslow broke through her thoughts. Jenny was a pleasant girl from New York who was staying at school over Thanksgiving.

"Yes, I'll be right there," Caroline called.

She tried to remain cheerful during Thanksgiving while she and six other girls occupied the dorm with a lonely housemother. She took long walks across the campus making plans, dreaming dreams. But Ryan kept sneaking back into those dreams. Even though Ryan seemed to like her, she knew there was no future with him. Because of that, she tried not to get serious about him.

On Sunday the girls and their housemother attended church near the campus. When they returned to the dorm, Caroline saw the carriages and buggies returning girls to the dorm.

She hurried around, looking for Emily, but she had not returned. Claire had arrived with stories of Christmas shopping. Caroline and Claire waited on Emily until someone reminded them that lunchtime at the dining hall would soon be over.

When Caroline returned, she was surprised to see

Emily on her bed, crying softly.

"Emily, when did you get back? And where are your parents?"

Emily sat up, sobbing.

"What's wrong?" Caroline asked, hugging her.

"I had a fuss with my father," Emily said, her voice muffled as she sobbed against Caroline's sleeve.

"Tell me about it," Caroline said gently.

Emily pulled back and dabbed a handkerchief against her wet eyes. "Father forbade me from seeing Tommy and I refused, so he offered Tommy a menial job. Tommy said no. Finally, Tommy told me Father has tried to bribe him to leave Atlanta. Tommy refused his bribe, and I love him more than ever for it." She broke into another sob.

"Oh," Caroline said, staring into space. She didn't know how to comfort Emily. She wanted to tell her how often she had longed for her dead parents. Caroline thought about how she would feel if she and Ryan could have a future together, and suddenly she understood Emily's tears. "I'm so sorry," she finally said.

"I don't care if I flunk out of school," Emily wailed, sobbing harder.

"Yes, you do," Caroline said, gripping her shoulders. "Don't you see, now you *have* to show your parents you're mature enough to make responsible decisions. In time, they may give in to you about Tommy."

With those words of encouragement, Emily's tears ceased momentarily, but the bleak look still filled her wet eyes. "I don't know if they'll ever do that."

"We'll pray about it, Emily, if this is your dream. I

believe if we do the right thing and ask God, believing that He hears, He honors our prayers—and our dreams," she added, thinking of Ryan suddenly.

She had not asked God for Ryan, but she prayed for him to get over his bad cold, do well on his exams, and succeed in being a great doctor. She had never mixed their futures, for she felt they could not change directions in their life. She had to be true to herself, and she knew where she wanted to spend her life. Ryan, meanwhile, would be in Montgomery. She had to live with that.

"Maybe when you have your morning prayers, we can start praying together," Emily offered, startling Caroline. "I never was very religious, but you're the kindest, most genuine person I've ever known. If being a Christian makes you that way, I want to be like you. I want to start reading your Bible."

"You read my Bible anytime you want," she said, hugging her again.

The next morning, Emily sleepily listened as Caroline read aloud from her Bible. Then they prayed together, hurriedly dressed, and rushed to class.

The following week Ryan seemed to have recovered from his cold, and his eyes were glowing again. "You look rested from the holidays," she said.

"I am." He reached out, clasping her hand as they walked to class together. "I was tempted to bring you a plate of food on Thanksgiving Day, but Mother said you were probably with friends."

Caroline wondered how his mother felt about her, or what she knew. She looked at Ryan. "What did you tell her about me?"

"Everything." He grinned.

"What exactly is *everything?* And had she ever heard of Pine Ridge?" she asked casually as they entered the brick building that housed their English class.

"No, but my father has."

"And what does he think?" she asked guardedly.

"They both think it's wonderful that you're going back there to teach."

"Oh." Maybe she could look forward to his Christmas party, after all.

six

Emily insisted on giving Caroline a red velvet dress with a lace sash and flowing skirt. "I want you to wear it to Ryan's party," Emily insisted.

Emily was much happier since a letter from her mother indicated her parents were going to give Tommy a fair chance.

"Emily, this is the most beautiful thing I've ever seen!" Caroline trailed her fingers over the soft velvet. "I can't—"

"It's Christmas and I can do whatever I want! I've had that dress a year and have never worn it. Fortunately, the style is still in fashion."

Caroline hugged Emily, unable to say more as she hung the dress in her closet and began to dream about Ryan's Christmas party.

The campus held glowing candles in all the windows, and the girls in the dorm had spent a wonderful weekend decorating the parlor Christmas tree. Caroline donated a small angel doll to sit on top, one she had been sewing on for weeks. Although Amelia and her friends sneered, everyone else was impressed.

The Blankenships' Christmas party was scheduled

for three o'clock Friday afternoon in order to give everyone time to return to their dorms to prepare for a Saturday departure. When Caroline made her train reservation, however, the last one available was the five o'clock train Friday afternoon.

Ryan assured her he could get her to the station in time, since his home was only fifteen minutes away.

The last exam was on Thursday, and Caroline was happy as she walked back to the dorm. Her exams had been easy, and she had straight A's for the semester. Emily's parents had come for Emily, and they appeared to be in a good mood. Emily hugged Caroline and wished her a Merry Christmas, and Caroline stood outside and waved as they departed.

On Friday she took extra care in dressing, styling her hair in a thick chignon at her nape, securing it with a red velvet ribbon. Then she went to the parlor to wait for Ryan.

He was more handsome than ever in his black frock coat and pants with a white shirt and red cravat that set off his dark hair and eyes. She could feel the envious stares of the other girls as he draped Claire's borrowed cape around Caroline and they walked to his carriage.

A handsome carriage complete with driver awaited them, and he glanced at Caroline, looking sheepish.

She smiled at him, aware of what he was thinking. "Be proud of what you have, Ryan. It hasn't turned your head one bit. And besides," she said her blue eyes twinkling, "I'm going to enjoy the ride."

They laughed together over things that had happened during the week, and soon she was gazing out at sprawling estates with enormous front lawns.

"My goodness," she said, turning to Ryan, "what do these people do for a living?"

"Some own large businesses downtown. Some are doctors," he added quietly.

"Doctors?" She smiled at him. "Then I imagine we must be in your neighborhood."

"Caroline—"

The carriage made a wide turn and she gripped the armrest and stared through the window. Gas lanterns topped brick posts at the entrance to the driveway. A huge lawn held marble statues and even a miniature Christmas tree had been decorated for outside.

Her eyes widened. Ryan was saying something, but she didn't hear. She had never seen such a grand estate in all of her life; she had never even imagined one like this existed. The drive curved again, ending before a three-story stone house with gabled roof. Candles glowed in every window, dozens of windows, and the front porch was covered with holly and velvet bows and bright tinsel.

She felt Ryan's fingers pressing her arm through her cloak. "It's my home, and I want you to feel welcome."

"It's beautiful," she said, then swallowed hard, dreading going inside.

The driver opened the carriage door and unfolded the steps while Ryan got out to assist her. Carefully, she descended and with her fingers gripping his arm, they climbed the crescent steps of the impressive house; then Ryan opened the front door.

A dozen wonderful smells greeted her—food, spices,

perfume. He escorted her into the parlor, which was already filled with beautifully dressed people. She recognized a few faces from school interspersed among adults who talked in rich voices and laughed softly, oozing the kind of sophistication she read about in novels. She felt like a creature from the forest that had been plucked up and set down on a foreign beach. Her eyes moved to a Christmas tree at the far end of the room, and she could only stare. It was a perfectly shaped evergreen that reached all the way to the ceiling and was decorated with garland and ornaments in all sizes, shapes, and colors. Beneath the tree there must have been a hundred gifts.

"Let me take your cloak," Ryan said.

She untied the strings and felt it lift from her shoulders although her eyes never left the room that held oil paintings, antique furnishings, and fancy little sculptures on marble-topped tables.

"Hello."

Caroline turned to see a middle-aged woman wearing a lovely green gown; she had dark hair and eyes and resembled Ryan.

"Hello. I'm Caroline Cushman," she said, offering her hand.

"And I'm Ann Blankenship. We're so glad you could come."

"Oh, you two have met," Ryan said, joining them.

"Yes, and she's even prettier than you told us." Mrs. Blankenship smiled at her son.

"Now get her some refreshments, dear."

Ryan and Caroline walked out of the parlor into

the dining room, where a long table was covered with silver trays of food, candles in silver candleholders, and a cut glass crystal punch bowl and matching cups. Caroline stared at the punch; *red again.*

One maid served their food; another ladled out punch. Caroline took a firm grip on the plate and cup.

Voices filled the house as more people arrived. Glancing back, she saw Amelia enter the dining room. Caroline's back stiffened, but she held her smile, determined to be polite. Behind them, other young people mingled, although she didn't recognize anyone.

"Merry Christmas, Ryan!" Amelia linked her arm through his. She looked stunning in a white velvet dress with an ermine collar. Diamonds glittered on her earlobes, and her cheeks and lips were painted a soft, delicate pink. Her hair was swept up in a crown of blond curls.

"Merry Christmas," Ryan said, smiling down at her. Caroline watched his face and felt her heart sink. He was staring at her as though entranced by her beauty.

Caroline heard the clink of glass and realized, with horror, that her fingers were starting to tremble. The sight of Amelia was a challenge to Caroline's nerves.

"Amelia, good to see you," a man's voice boomed across the room.

"You too, Mr. Blankenship." She released Ryan's arm and extended a dainty gloved hand.

"I had lunch with your father at the club last week. I understand we're all getting together for dinner."

"Yes, Ryan suggested it," she said, giving Ryan a radiant smile before her eyes slipped to Caroline.

Caroline realized the trembling had moved up her

fingers to her palms. Desperately, her eyes flew to the table, and she quickly set down the plate and cup in an empty space—before she could drop or spill anything.

Ryan was turning toward her. "Father, I'd like you to meet a friend."

Caroline turned to face a tall, gray-haired man.

"This is Caroline Cushman," he said.

"How do you do?" Cool blue eyes swept her. "You're the young lady from Pine Ridge?"

Caroline felt her stomach tighten even more. "Yes, I am."

"I'm sure your community is proud of you." He glanced over her shoulder. "Oh, excuse me, please. I see someone I must speak with. Nice meeting you." He smiled briefly, then rushed off.

Caroline couldn't decide if he was reserved or if he disliked her. She tried to keep her smile in place as Ryan took her elbow and escorted her into the living room.

Her stomach was now balled as tight as a fist as Amelia's words echoed in her mind. Ryan had suggested their families get together. He *did* like Amelia. Why else would he suggest that? She glanced over the strangers. She had never seen so much jewelry, smelled so much perfume, or felt so drastically out of place.

Ryan introduced her to a gracious older couple who peppered Ryan with questions about school. Half listening, she let her eyes sweep the room. She spotted Amelia chatting with Ryan's mother and a young girl who was dressed in a beautiful blue dress. Suddenly, the girl turned and looked directly at Caroline. What were they saying?

Caroline's stomach lurched. She had to find a lavatory. She was going to be sick. The nervous stomachache that had been troubling her for months increased to severe stomach cramps when she got nervous. She knew, in just a matter of minutes, she would be throwing up.

Before Ryan finished his conversation, she tapped his arm. "Excuse me," she said, lowering her voice. "Could you point me to the lavatory, please?"

"Oh, of course." He detached himself from the older couple and directed her down the hall to the first door on the right.

She rushed in that direction, relieved to see it was a large room and that the two ladies present were primping before a gold-framed mirror. She smiled briefly and rushed into the toilet, which, to her enormous relief, had a door to close. The women's voices floated away as the outer door opened and closed.

Enormously relieved to be alone, she gripped the wall and gave way to the heaving nausea. In the midst of her spasms, she heard the door open again. She tried to muffle the sound, but how could you be quietly sick?

"What is that?" a younger voice asked.

"Sounds as though someone drank too much of that special punch your father stashed in the kitchen."

If she felt sick before, it was even worse now. For the voice was Amelia's and Caroline knew she would rather die than go out and face her.

Fear had ended her spasms, and at least she was no longer heaving, but now she felt cold to the bone and dizzy with apprehension.

"Could you please hurry up in there?" a younger voice pleaded.

Taking a deep breath, running a hand over her face, and checking her dress, Caroline opened the door and stepped out.

Amelia stood beside the young girl studying Caroline curiously.

"Oh, Caroline," Amelia said patronizingly, "you know you shouldn't start drinking this early in the day."

Caroline's mouth fell open, and for a moment she was too startled to reply.

"Eugenia, this is Caroline Cushman. Caroline, this is Eugenia, Ryan's sister."

The girl's pale blue eyes were filled with scorn as she looked Caroline up and down.

Then she struck the worst blow of all. "How dare you get drunk at my parents' party. I think you're disgusting." She turned and entered the toilet.

Amelia was eyeing herself in the mirror, adjusting a curl. Caroline walked over to the faucet to rinse her hands. She dried them carefully, then turned to Amelia.

"I do not drink, and you have no reason to slander me," she said to Amelia, who was trying to ignore her.

Amelia had turned to face her, her chin lifted, her blue eyes cold. She said nothing.

"You've done your best to make me feel inferior since that day at the dorm when you deliberately bumped me so I would spill my punch," Caroline continued, "but you've only made me more determined to succeed. And I'm proud of where I come from and the people there;

we are good, hard-working people who try never to hurt another human being."

She heard the door open behind her and realized that Eugenia was walking around to face her.

"You're mistaken, Caroline." Amelia pushed a little smile onto her lips while Eugenia stared. "It wasn't my fault you spilled the punch. I think you're just upset because Ryan is seeing me again. In fact, I would have been his date today if he hadn't invited you. He gave me a special invitation to come anyway, didn't he, Eugenia?"

The girl nodded, looking from Amelia to Caroline.

"And for your information, we're having dinner together tomorrow night. He told me he felt sorry for you, knowing you had nothing to do."

"I *do* have something to do," she said calmly, looking back at Eugenia. "I am glad to have met you," she said. Then she lifted her chin and left the room.

Yes, she had something to do. She had a train to catch and she wanted no part of this social world ever again. She practically bumped into Ryan's mother as she turned a corner, looking for the coat closet.

"I hope you are having a good time," the woman smiled.

Caroline nodded. "Yes, ma'am. I've enjoyed your party, Mrs. Blankenship, but I have a train to catch. Could you please tell Ryan I had to leave?"

She hurried past her to the next room. She had no trouble locating her simple cape among the others as the grandfather clock in the hall struck four. She remembered Ryan had said they could get to the train station in fifteen minutes from his house. With an hour, she would have no trouble getting there on her own. She cast one last glance across the room, seeing Ryan with his father and an older man. He wasn't even looking her way; he seemed to have forgotten her completely. She turned and opened the door, stepping out into the cold gray day.

Carriages filled the drive, but she knew she could easily locate the Blankenship carriage; it would be the only one with a battered cardboard suitcase on the seat. Soon she had her suitcase and was hurrying down the driveway. Fueled by anger, she walked fast and hard. She glanced around her, trying to forget what had happened. On the contrary, the opulent estates merely reminded her of the Blankenships. And Amelia. The pain of Amelia's insults, Eugenia's scorn, and Mr. Blankenship's subtle indifference was mild compared to the raw ache of Ryan's deception. Or was it deception? He had never said he liked her, but she had assumed. . .

Was it true he felt sorry for her, thought she needed a friend? He was kind to everyone, and he had been fascinated by Pine Ridge. Maybe that was why he had been nice. Emily thought he was crazy about her and Caroline had wanted to believe that; but now she knew they were both wrong. She had seen for herself that Amelia was really his girl. She fit perfectly into his world. And now she had no one but herself to blame for her broken heart.

The wind picked up, making the day feel even colder. On the street corner, carolers huddled together, their breath making tiny circles of fog as they sang.

165

Her eyes watered and tears trickled down her cold cheeks. Lowering her head, she hurried on, forcing her thoughts toward home. It was the only way she could survive the terrible hurt inside. She thought of the community church on Christmas Eve, with home-made candles in every window, the handmade gifts folks passed out, more precious than those fancy ones under the Blankenship tree.

Deep in thought, she had walked for blocks and blocks until she suddenly stopped and looked around. Nothing was familiar. She thought if she merely headed straight back, she would pass the train station. With a sinking heart, she realized there must have been another street that led to the station, and somehow she had missed it.

With lips trembling from the cold, she stopped a passerby.

"Could you please tell me how to get to the train station?" she asked.

"Miss, you're ten blocks too far north."

She gasped. Ten blocks! Had she walked ten blocks out of the way?

"Thank you," she said, whirling around.

"When you get to Fifth, you have to take a right and go straight west four blocks."

She nodded, wondering about the time. She regretted not taking her father's watch out of its safe place in the bureau as Granny suggested. Walking faster now, reading the street signs, she regretted her impulsiveness. Why hadn't she asked directions before rushing off? *I will find it on my own,* she told herself.

She didn't need anyone's help.

Gripping her suitcase tighter, she was practically running by the time she reached Fifth. She made the turn, stopping beside an old man selling newspapers. "What time is it, please?"

Stiff fingered, he fumbled in his pocket for his watch. "Twenty till five."

I can make it, she told herself. With one hand, she lifted her skirt and began to run the four blocks. The frigid air poured through her open mouth as she panted for breath. She could feel her hair slipping out of the chignon, tumbling about her face. *How could four blocks take so long?* she wondered, gasping for breath. Just when she thought she would pass out, she saw the outline of the train station and she tried to calm herself. The dull pain in her side had become a searing ache that warned her to slow down or fall flat; still, the whistle of a departing train quickened her steps again. *More than one train left the station*, she reminded herself as she entered the station.

She could hardly bend her cold fingers, but she managed to open her purse and find her ticket. "Pine Ridge," she gasped to the little man taking up tickets.

He looked up in surprise. "Just left. Sorry."

She stared at him. "Are you sure?"

"Yes'm, I'm sure."

"Then can I trade my ticket for a later—"

"Every train seat is booked for the rest of the holidays."

His words were blows to her frozen ears.

"Hurry up, miss," someone nudged her.

Dazed, she stepped out of line and collapsed on the

nearest bench. Her bottom lip began to tremble. She wouldn't be going home for Christmas! She sat there, hugging her useless ticket, as voices rose and fell in harsh cadence. She looked bleakly at the crowd and shivered into her cape.

There had been times when she had thought she was lonely, sitting alone on a creek bank, tossing pebbles in the pond. But *this* was loneliness—surrounded by strangers at Christmas, with nowhere to go and no one who cared.

Then she felt a hand on her shoulder, suddenly aware that someone stood behind her.

"Tell me what happened." She lifted her tear-stained face and looked into Ryan's troubled eyes.

seven

I missed the train," she said.

He glanced quickly toward the ticket counter, then sank into the seat beside her.

"That's not a problem. What caused you to leave my house?" He pushed a trailing strand of hair back from her face. "Your face is frozen. Surely you didn't— did you walk?" he asked, looking horrified.

"What difference does it make? You had more important guests."

"That's not fair," he said, reaching for her hand.

She tried to hold back, but his touch was gentle, yet insistent.

"When Mother told me you had left, I was puzzled, but I thought you must have left with friends from school. Father saw you leaving and found me; I couldn't believe you would leave like that. I knew something had gone wrong. As I was getting my coat, Eugenia rushed up and told me about Amelia. That explained everything," he said, his voice edged with anger.

He paused, shaking his head. "Amelia has misled you and everyone else into thinking I care for her. We have been friends since childhood because our parents are close friends. Naturally, I asked her if she was coming to their annual dinner party of close friends. As for today's gathering, Mother insisted I invite her to the party, but my friendship with Amelia has ended. She lied to you."

Caroline stared at him, not wanting to hope, and yet she could feel something deep inside warming, just as he was warming her hand with his own.

She stared at him, considering his words. If his family didn't like her, why would they help clear up the misunderstanding? And if Ryan didn't care, why didn't he stay with Amelia? Why had he come here for her?

"Look, there's plenty of time to explain. The carriage and Felix are waiting outside. I was going to insist on taking you home; now you have no choice."

His warm smile reached out to her, and she felt her reserve topple. "Guess I can't say no," she replied.

Later, after they were settled in the carriage with a blanket wrapped around her, Caroline thought she must be dreaming. Was Ryan really saying these things to *her*?

"I have liked you since the first day I saw you. And now I think I've gone beyond the liking stage and—"

"Ryan," she sighed, "I don't fit into your world."

"Who said so? My mother adored you, my father liked you—if you understand that he's always a bit preoccupied, even with me. And once Eugenia's eyes were opened to the truth, she liked you too. My parents and sister are good Christian people; they are not snobs."

"No, they were very nice to me," she said, regretting her rude departure.

He reached across and pressed her head against his shoulder. "You look exhausted. Why don't you rest until we get there?"

"I am tired," she admitted. The warmth and the gentle rocking of the carriage had worked its magic as she nestled against Ryan and felt the sweetest peace she had ever known.

A gentle hand on her shoulder brought Caroline out of an exhausted sleep. She opened her eyes and looked around. The curtain was drawn back on the carriage window, admitting a soft, yellow light from the candlelit shops in Pine Ridge. Ryan's face was profiled against the light, and he was smiling down at her.

"We're here," he said, turning toward the window.

Caroline looked out at the place she loved and had dreamed of for months.

A full moon streamed pure silver over the small shops and log cabins where homemade candles twinkled in the windows. Wreaths made from pine cones adorned the doors, and in the soft night she could hear the peal of the church bell.

"They're having a service tonight, Ryan. Could we stop?" she asked eagerly.

"Of course." He looked out at the sleepy little community and sighed. "Caroline, I feel like I've landed in a Dickens novel. This is the most beautiful little place I've ever seen."

The carriage slowed to a stop. Felix got down and came to open the door. "Where are we going, Mr. Blankenship?"

He looked at Caroline. "Which church?"

171

She smiled. "There's only one. The little church straight ahead."

Felix nodded. "Thank you." He closed the door, and Caroline looked back at Ryan.

"Ryan, I can't thank you enough." Her eyes filled with tears.

"The opportunity to come here is my thanks. Where is the doctor's clinic?"

She frowned. "Dr. Felts? Why, he has a clinic in his home. In fact, we'll be passing his house in just a minute. He lives across from the church."

Her heart jumped at the question. Why had Ryan asked? Was it possible——?

"There. That's his house," she pointed. "Dr. Felts wanted to blend into Pine Ridge, and so he built a log cabin, as well. His, of course, is larger and nicer."

Tonight, dozens of candles twinkled in the windows, giving Pine Ridge the kind of storybook beauty Ryan had mentioned earlier.

"I can't believe anyone can live like this," he said, staring at the house.

Caroline's heart sank. "I guess it does seem remote and——"

"Stop it." His hand squeezed hers. "I can't believe anyone could have such a peaceful, beautiful life."

Caroline stared at him for a moment, seeing the fascination in his face. He meant what he was saying, but why had she ever doubted him?

The pealing of the church bell was closer now, and she looked out on the cemetery across from the church as the carriage rolled to a halt.

Ryan was following her eyes and asked gently, "Do you have family members buried there?"

She nodded. "My parents. They were killed in a house fire. I escaped because Daddy handed me through an upstairs window just before the roof collapsed."

Ryan pulled her into his arms, saying nothing. Then he tilted her chin back and kissed her gently.

She had never been kissed before, and the feel of his lips on her own brought a joy she had not thought possible.

The sound of Felix's hand on the door brought them apart as he opened the door and withdrew the carriage steps.

Ryan smiled into her eyes, then he stepped out and turned back to hand her down.

"Felix, will you join us?" she asked, smiling at the older, white-haired man.

"I would be honored."

She pressed her gloved hand on Ryan's arm and turned to face the white clapboard church with its spindly steeple. Candles filled the windows, holly framed the front door, and the sweet smell of home-baked cinnamon and spice wafted on the air. "I guess they're having refreshments after the service," she said and smiled.

So many memories filled her mind at the sight of the church that she decided to share her thoughts with Ryan, since he seemed to share her affection for Pine Ridge.

"When I stand here, so many thoughts rush to my mind." She smiled up at him as they crossed the street to the church. "All-day singings, dinner-on-the-ground—we called it that, although the men built a long pine table for the meals. And Ryan, there's a little creek behind the church where everyone is baptized. I can still feel the freezing water on my skin; in fact, I had croup for weeks, but it didn't matter. I wasn't afraid of dying; I was afraid of living without God to guide me."

He put his arm around her, and this time there were tears in *his* eyes. "That's what makes you so special, Caroline. From the moment I saw you, I was drawn to you. And then when you told me about Pine Ridge and your dreams of returning, I felt a respect for you that I've never had for another human being. Those feelings of respect have grown into love. I love you, Caroline. And I think I want to spend my life with you here."

She gasped, staring up at him, almost stumbling over the small church step.

He steadied her and smiled. "We can talk later."

Felix was opening the door for them, and through the golden light of numerous candles she could see her friends and neighbors, hear their voices singing a stanza of "Silent Night."

"Welcome home," Ryan said as he lifted his voice and joined in on the chorus.

Caroline began to sing as well, while Felix closed the door behind them, and a hundred merry voices filled the night.

Peggy Darty

Peggy has been spinning wonderful tales of romance for several years—and winning awards along the way. She had her first inspirational romance published by Zondervan in 1985. She started writing articles of inspiration about family life, but fiction was her real joy. After an editor suggested she try inspirational fiction, she found it to be a way to share messages of hope and encouragement that she feels are desperately needed in these difficult times. She loves to hear from her readers and says, "When I get a letter from a reader who tells me one of my books touched their heart, lightened their load, or helped in some way, I feel my goal has been accomplished." At home in Alabama, Peggy has been married to her college sweetheart for more than 30 years, and she is the mother of three and grandmother of two little boys.

EYES
OF THE
HEART

Rosey Dow

Dedication

In memory of Miriam Dow,
my mother-in-law, mentor,
confidante, and friend.
I still miss you, Mom.

I was sitting in the library in my favorite oversized chair when I felt a blast of cold wind. Someone had thrown open the front door. My heart lurched. I was afraid that this Christmas of 1925 would be one I'd never forget.

Eighteen-year-old Millie Box squeezed into the chair with me so she could peek around its high back and spy into the foyer.

"Is it them?" I asked.

One glance and she whispered, "It's them all right, Julie. All of 'em red and chapped with cold." She giggled. "I wonder which one is Honey's beau."

"Sh-h-h! They'll hear you."

"Help me off with this coat, Bob," a shrill voice whined, "so's I can go in by the fireplace. My toes are icicles."

I stiffened. Would they choose the library or the parlor across the hall? Both had blazing fires.

"I'll help you, Lucy," boomed a mellow male voice. "Bob's busy with his own coat." He sang off key, "Oh, you beautiful doll. . ."

"Cut it out, Tubby," the girl said, exasperated. "We've

listened to you for three hours straight. You should be on the radio. . . ."

"Then we could turn you off." A tenor male stole the punch line. Several people groaned.

Millie giggled. I jabbed a forefinger toward her middle. "You'll give us away, goosey."

Just then I heard Mother's heels clacking on the oak floor as she bustled down the central hall. Short and wide with a sensible manner, she might have been a matron from a girls' school. "Honey, dear!" she cried.

Millie whispered to me, "She's hugging Honey and snifflin'. Say, Julie, Honey got her hair bobbed. She's got bangs and red lipstick."

In a moment, Mother said, "Come into the parlor and get warm." She called loudly, "Millie!"

Millie scooted away, leaving me to eavesdrop alone. Millie was more of a little sister to me than Honey was, though they were the same age. When Millie's mother, our cook, died eight years ago, Mother kept orphaned Millie and trained her as a housemaid. Millie and I were pals. Honey and Millie had never been close.

Honey had just arrived home for her first Christmas holiday since she'd entered the University of Vermont. Being Honey, she'd organized a house party at the last minute. With five friends in tow, she phoned a message to Shegog's Grocery, telling Mother and Dad of her plans. Shegog had the only telephone in the village. Lucky for us, it was a five-minute walk away.

Honey's message arrived with the meat delivery. Mother threw up her hands and scolded, but an hour later she was making lists and chattering about gifts and activities.

Our cook, Esther Quin, grumbled through the menu planning, the pie baking, and the cookie cutting. But that was nothing new. Esther was forever grouching about something.

Dad took the news in stride. A family crisis rarely rattled him. He spent most of his time at his sawmill across the road from our house. He left most things to Mother—especially Honey.

I wished I could overlook Honey's shenanigans, too. I should be used to her scheming by now. When she was ten and I was twelve, she got inspired to start a glee club in Athens, our tiny village. Worst of all, she made her big sister sing "Snookey Ookums."

I hated every note. I still sang, of course. I was dying inside, but I sang with all my might. Maybe that's why the glee club dissolved after its first performance.

The next day Honey apologized for embarrassing me. Then she started planning a backyard rendition of *Romeo and Juliet*. Guess who got to be Juliet?

I pressed my head against the upholstery and closed my eyes as Honey said, "Mother, meet Lucy McDowell and Alice Stuart."

Then a deep, resonant voice said, "Good evening, Mrs. Simmons. I'm Jim Clarke."

"I'm Tubby. . .uhm. . .Michael Adams." The singer.

"Bob Barton," said the tenor, sounding younger than the others. He spoke like he'd practiced every word in front of a mirror.

"Honey," Mother said, "after your friends warm up,

take them upstairs to their rooms—the boys in the back and the girls in your old room. You'll be in with Julie."

Her voice faded as she called, "We'll have dinner in an hour."

I chewed my lip. An hour till dinner wasn't nearly long enough. If only I could get upstairs to my room. Too late now. Someone would surely meet me on the stairs or in the upper hall. So I held my breath, dreading the inevitable.

The farmhouse smelled rich with mingled scents of linseed oil, the giant fir tree in the parlor, wood smoke from two fireplaces, and tantalizing aromas wafting from the kitchen.

Twenty minutes later, a man's expensive cologne touched my sensitive nose. I tensed.

"Pardon me. I didn't know anyone was here." It was the gent with the deep voice. "Mind if I sit near the fire? This cold gets into one's bones."

"The blue armchair is comfortable," I said, gulping, "and it's near the hearth."

Across from me, the chair made a faint scrishing sound. "I'm Jim Clarke. You must be Honey's sister, Julie."

I wet my lips. "Yes."

"She told me about you. I'm glad to know you."

I scraped together my manners and asked, "What are you studying at the university, Mr. Clarke?"

"Please call me Jim. I'm a senior at pre-law. My father wants me to join his firm. My brother Peter is a partner, and it looks like my younger brother Ron will be one, too." His words tightened. "I'm supposed to make it a happy foursome."

"You don't want to?"

He chuckled. "You have your sister's knack for cutting to the quick."

The dinner bell tinkled, and the chair creaked. "May I escort you to dinner?"

"Why. . .surely. Thank you." His warm hand gently lifted my fingers and placed them on the sleeve of his dinner jacket. It was then that I knew that he knew. . . that I was blind.

✻

I knew the big farmhouse inside and out, every inch of polished walnut flooring, every piece of antique furniture, every shrub and tree in the yard. Five years ago, I was an average girl in every way. Then a skating accident left me in a coma for days. On my fifteenth birthday, I awoke to a dark world. Only the brilliance of sun on snow could turn my eternal midnight into dense gray fog.

Three years at Perkins Institute for the Blind had taught me how to cope with everything, except strangers. Strangers seemed to think my injury had also dulled my ears and my mind. Strangers my own age were the worst. Why had Honey brought so many of them home for Christmas?

I'd much rather have a house full of rollicking village children. Their spontaneous questions and loving touches warmed my heart. That's why I taught Sunday school for grades four through six.

As Jim led me through the parlor into the dining room, his sleeve felt rough under my hand. His palm lightly covered my fingers.

I pulled in my lower lip. Had my brown curls gone wild while I hid in the chair? My hair was bobbed above my collar with clips at each temple to keep it controlled, but sometimes it felt like a lion's mane. I was afraid to reach up and find out.

"There you are, Jim," Honey called from behind us. "I was looking for you."

"I found Julie in the library," he answered easily.

"Hi, sis," she said, giving me a short squeeze. "I've got tons to tell you later."

Mother broke in with instructions. "Julie sits there next to you, Jim, with Honey on your other side." She seated the other guests opposite us, with Mother and Dad at each end of the table.

After Dad ground out thanks for the food, Millie served my plate and cut my meat. She leaned over me from behind to whisper, "Roast beef at ten o'clock, potatoes at two, peas and carrots at five."

Afraid of who may be watching, I lifted my fork, found a cube of meat, and jabbed it. Success.

A clink and a gasp next to me. "Oh, no. It slipped out of my hand," Jim said. "Pardon me, Mrs. Simmons. I'm clumsy tonight."

"Esther, get a cloth," Mother ordered calmly. "And another plate for Jim."

He chuckled. "My beef's swimming in grape juice. A new delicacy."

Tubby sang, "I'm forever blowing bubbles. . ."

"Tubby, please!" Alice stage-whispered.

"Oops, sorry, Mrs. Simmons. I forgot myself."

184

"Michael," Mother said, a smile in her voice, "after dinner you can sing to your heart's content. . .in the parlor."

Honey added, "Julie can play the piano for you!"

My face grew warm as I reached for my glass. My fingers bumped it over. I felt Jim lurch back.

"Jim, your white shirt!" Honey cried.

Esther tsked. "And I just brought you a new plate, Mr. Jim."

"It's no worse than what I did," he said.

I couldn't breathe. I dropped my napkin on my plate. "Excuse me, please. I'm not feeling hungry." I scraped back my chair and aimed for the kitchen door to make a quick escape.

Millie was at my heels when I reached the hall. "Julie, don't run away. It was just a little accident."

"Please, finish your dinner, Millie. I want to be alone."

Running my hand up the wide banister, feeling the pine garland tied there, I climbed the stairs and shut myself into my bedroom. If only I could stay here until they went away.

I sat on my bed and felt the texture of the quilt. Of all the awful things that could happen, spilling something on a guest had to top the list. My stomach clamped down until I felt sick.

A few minutes later, the door softly opened and Millie's shoes scuffled in. "Julie? You okay?"

"I'm perfectly fine."

She sat in the chair without saying more. She knew how I hated to be fussed over.

I thumped my pillow and pulled it into my lap. "What are they like, Millie?"

"They're silly college kids."

"But what do they look like?"

She moved next to me, her voice warming. "Lucy is a pudgy girl with a shingled bob that makes her look like a boy. She wears red lipstick and orange-colored rouge. She'd be cute if her mouth wasn't always in a pout. She constantly whines at the fellows. I wonder how they put up with her.

"Alice is thin as a bean stalk with frizzy red hair and lots of freckles. Her clothes are from *Vogue,* her face is from Max Factor, and she talks like her head's full of air."

I smiled. "What about the fellows? Is Tubby as big as he sounds?"

"Bigger. He's got a round face and teeth like a picket fence. He needs a haircut, too. The other boy reminds me of a soda jerk in Stowe. He'd steal the shirt off his ailing grandfather."

"Millie! You don't even know Bob."

"He has shifty eyes, Julie. And he's got a sort of pasted-on smile too."

"What about Jim Clarke?"

"Honey's beau?" Millie's voice became dreamy. "Six feet tall, sandy brown hair, and eyes that look right through ya. And Honey looks at him like a cat sizing up a fat trout."

I laughed. "Millie, you're the limit."

The door opened, and Honey skipped in. "We're going to listen to the Happiness Boys on the radio and

186

play some games. Come and join us, Julie."

"I need to practice my offertory for Sunday." I hugged my pillow hard. "Maybe another time."

"Suit yourself." She went to the dresser and sprayed L'Heure Bleu until it filled the room. "I see you met Jim. He's a sheik. And rich as Croesus." She laughed softly.

"Did he give you a ring?" I asked.

"Not yet. But he will soon." Her heels tapped across the floorboards. "See you later."

"Why do you have to practice?" Millie demanded as soon as Honey left.

"Because I don't want to play with them."

"I never knew you were such a spoilsport, Julie Simmons." She stood. "I've got to help Esther wash up." She banged the door behind her.

I picked up a brush and dragged it through my curls. Alice and Lucy were in their room. The connecting door was shut, but I could hear their muffled voices, their laughter.

Soon they shuffled downstairs, and the second floor felt like a tomb. Why not play Mah-Jongg? Dad had carved me a set so I could distinguish the pieces. I loved to play with Millie. But with strangers?

When I couldn't bear the quiet any longer, I slipped down to the library where my baby grand sat in the corner. The smooth bench felt good. My feet automatically found the pedals. My fingers skipped across the keys, playing "The Skater's Waltz" without conscious effort, the tune so familiar that my mind wandered to happier days full of light and laughter.

two

J im, would you like to play Mah-Jongg?" Honey asked me, leaning over my chair. Light from the parlor fire danced off her golden hair, which hung forward onto her cheeks. Her wide blue eyes looked deeply into mine. Honey had style. She was a unique person who could follow the latest fashions without the gaudy extremes of the flapper.

I was a lucky man. She could have chosen any fellow she wanted. She'd even charmed my father when I took her home for Thanksgiving. Before we left, he told me she was a perfect match for a rising young lawyer— vivacious, beautiful, and not above a daring, inviting look now and then. The better to charm stuffed shirts and politicians. He told me to give her a ring—the sooner the better, like it or not.

I didn't mind. She sure was beautiful.

"Mah-Jongg or charades?" she asked, raising a shapely eyebrow.

"You choose," I said. I didn't feel like playing anything. After driving most of the afternoon, I'd much rather put my feet up and relax.

"I'm turning in," Lucy said. "My head's killing me."

Tubby hooted. "It's hurting me, too."

She threw a small pillow at him on her way out.

On the sofa, Alice snapped her chewing gum. "Not charades. We won't be able to hear the radio." Her red hair billowed around a gold cord she'd tied across her forehead, its ends dangling by her left ear. Cute, if you liked the type. I didn't.

Bob Barton pressed his ear to the radio cabinet, fiddling with knobs. Static hissed into the room as Honey moved to a corner cupboard and pulled out a flat mahogany box.

"This Mah-Jongg game is the only one of its kind. Dad made it." She set the box on a long, low table in front of the sofa.

"Partners," Tubby called, sliding closer to Alice.

"Without Lucy there are only five of us," Honey said, kneeling on the rug to set out the tiles. "We can't play partners."

"I'll sit out this time," I said, ignoring Honey's surprised, hurt look. "I'm tired from driving all day. I'll catch forty winks in the library."

The moment I crossed the hall, the fireplace lured me back to the blue armchair. I slid down until my neck rested on the back cushion. Warmth seeped into my cold joints until my eyes felt deliciously heavy.

A few minutes later, light fingers playing "The Skater's Waltz" made me blink. I sat up and saw Julie at the piano, a soft smile on her lips. I studied her eyes, so clear and liquid brown. How could those beautiful, perfect eyes be useless?

I didn't move. She was just as lovely as her sister,

but what a contrast. Honey knew she was beautiful. Julie didn't. Were there other differences beneath the surface? Intriguing.

At the end of the song, I couldn't keep from clapping. She played wonderfully, effortlessly.

She froze like a frightened bunny.

"That was marvelous," I said, trying to put her at ease. "One of my favorite pieces."

"I–I thought everyone was in the parlor."

I wracked my brain for an answer that would keep her from bolting. "Do you play Mah-Jongg?" It sounded lame even to me.

"A little." She absently stroked the black keys.

"Why don't we join the game? We'd make a third team."

Her cheeks turned pink. "I'd rather not, thank you."

"Why not? The gang is in fine fettle tonight. We'll have a blast." A burst of laughter came from the parlor, proving my point. I waited, fully expecting her to refuse, but she surprised me.

"Well. . ." She sighed, and a look—half hope, half fear—flitted across her features. "Maybe one game."

"That's the spirit. Let's show 'em how it's done."

"Wake up, Julie!" Millie shook me the next morning, excitement in her words and urgency in her hands. "The kids are going skating. I'm going too. Will you come? You had such a lovely time with them last night. Please, say you'll go."

I pushed away her tugging fingers and sat up, rubbing hair from my face. "I can't, Millie. Go ahead without me."

"But why not? I'll skate with you. It'll be the cat's pajamas."

My skates were hanging in the back of the closet. Five years they'd hung there. The leather had probably cracked by now. I used to be a champion, but the accident had changed all that. Last year I'd slipped them on, but they brought up such painful memories that I'd put them away.

"Ask Esther to bring me a tray, Millie. I'll stay upstairs this morning."

"I wish I could change your mind."

As I slid deeper under the covers, I could hear Honey's friends in the front hall.

Tubby sang loud and long until Lucy made him

191

stop. His booming laugh filled the house.

"Let's take a rope and play windmill," Honey cried. "Millie, can you find one for us?"

"There's one hanging by the back stoop," she called from the top of the stairs.

I pulled the pillow over my ears to block out their voices.

Last night Jim and I had won two games. He was a sharpshooter. I smiled. I wasn't a slouch at memory games either. We made such a good team I forgot to be shy.

A few minutes later, Esther huffed, "Here's your breakfast, Miss Julie. You'd best come down for lunch. My poor legs can't take those stairs twice in a day."

With a murmur of thanks at her retreating back, I bit into a warm blueberry muffin soaked in melted butter.

I finished off the last crumb and drained my teacup. Setting the tray on the floor, I reached under the bed for a shoe box carefully tied with a red ribbon. Inside lay a stack of letters written on crackling paper. I couldn't read them, but I still loved to hold them and smell them, remembering the boy who wrote them to me more than five years ago.

Puppy love, father had called my feelings for Tom. I guess he'd been right. After twenty-three letters describing my charms and declaring his devotion, darling Tom visited me twice after my accident, then faded away. I never heard what happened to him. I only knew he hadn't really cared.

In spite of that, I loved to remember that he'd

found me appealing. Since my blindness, I was so clumsy. My curly hair felt like a tangle. My face seemed so stiff. What man would ever look at me twice?

I fingered the letters, remembering the look in Tom's eyes when he told me he loved me.

The click of an opening door jerked me to reality.

"You're not dressed yet?" Mother asked. "If you don't want to go skating, at least you can come downstairs and help poor Esther roll out the biscuits."

I threw back the covers. "Sorry, Mother. I was daydreaming."

"What's that box?"

I shoved it under the bed. "Just some old letters. It's nothing important."

"Here's your plum-colored dress." She spread it on the bed beside me. "Please hurry. Esther's in a dither. I'd best get back to the stove before my creamed onions burn." She trundled away.

How could I manage my hair without Millie? I wanted to clip it back with the pearl barrettes Dad had given me last Christmas.

Twenty minutes later, the aroma of sugar-cured ham from our smokehouse made my mouth water. Esther greeted me with a sniff. "I could swat that Millie for running off this morning and leaving me with all the work. Here's the biscuit dough, Miss Julie. I floured the board for you, and the rolling pin's beside the bowl."

Mother wrapped a wide apron around my middle. I felt the floured board, used a wooden spoon to scrape out the dough, and sprinkled more flour on top. "Don't blame Millie, Esther," I told her. "Millie doesn't have much time for fun."

"Seems to me that's all she does have time for." The cook thumped a pan to the worktable. My fingers found the biscuit cutter, and I punched it into the dough with practiced rhythm.

The front door groaned.

"I wonder who that is," Mother said, heading for the hall. "The young people aren't due until lunchtime." Her voice drifted back. "Why, Jim, are you hurt? You're limping."

"It's nothing, Mrs. Simmons. I broke my ankle while playing tennis last summer, and it's still weak. I'm afraid I tried to do too much today. Don't worry. A little rest and I'll be good as new."

"Here, come into the library. I'll pull an ottoman near the fire for you."

"That's very kind."

I dropped the last limp circle to the pan and dusted my hands as Mother hustled into the kitchen and straight to me. "Julie, go and entertain Jim. He's hurt his ankle."

"Me? What will I say?"

"He's a polite young man. Ask him questions, and let him do the talking." She untied my apron. "It's the least we can do for Honey's young man." She sighed. "I wonder why Honey didn't come back with him."

"It's her party, Mother," I said, washing my hands at the sink. "She has to stay with the group to keep everything organized."

"You have a flour smudge." A soft towel touched

my cheek. "There. It's gone."

"Is my hair okay?"

"You look fine," she said quickly. Had she checked?

I walked the ten steps down the hall, trying to think of an interesting question. I'd already asked about his schooling. It wasn't polite to ask too many personal questions, was it? My brain filled up with limp cotton.

"Good morning, Julie," Jim said when I reached the door. "Do you feel like playing something with a poor cripple?"

Suddenly I was glad I'd agreed to spend time with him. "Do you mean a game or music?"

"You choose."

I stepped inside the library door. "I play a mean game of checkers."

"You're on. Where's the board?"

"In the cupboard under the window seat. I'll get it." I knelt before the cupboard and reached inside. "My father carved these for me. One side is domed, and the other is flat. The pieces have the bottoms indented so they can hold a king, and the board has wooden strips between the squares to hold the pieces secure."

Holding the game, I crossed the room to a square table against the wall near the piano. "We'll have to play here. Can you walk over?"

"Sure. I'm not an invalid. I just need to rest the old ankle for a while. Most likely I'll be able to skate again before we leave, if I take it slow." He paused. "It's not easy to accept one's limitations, is it?"

I turned toward his voice. "No. It's not."

In a moment, I felt his presence across from me. It's

strange the sixth sense God gives to those who need it most.

His chair scraped the floor. "Which set would you like?"

"The flat ones. I always win when I play with them."

He chuckled. "Quite the competitive type, aren't you?"

"It's in my blood, I guess." I set my pieces on the board. "I used to enter tons of sporting events: tennis, gymnastics, figure skating."

The pain must have shown in my face. His voice changed to a soft pitch that made me want to answer his next question. "Why didn't you accompany us this morning?"

"The last time. . ." I drew in a breath. "Last time I skated on the river, I had a dreadful accident. I can't bear to go out there again." He didn't speak, and wanting to explain, I hurried on. "The last thing I ever saw was gray sky and a white snowbank as my feet flew out from under me." I shivered. "The very thought of going back there makes me shaky."

I felt the gentle drumming of his fingertips on the table. Without missing a beat, he said, "You get the first move."

We played until we had three pieces left on the board—two of mine and one of his, all kings.

"You must play frequently," he said while I studied out my next attack.

"Millie and I play most evenings. But it's Dad who taught me all the good moves. He's the only one I can't beat." I set the left king forward three spaces. "I don't like to pry, but. . ."

196

"But you're going to anyway."

He was laughing at me. I hesitated.

"I was teasing, Julie. Ask me anything you like."

I plunged ahead. "If you don't want to be a lawyer, what do you want to be?"

"You'll laugh. Honey does."

"I'm not Honey."

"I knew that the first time I met you." He moved his lonely king, and my hand reached out to find it.

He said, "I want to work with city children. To lead them to Christ and give them hope for the future. With proper encouragement they can become useful citizens. Without help, they'll almost certainly end up in trouble. I've spent the past two summers volunteering at a Brooklyn YMCA. I love it."

"You're a Christian." It was a statement, but a surprised one.

"Dave Yancy, one of my roommates, made a big impression on me. He had a gentle strength that I'd never seen before. And he wasn't afraid to talk about God. Dave had me primed when William Jennings Bryan spoke at the university. I asked God to save me right there in my seat at the end of Bryan's speech." He paused as I made my move. "Dave went to seminary last year. I miss him. My life's been sort of unfocused ever since."

Wood bumped wood. "Your turn," he said.

"I received Christ in the same Sunday school class I'm teaching now. When dear old Miss Susan went to heaven three years ago I took her place. I don't know how I'd get through a day if I didn't know the Lord. . . especially now."

"What about Honey?" he asked.

"Honey's a Christian, but she doesn't think much about it."

He said wryly, "She calls my YMCA work slumming."

I made a sweeping move. "Got you. I win!"

"Well, what do you know? Beat by a girl." He chuckled. "Don't tell the fellows. I'll never live it down."

"Don't tell the fellows what?" Tubby boomed from the hall. The cold from the open door reached the back of my neck. I drew my arms closer to my body.

Tubby went on without waiting for an answer. "Look at you, Jim. We're out there turning into blocks of ice while you're roasting your toes by the fire and playing checkers with a pretty girl." He stamped and called, "Hurry up, slowpokes, or I'll shut the door on you."

The hall filled with gasps and groans about the cold. Millie called over the noise, "I'll bring hot cocoa to the parlor. Esther has some ready for us, I'm sure."

Honey swept into the library, out of breath with exercise and excitement. "Jim, Julie, I have some wonderful news. The parson stopped me on the way home and asked me to organize a Christmas pageant. It's sort of last minute, but he said we can practice with the children Sunday afternoon and—since school is out— several times next week. We'll perform it at the church on Christmas Eve."

"That's great," Jim said. He seemed pleased.

I froze, dreadfully certain that her next statement would involve me.

"We're doing *The Byrd's Christmas Carol.* Julie, you can be Carol Byrd. All you'll have to do is sit in bed and look adorable. It's perfect!"

Honey's announcement confirmed my worst fears. How could she do this to me?

Full of plans and brilliant ideas about props and costumes, Honey scurried to the parlor, where the others had gathered around the fire. My heart beat heavily against my ribs as I dropped the checkers into their box.

"What is it, Julie?" Jim asked.

I didn't say a word. I couldn't or I'd burst into tears. I shook my head and didn't answer.

Mother used to read the old classic about Carol Byrd every Christmas Eve until we got old enough to read for ourselves. It was about an invalid girl who tried to help a poor family have a merry Christmas. I always cried when she died at the end. I loved the story, but I did not want to play the part of Carol Byrd.

Since we had only one copy of the play, the girls spent the evening taking turns typing extra copies of the short script while the others played Mah-Jongg and talked about the pageant. I heard them from my room, where I lay with my cheek on the goose-down pillow.

"Well, what's this?" Millie demanded. "I missed you after dinner so I came to see what's up. You sick or something?"

"I'm fine," I lied.

"Oh, pouting, huh? You should be down there playing Mah-Jongg and beatin' the socks off them, Julie."

I turned my face away.

When the chair creaked, I said, "You don't have to baby-sit me, Millie. Go down and have a good time."

"Not with you in a fret. I want to know what's wrong."

"If you must know, it's the pageant."

"Is that all? I looked over the script. You only have a dozen lines. You'll be the first to memorize them, Julie dear. I think you'll make a lovely Carol Byrd."

"With everyone staring at me like some sort of wax museum figure? I hate to be on display like that, Millie. And I can't even read the script myself."

Honey called up the stairs. "Millie, Julie, we're ready to get started. Come on down."

"Come on, love," Millie encouraged with a resigned sigh. "Let's go face the lions."

"I'm not going."

"Well, suit yourself, but your mother will have something to say about that. She's always talking about how you hide away too much." She went out with her usual flounce and bounce.

I gnawed my lower lip. Was a ten-minute delay worth a fifteen-minute lecture from Mother?

Taking my good old time, I eased downstairs.

"Sit on the sofa by me, Julie," Mother said. "I was

just about to come for you."

Honey stood in front of the fireplace. "I'm going to assign parts tonight," she said, "so everyone has time to look over their lines before practice tomorrow morning.

"Alice is Mrs. Byrd; Jim, Mr. Byrd; and Millie is the cook. Tubby can be Uncle Jack. Bob is Peter Ruggles."

"What about me?" Lucy asked. "I don't want a long part. My head aches if I have to memorize too much."

"You'll be Mrs. Ruggles."

Jim spoke from the window seat. "That accounts for everyone except you, Honey."

She laughed. "I'm the narrator, silly." Her papers rustled. "Besides playing Mr. Byrd, Jim, you'll lead the children's choir. Julie will play for you."

She spoke louder. "The pastor will make an announcement Sunday morning, and we'll have our first full practice Sunday afternoon. Tomorrow we'll practice here. On Sunday, I'll recruit children to play the rest of the Ruggles family. They won't have much to memorize."

"What about costuming?" Mother asked. "That could turn into quite a job."

"I'll dig through Grammy's trunk in the attic," Honey said, her pencil scratching as she made a note. She shoved some pages into my hands. "Here's the script, Julie. Get Millie to go over it with you tonight so you can be ready for practice tomorrow."

"Honey, I can't learn my lines in one night. It's already eight o'clock."

She waved aside my protest. "Millie will help you tomorrow."

"Now that the play's all settled," said Bob, "how about another game of Mah-Jongg? The night's young."

"You're on," Tubby said. They moved to the game table; Alice and Lucy joined them.

A few minutes later, I escaped upstairs and dropped the script to the floor. With angry fingers I tore at my buttons. I was wriggling into my nightgown when Millie came in.

"Don't get yourself in a stew, Julie," she scolded. "Honey gave you the best part. I've got to borrow one of Esther's dresses and stuff it with pillows." She giggled. "I'll be a sight."

"I don't appreciate the way she manages me. Like I'm a checker piece." My voice grew shrill. "Julie will play piano for you."

Millie sat beside me on the edge of my bed. "She thought she was being nice by including you. I wish you wouldn't take on so."

I didn't sleep well that night. I knew I was being stubborn and unkind, but I couldn't shake my grumpy mood. By morning I had a headache.

Honey was in high spirits. She woke me with cheerful singing that made me want to stuff my handkerchief in her mouth. She buzzed between the adjoining rooms, chattering like a spring blue jay. As soon as she finished dressing, she and Alice scampered upstairs to dig around in the attic.

Lucy strolled in to borrow Honey's lipstick and stayed to chat about her boyfriend. I didn't want to socialize. Finally, she climbed the attic stairs to find the girls.

I didn't feel like eating breakfast, but I went to the table anyway to keep Mother from fussing over me. When Honey clattered down the stairs, I could hardly swallow my eggs.

She swept into the dining room and cried, "Guess what! There's an iron bedstead in the attic that will be perfect for the pageant. You fellows must haul it down. We'll make it up, and Julie can sit in it for practice this morning."

I stiffened. "Can't we put some pillows on the sofa and pretend?"

Honey bore down on me. "C'mon, be a good sport, Julie. The bed will give atmosphere to the whole room."

Her tone told me arguing was useless. If I called attention to myself, she might get inspired and make me go upstairs and change into my nightgown for "atmosphere." Millie squeezed my hand beneath the table. I couldn't tell if she wanted me to keep quiet or if she was sympathizing with me.

Play practice was agony. Millie read my lines for me while I sat in the middle of the library on a lumpy cotton mattress with a quilt over my legs. Worse, I started thinking about the thousands of spiders living in the attic. What if one had gotten on the mattress? I'd always been terrified of them, but since my accident the idea of a creepy thing crawling on me was unbearable. Somehow I held on and didn't make a fool of myself.

I was tired enough to cry by the time Mother called us for lunch. Afterward, I took a nap and woke up to a quiet house. The gang had gone out for another skate-fest.

I dragged a brush through my hair and went down to the library for some time alone with my piano.

"There you are," Jim called, when I reached the bottom step. "I've been waiting for you."

I touched my curls, wishing I'd taken more time with them. "You didn't go skating?"

"You forgot my bad ankle. I'm afraid you'll have to endure my company again this afternoon."

I went to the piano and flicked fingers along the keys. "Would you like to hear anything in particular?"

"Play the one you did before."

" 'The Skater's Waltz'? It's my favorite piece." As I swept through the melody, I said, "You haven't told me where you're from. Do you live in Vermont?"

"Connecticut. Just outside New York City. My father's practice is in New York, but Mother always hated the city. Ten years ago, we moved to a hundred-acre estate named Thornton's Hill." He leaned against the baby grand. I could almost feel his breath when he spoke. "It's a rambling place with wide fields on each side of the house and white fences dividing the horses' paddocks. Two tennis courts. A small lake on the west side. The house is a three-story Victorian with massive pillars in front."

"Sounds frightening."

He chuckled. "It's a museum, not a home. Especially since my mother died. To be honest, I'd rather be at our bungalow on Long Island. No stress, no neighbors, no telephone for miles. It's lovely, especially in the fall."

I struck the last notes of the song.

"Say," he said, "would you like to practice your lines

with me? It's a shame to waste this quiet while the gang's outside. A person can hardly put two thoughts together with Tubby's singing and the girls' chattering."

"If I translated my lines into Braille, I could read them during practice."

"That's a great idea."

"I'll get the slate from my room." My heart felt curiously light as I came back down, the metal rectangle and stylus in one hand, two sheets of stiff paper in the other.

I sat at the table. "Please, read me the words, and I'll punch them."

" 'I want to tell you all about my plans for Christmas this year, Uncle Jack,' " he read, pausing every few words until I got them down.

Before I knew it, the gang was back and we were drinking cocoa in the parlor. Honey could talk of nothing but the pageant. As usual, her enthusiasm wore everyone else to a frazzle, and she was still going.

That evening, practice went much better. I still felt stupid sitting in the bed, but the covers hid my hands, and I didn't miss a word.

Sunday morning, Millie helped me into my navy dress with a white sailor collar and red tie. Except for Jim, all of Honey's guests wanted to sleep in.

The weather was clear with an icy breeze when we left the house. Of course, Jim escorted Honey. I was close behind them, holding Dad's arm with Mother on his other side. Millie stayed behind to help Esther.

We headed down the lane to the gravel road. Ahead on the left lay Shegog's Grocery, a squat building with gray shingled siding. When I was six, it already looked as old as Moses. On the other side of the road the clapboard church had a spire but no bell.

The ice-covered river ran parallel to the road until it veered east just before the church, leaving enough space between the road and the river for the church property.

"You're looking smart this morning, Mr. Clarke," Honey said, a lilt in her voice.

Jim chuckled. "Are you fishing for a compliment?"

Usually I smiled at my sister's flirtatious nature, but today I didn't feel like smiling. Once we reached the church, I went straight to my classroom. "Good morning, girls," I said brightly when I reached my room. "Have you heard about the pageant?" My scholars peppered me with so many questions, I could hardly get through my shepherds-and-wisemen lesson.

The day was full with an afternoon of play practice—squirming kids everywhere—followed by the evening service. That night I fell into bed too tired to stay up for the Will Rogers radio program, the family's favorite ending to a Sunday night.

On Monday after lunch, the gang suited up to go skating again. I was looking forward to a quiet afternoon in the library with Jim and his sore ankle. Today, I'd ask him to read my favorite passage from *Jane Eyre*. Instead, he made a suggestion that gave me a shock.

five

W hen Julie came downstairs with her head tilted in that charming way, listening to find out who was there, an idea flashed through my mind. It probably wouldn't work, but I had to try.

I waited until she sat on the piano bench so no one else could hear. Then I knelt beside her and spoke softly. "Julie, won't you come with us to the river?"

Her chin jerked. Her face turned pale. She didn't answer.

I leaned closer. "My ankle won't let me do any fancy footwork today, but it has improved enough so I can do some simple skating with the others. Won't you come out with me? I'll stay beside you every minute. Please come."

She wet her lips. "I can't," she whispered.

"I won't let you bump your nose. Promise." I gulped some air and pushed harder. "You've got to face your fears someday, you know. If you don't, you'll grow old in this cocoon of a house and never know true happiness. I know it's painful, but please try."

She pressed her tiny teeth into her bottom lip until

I feared I'd see blood. Her chest rose and fell. I waited, hardly daring to breathe, praying like I hadn't done in months.

"I'll have to change," she whispered.

I touched her hand. "I'll wait for you."

With new starch in her backbone, she climbed the stairs like a queen. I cheered every upward step.

Honey touched my arm. I looked at her, startled to see the others had already gone. "Are you coming, Jim?"

"Julie's coming with me to the river."

Her eyes widened. "You must be a miracle worker. She hasn't set foot near the river since. . ."

"I know. It took some persuading, but I talked her into it."

She lifted a plaid scarf over her chin. "There's no sense in my waiting, too. I'll see you there." She strode through the door, skates dangling over her shoulder. Her green ski hat and that blonde hair made me wish for my Brownie camera and a wide-angle lens.

Fifteen minutes later I was still waiting. Had Julie lost her nerve? Finally she stood in the hall holding out her skates. "Are these still wearable? It's been so long, I'm afraid the leather is cracked through."

I took them from her and turned them over. "They're sound enough. I'll carry them with mine. Which coat is yours?"

"The black wool with a sheepskin lining."

Buttoned up to her chin with her curls bobbing beneath a black cloche hat, she looked like a pixie. I grasped her mittened hand and placed it inside my bent elbow. "Miss Simmons, let's cut some ice."

She smiled, but I could feel her tremble.

When we stepped onto the porch, the sun glaring on the mill's tin roof made me squint and turn away. We crossed the gravel road and reached the river in two minutes.

The gang had vanished by the time we changed into our skates. I could hear Tubby shouting and Alice squealing. Bob called Honey's name as their voices faded on the faint breeze.

"I feel so wobbly," Julie said, clinging to my shoulder as she stood. "Maybe I've forgotten how. I never used to skate with my eyes closed."

"Give yourself a chance to get a feel for the skates. Here, let's get set. Cross your hands and hold on to me." I put my right arm around her waist. My left hand clasped her right and my right hand held her left. She fit into my shoulder like she'd been carved to match. Her hair tickled my cheek. She smelled like a summer meadow.

"Now let's get in stride. Lead with your left." Slowly, jerkily at first, we headed for the center of the ice. After ten strides, she found her rhythm and seemed to anticipate my moves. We picked up a little speed.

"I can't believe I'm doing this." She blinked hard. "The sun is so bright I can almost see it." Energy swelled inside her until she glowed. "The sawmill is on our left, isn't it?"

"Yes. Another river branches off to the west just ahead."

"Let's take the branch, Jim. I used to love to go that

way. Some days I'd skate all the way to Nebraska Valley."
Her feet moved with natural grace.

"Say, you're pretty good."

A gleam of pride shone in her smile. "I won first
at state figure skating two years running. Where are
we now?"

"Just beyond the sawmill. I can see a wall of moun-
tains in front of us. They're splotchy with bare trees and
evergreens and patches of white."

She nodded. "We haven't had much snow this year.
I hope we get some soon or tourist season will be a
washout. Dad depends on tourism in the winter." She
tilted her head. "There's a cardinal in the woods over
there."

I listened. The birdcall came from the pine forest
rising on our left. I hadn't noticed it before. The river
ran between the mill and Shegog's store, giving me a
splendid view of their backyards. Further on, the woods
surrounded us.

"Maybe we ought to turn back," I said. "I don't
want to tire you out the first day."

"But I don't want to go back yet. I'm having too
much fun."

"Why don't we sit and rest a while, then. My ankle
is starting to talk to me."

She turned her face toward my cheek. "I forgot
about your ankle! Let's go back."

"All it needs is a little rest. There's a ledge ahead.
We'll sit down." A piece of gray slate, about three feet
wide and a foot deep, extended out from under an old
spruce. We reached it in two glides.

"Whew! I'm warm," Julie said, puffing, as she pulled off her hat. "That was great fun." She tilted her face toward the sky. "I love the crisp feel of a winter breeze."

A masculine shout came from the east.

Julie turned to me. "You'd rather be with Honey. I'm beginning to feel terribly selfish."

"Don't give it a second thought. There'll be plenty of time for me to be with the others. It's your turn, Julie. You deserve it."

She relaxed against my side, contented. The trouble was, I was feeling pretty contented myself.

"Too bad we can't stay here," I said. "It's so peaceful. No problems or worries."

"Like law school?"

"How'd you guess? My father is a good man by most standards. He cares about his sons. He just has his own ideas about what's good for them."

She shifted positions, and her hair brushed my ear. "What are you going to do?"

"Go to law school, I guess." I drew in a slow breath. Cold air made my lungs ache.

Her face crinkled around the eyes and forehead. "Can your father's approval make your life fulfilled forever? Is it enough?"

"That's the question I keep coming back to. Sometimes I see faces when I close my eyes—Ricky, whose father left before he was born; John, who lives in a ratty tenement with no running water; Tommy, who's lived on the street for as long as he can remember—dozens of them, Julie. I can't get them out of my mind."

"Do you really want to?" She turned toward me, her face inches from mine. "If you forget them, something inside you will be gone."

I squeezed her mitten. "How'd you get so smart in a backwater place like this?" I stood and brushed my pants. "We'd best get moving. A few more minutes and we'll freeze to that stone." I gave her a hand up, and we set off.

At the time I didn't stop to analyze the situation, but when we reached the others half an hour later, Honey's arched eyebrow and silent look brought me back to reality with a thud.

six

"Julie? Are you awake?" Honey asked from the other bed.

Under the quilt, I stretched and sighed, enjoying a strange, sleepy excitement. Was it because I'd faced the river and returned triumphant? Or was it something more?

"What time is it?" I asked.

"Seven. I'm thinking of knocking on Jim's door and asking him to go for a walk."

"Honey, you shouldn't knock on the fellows' door. Mother and Dad wouldn't like it."

She scuffed on her slippers and stood. "I'm not a child anymore, Julie. And besides that, Jim and I have an understanding." Her voice softened. "I wouldn't be surprised if he gave me a ring for Christmas."

"Do you really love him, Honey? You've had so many beaux. How do you know it's real this time?"

"Two good reasons, child. First, he's a sheik, and second, he's worth twenty-five thousand a year on his allowance. Just wait till he gets his inheritance."

"Honey! That's not love." I sat up. "How would you feel if he had an accident that disfigured him or paralyzed

214

him?" I reached for her. "Don't do this, Honey. You'll regret it all your life."

She ignored my hand. "Save the sermon, sis. I know what I want. And what I want right now is Jim Clarke." She shuffled to the closet.

A moment later Millie burst in. "Oh, you're awake, Julie. I came to help you dress. Esther gave me a black dress to use for the play." She laughed. "I could put two of me in it and still have room left over. What a lark!" She headed toward the closet. "Say, I like that maroon sheath, Honey. It makes your hair glow."

Honey opened the adjoining door and called, "Lucy, Alice, get up! We have to work on our costumes today."

Alice mumbled, "Go away!"

"It's after seven," Honey said. "You've got two minutes to roll out, or I'm going for some cold water."

Lucy giggled. "This could be interesting, Alice. I wonder if the boys are up yet. We could get some glasses and. . ."

Millie said, "They went out for an early fling on the ice, all three of them."

Honey sat in the chair and ticked off the day's agenda. "Millie's dress is ready. Jim and Tubby can wear their usual clothes. Bob has a pair of knickers to play Peter Ruggles. Mother's white nightgown will do for Julie, but we ought to make a nightcap for her, too."

I pulled on a corduroy jumper, biting my cheek to keep from commenting on the nightcap idea. Arguing with Honey only made her more determined to have her way. I finished dressing, then hurried downstairs to

215

help Esther knead bread dough. Better the kitchen than Honey's endless plans.

The men arrived at the breakfast table on time. Dad was already at the mill and Mother had walked to Shegog's for some thread, so the meal was livelier than usual.

"Throw them hotcakes on over, Bob," Tubby said. "On second thought, maybe I should just exchange plates—my empty one for the platter."

Lucy cut in. "Don't forget us girls, you hollow legs. We're hungry, too."

Esther trudged in, bringing the pungent smells of coffee and sausage with her. "Here, Millie, help Miss Julie." She set a platter beside me, poured my coffee, and hurried out, saying, "I've got more hotcakes on the griddle."

"What are we going to do while you ladies sew?" Bob asked between bites.

Honey said, "You can carry props from the attic. And we need a Christmas tree at the church. If we finish the dresses in time, Lucy, Alice, and I will go over and decorate it later today."

"I want to do my nails this afternoon," Lucy complained. "All this practicing is wearing me out."

Tubby sang, " 'O, Christmas tree. . .' Where do we find one?"

"Cut one down in the woods out back," Honey told him, as though it were a dumb question. "There are plenty of small spruces around."

Bob's voice dripped sarcasm, "This is getting better all the time. You think it's easy to chop down a tree?"

"You'll live, Bob dear," Honey told him. "After all, you and Tubby can take turns."

The big fellow sputtered. "What about Jim? What's he doing?"

A fork clinked on a plate. "Jim will be driving around Athens, collecting things." A paper rustled. "Here's the list."

Jim read, "A table and chairs from the parsonage, lamps and rugs from Mrs. Anders—"

"I found some darling old ornaments in an attic box," Honey interrupted, "and Grammy's old china set. We'll bring them down today."

"Hunky-dory!" Bob said. "Be careful today, Jim. You don't want to strain yourself with all that heavy work."

Honey answered before Jim could. "Cut it out, Bob! The pageant is tomorrow afternoon. Don't start griping now."

Bob and Tubby were unusually silent for the rest of the meal. At eight-thirty, we went our separate ways: the fellows outside and the ladies into the library.

Honey pushed a wad of flannel at me as soon as I stepped through the library door. "Put on this night-gown, Julie. I'll close the doors. You can change in here to save time."

"Why do I have to put it on now?"

"Just do it," she said sharply. "I want to see it for myself."

"Let me help you." Millie came behind me and pulled at the fastenings on my dress. Minutes later, I stood in the center of the room with soft flannel brushing my bare feet. After pulling two garments over my head, my hair felt like a tumbleweed.

A light knock sounded at the door.

Jim called, "Honey, I need directions to Mrs. Anders's house."

"Come in, Jim. Everyone's decent."

I whispered frantically, "Honey! I'm not decent."

The door slid back as she said, "Silly, tomorrow you'll be wearing that in front of a whole crowd."

"It's not the same." I wanted to die.

Too late. I could hear Jim's voice saying, "Just sketch a map on the back of your list, and I'll be on my way."

As soon as Jim strode out, Honey said, "I think we can make a nightcap from one of Dad's big handkerchiefs. I'll go up and fetch one."

I couldn't stand it any longer. "Why do I have to wear a nightcap, Honey? No one wears those anymore. I'll look ridiculous."

"The play was written in the 1800s, when girls wore nightcaps." She trotted away. The next moment I heard her shoes on the stair treads.

"Don't worry so much, Julie," Alice said around her wad of gum. "None of us are going to be fashion plates for this thing, you know."

I blinked back frustrated tears. "I just wish she'd listen to me sometimes. She acts like I don't have a brain."

Millie hugged me. I returned the hug, thankful for her concern but still uncomforted.

Honey came whizzing back and set a soft cloth on

my hair. "Isn't Jim sweet? Whenever I ask him to do something, he does it right away. He's one in a million."

Alice giggled. "One with a million, you mean."

"Don't be crass." Honey laughed deeply.

"He's thoughtful and kind," I said softly.

"And he's mine." Honey snatched the cloth from my head. "Everyone had best remember that."

I reached for the buttons on my gown. "Are you through with me now?"

"Yes. You can run and play." Honey moved to the game table, where Alice and Lucy were working over their gowns.

"This is boring, you know that, Honey?" It was Alice and she wasn't kidding.

I groped to find the sleeves in my jumper as Millie said, "I'll go up and help your mother sew rings on the stage curtain. She must have a hundred left to do."

"I wonder how Tubby and Bob are doing." Alice cracked her gum and snickered. "I wish we could take a little hike and spy on them."

Lucy spoke up. "You'd be a dead duck. If you laugh at Bob while he's in a grump, he may break some ice and stick your head in the river."

"Now that would be a sight," Honey said as I reached the stairs. "I'll get my camera. Let's go."

Even Millie laughed that time.

seven

I couldn't believe how callous Honey was acting toward Julie. As I headed out to my car, I thought about the scene I'd just been through in the library. I'd been almost as embarrassed as Julie when I stepped inside the library and saw the poor girl standing there in a nightgown. Her face could have lit a town square.

As soon as Honey drew the map, I'd hurried away. What could explain Honey's behavior? Ever since we'd arrived, I'd been picking up little hints that things were strained between the two sisters, but I didn't think much of it. I'm not that close to my brothers. Those things happen in families.

The Oldsmobile purred like a warm cat as I headed down the gravel road. Shegog's Grocery loomed just ahead. On impulse, I parked in front.

The place smelled of freshly ground coffee and the coal smoke belching from the rusty potbelly stove in the back corner. It was a mom-and-pop affair with farm equipment on one side and dress goods on the other.

"He'p you, mister?" a grizzled old codger asked. His whiskers touched the top button on his faded flannel shirt.

"I'd like to make a phone call. I'll reverse the charges."

The shopkeeper nodded to the wooden box on the wall near the end of the counter. "There it is."

Our butler, James, had Dad on the phone in less than a minute. "I just wanted to check in," I told him. "We're having a swell time."

"Did you give that girl a ring yet?" The old man had a mind like a vise. Once it clamped on to something, it wouldn't let go.

I sighed. "No. I haven't found the right time." The diamond lay deep inside my inner coat pocket in a velvet pouch. I hadn't touched it since we arrived.

"Well, see that you do. With her pulling for you, you could be a senator someday. She'll charm fat accounts out of the woodwork."

"Dad, I'm not sure I want to join the firm. I've been doing some serious thinking—"

"Well, think about this, then. I've spent a small fortune on your education, and I'm willing to spend more. But if you welch on my investment, you're going to regret it. Do you understand me, son?"

"Yes, Dad. I understand." I held the silent receiver a moment, then said, "Have a Merry Christmas."

He grunted. "Pete and his wife are in the country, and Ron is at a house party for the holidays. I'm alone with James and the cook. Call me before you leave Vermont."

"I will, Dad. Good-bye."

I left the store wishing I hadn't called. Dad had his ideas and I had mine. What was I going to do?

I aimed my roadster toward Stowe. Mrs. Anders

221

lived near the north end of the narrow road in a square cottage with frost-killed marigolds lining the walk. My breath came out in white billows as I knocked on her door.

A rawboned woman opened it and looked me up and down. "Yes?"

"I'm here to collect the lamps and rugs for the Christmas pageant. Honey Simmons sent me over."

"They're right here." She pulled the door wider.

I had everything loaded and delivered in an hour. On the way back the roadster suddenly developed a cough. I reset the choke and listened closely. I'd have to check it out before Monday.

My thoughts drifted to Julie. Maybe I should talk to Honey about her sister. Maybe if I told her what she was doing to Julie, she'd ease up a bit.

I saw my chance when I reached the house and she said, "Let's go to the attic. I'll show you the boxes I need."

I dropped my leather cap on the newel post and followed her up two flights. The attic covered half the house. It was dusty, organized, and cold as the Arctic.

"That box," she said, pointing to a cardboard carton on the floor, "is the china."

"Honey." I ignored the props and turned her to face me. The look on her face said she expected me to kiss her. "It's about Julie," I said.

Her mouth tightened. "I've noticed you're spending a lot of time with her."

"Please try not to embarrass her." I wanted to smile, to ease the tension, but my lips felt stiff. It must have been the cold.

"I haven't embarrassed her." She sounded indignant.

"I can think of several times when you have."

"When?"

"Making her sit on the bed for practice when none of the rest of us had to get into our parts. Calling me into the library when she was wearing. . . Honey, you can't be so dumb that you don't understand what I'm trying to say."

"Jim, darling, I haven't asked her to do anything that she's not going to do in front of a hundred people during the pageant."

"Just giving her the main part embarrasses her."

"I was trying to be nice to her."

"It's not working." I lifted the carton. "Let's go down. You're shivering."

"Wait a second. Why are you so interested in Julie?"

"She's vulnerable. I don't want to see her hurt."

"I wouldn't hurt Julie for anything. She gets stubborn sometimes, and I have to give her a little push." Her eyes narrowed. "You did the same thing when you took her to the river."

"That was different. She had a great time skating. She's miserable about the pageant. Can't you see that?"

"You like her, don't you." It was an accusation.

"Of course I like her. She's your little sister."

"She's two years older than me. And she's not the fragile flower you're making her out to be."

I bit back a sharp reply. "Forgive me for mentioning it." I turned away. "I'll take these to the car."

She followed me downstairs and disappeared into the library. I stopped to catch my cap from the post.

Honey was usually so sympathetic. What had happened to her?

Two more lonely trips to the attic, then I drove to the church. With the pulpit to move and the props to arrange, I was busy until Bob and Tubby arrived—scratched and seething—dragging a four-foot spruce behind them.

eight

There you are, Julie!" Millie said. She pulled out my chair at the lunch table, and I sat. "Ham sandwiches and potato salad," she whispered, "at nine and three."

"I'm catchin' forty winks after this." Bob's lifeless voice was almost unrecognizable. "I'm beat. If I'd known we were going to be lumberjacks today, I wouldn't have gone skating before breakfast." Though I couldn't see anyone's face, when I'd come down for lunch I'd sensed that the party spirit had soured. The only one in a good mood was Millie, who seemed terribly amused.

"Don't fuss," Alice told him. "Exercise is good for you. Builds muscles."

"He's got plenty of muscles," Lucy said, "around his mouth."

"Can it, girls." For once, Tubby was serious.

"We'll all rest for an hour," Honey said. Her voice sounded dull. "Dress rehearsal's at two-thirty."

"I want to go shopping," Alice said. "I haven't bought a single Christmas present yet."

Even Jim sounded subdued. "After practice I'll take

225

everyone on a drive to Stowe. I'd like to look around myself."

I leaned toward him. "Will you have room for me?"

"Certainly." His voice lost its apathy when he said, "Delighted to have you aboard."

We all filed upstairs when Millie started clearing the table. It was the first time my sister had been silent since she'd arrived.

"What's wrong, Honey?" I asked, lying back on the bed. "Did you quarrel with someone?"

She punched her pillow. "Tubby and Bob have turned into two spoiled cabbages, Alice is bored, and Lucy whines until I want to slap her. Even Jim's in a bad mood." The bed creaked as she moved. "The house party has gone wrong, and I'm not sure why."

"Maybe you're expecting too much of everyone," I said carefully, not wanting to rile her. "They came here for a good time, and you're putting them all to work."

"Well, that's just too bad, Julie. The pageant is tomorrow, and we have to see it through—no matter who likes it and who doesn't."

I turned away from her and closed my eyes. How could anyone get through to her? Sometimes her mind wore armor plating.

❄

Since we had to change into our costumes, we girls walked to the church half an hour earlier than the fellows. My tiny Sunday school class acted as a dressing room. We were constantly bumping elbows and losing things.

Honey flitted from Alice to Lucy, helping them

with buttons, joining in their snickers, reassuring Lucy on the fit of her gown. Finally, Honey said, "I'm going out to see if the children playing the Ruggles family are here yet."

"Millie!" Alice yelped. "That dress makes you look like a pregnant elephant." She giggled. "Isn't this a panic?"

Millie laughed. "I put powder in my hair to make me look older. I'll be the first pink-haired cook in history." She pulled the nightcap over my curls and brushed stray strands away from my face. "You look like an angel," she whispered close to my ear.

I touched her hair. It was pulled back into a fat bun with wisps hanging down all around. Millie's springy mane was impossible to tame. How had she managed to fasten it up?

Honey opened the door and called inside, "Okay, gang. Let's go knock 'em dead."

"One look at us," Lucy said, "and they'll keel over for sure."

Dress rehearsal went surprisingly well. Only Bob had to be coached with his lines. Now that the props were in place and everyone in costume, I almost felt that I really was Carol Byrd. Despite the sad ending, it was a lovely story—one of my favorites.

At the end I sank into my pillow and closed my eyes.

From the audience Honey said, "Now the children sing, 'My ain Countree,' and the curtain falls."

"What curtain?" Lucy asked. Her voice echoed in the empty auditorium.

"Mother will have it ready by tomorrow morning. We'll run a wire from there to there and slide the rings over it."

"Shouldn't we do it today?" Jim asked. "There may be a slipup if we wait too long."

"Mother's not finished with it yet," Honey said.

"Let's get the wire up anyway," Jim said, stepping down to the lower level. "Where is it?"

Honey's shoes made the floor vibrate. "In that box by the organ."

The cast began to chat. I threw back the quilt and eased out of bed.

The children gathered around me. "You look beautiful, Miss Julie," little Mary Parks said, swinging my hand.

Her sister Maud said, "Get that bug away from me, Billy! I'll tell your mama!"

"What bug?" I tried not to flinch. If only I could see that rascal, Billy.

"Don't worry, Miss Julie," Billy Gates said. "I've got it in my pocket."

"It's a spider," Maud said.

Billy got louder. "No, it's not. It's just a beetle. They live in our basement when it's cold like this."

That was my cue to leave. "I want to change, Millie," I said reaching for her, "so I can drive to Stowe with the others."

"You want me to go along?"

"If you don't mind. I'd like to buy some Christmas presents. I haven't been Christmas shopping since. . . you know."

Millie gripped my hand, and we headed toward the classroom at the back of the church. Five minutes later, the other girls arrived, excited about our outing.

Jim's car had soft leather seats and a humming heater that reached to the backseat, where Millie and I stuffed in with Tubby and Bob.

"Meet back here at five-thirty," Jim said as he cut off the engine, "and I'll buy supper. There's a nice place just down the street, The Snow Goose."

"That's a lovely café," I told him when we reached the sidewalk. "I haven't been there in years."

Millie was buzzing inside. I could feel it.

Jim said, "Honey, I'm Christmas shopping this afternoon. Would you mind going along with the girls?"

"Of course not." The lilt was back. "See you in a while." She and her friends moved ahead. Her voice drifted back. "Where do you want to go first?"

"A dress shop," Alice said. "Do they sell glad rags in this hick town?"

Lucy added, "I want some chocolates. Big fat ones."

I turned toward Millie. "Let's go to Smithy's, Millie. I'd like to find a hand mirror for Mother."

An hour later, Millie and I were loaded down with packages.

"We'd best get back, Julie. It's five-twenty."

"Already? I've hardly gotten started."

"C'mon. I don't think I can carry any more."

I laughed, delighted. "I did get carried away, didn't I?"

"It sure is good to hear you laugh, girl. Here, hold my arm and let's go."

The wind had turned bitter. I tucked my chin deeper

into my sheepskin collar.

Jim greeted us with, "Two down and three to go. Have you seen the other girls?"

I smiled. "Not me."

He took my bundle. "The trunk's open. I'll lay these inside for you."

"We haven't seen the girls all afternoon," Millie said. "I heard they were going to look at clothes."

Tubby groaned. "They could be hours. I'm starved."

Jim thumped the trunk lid down. His keys rattled. "The Snow Goose is less than a block away. Let's go ahead. I'll leave a note on the window."

I felt Jim's presence beside me as we entered the restaurant. He had a special smell, a mixture of wool and that heady cologne he always wore.

"I'll take your coat if you'd like," he said, while we waited to be seated. His hands felt whisper light on my shoulders. "Party of eight," he told the hostess, placing my hand on his arm.

The smell of seasoned steaks and coffee filled my senses. I sniffed hungrily. It felt so good to be out again. Jim read me the menu and placed the order moments before the tardy girls arrived.

"Sorry to be late," Honey gasped, sliding into a seat across from Jim. "We found a luscious place full of handmade, hand-painted carvings." She laughed. "The girls had to drag me out."

"We weren't trying too hard," Lucy said. "I spent two month's allowance. Give me a menu, Tubby. I'm famished."

The conversation turned toward Christmas plans.

Tubby and Lucy had to leave right after the pageant so they could be home in northern Vermont for Christmas. Jim would drive them to the train in Waterbury. Bob and Alice would stay on. Alice's parents were in Italy, and Bob's single father was living it up in California—two poor little rich kids with no place to go for the holidays.

I listened to their insolent attitude toward their parents and thought of Mother and Dad. Maybe there were some things worse than a physical injury.

Christmas Eve was a miserable day. During the night the temperature rose to 35 degrees and rain came down in sheets. It beat against the windows and drove a chill into the house that the fireplaces couldn't chase away.

Lucy spent the morning packing her bags and worrying over a lost sash. Honey paced the floor with a case of nerves over the pageant that evening. I wasn't worried. Once she got to the church she'd be fine. As a matter of fact, I was feeling better about the pageant all the time. My part was easy, and the children had calmed my fears about how I looked to the audience.

While I was dressing, Mother came in. "Julie, I want you to put on this extra set of woolens. That flannel nightgown isn't nearly warm enough for the drafty church. And with this rain, it's worse. You'll catch your death up there in front. The heat never reaches up there. My feet turn to ice when I'm sitting in the choir."

"Mother, I hate those scratchy things. My long flannels will be enough."

"I'm afraid I'll have to insist, dear." She turned to Millie. "Help her with these, will you? I've got to put

231

the finishing touches on more pies for tomorrow's dinner. Those boys have completely emptied the pie safe." She hurried away, ignoring my objections.

Millie didn't move.

"What is it? What's wrong?"

"I wonder where she found these." Pause. "I suppose they'll keep you warm enough. That's what counts."

"Millie, tell me!"

She stifled a snicker. "They're striped like peppermint candy, the leggings and all. Patting my arm, she said, "No one will see them, love. It won't matter in the least."

"Won't they show through the white gown?"

"Not with three petticoats over them. Don't worry, I'll check you over before anyone sees you."

We decided to leave the house at five to give plenty of time for our hair to dry. With rain still pouring down, there was no way to keep from getting soaked.

We stood in the hall, screwing up courage to make a dash for the car, when Lucy whooshed open her umbrella and grumped, "I don't know why I'm bothering. With that wind, this bit of silk is just a token of despair."

My shoes got soaked in a puddle on the run from Jim's car to the church.

"Just take them off," Millie said. "No one will know your feet are bare. Your legs stay under the quilt. I'll put the shoes on the radiator to dry."

"And get wet again on the way home." I touched my hair. "This feels like a frizzy mop. Oh, I wish it weren't raining tonight."

Lucy said, "Get a shingle bob like me and you won't have to worry about it." She stepped closer. "Hey, what are those?"

Alice nudged in. "Are you playing the part of a candy cane tonight, Julie?"

My face grew warm. "Mother insisted I wear these because of the dampness."

Lucy said, "They're pippin. Wish I had a pair." Then she laughed.

I bit my lip to hold back a sharp answer.

Soon, children swarmed over the church like bees over a clover field. Not only the ones in the play, but all their brothers and sisters with some cousins thrown in. I heard Honey calling to them, frantically trying to keep order.

J im, please help me with the children," Honey said minutes after I stepped inside the church. Her face was flushed from chasing two speeders through the oaken pews. She pushed the delinquents toward me. "I've got to see to last-minute details, and they keep running around the church, yelling and knocking things over."

I took two grimy hands and said, "I'll put them all down front in the choir's chairs."

She smiled and touched my arm. "You're the greatest."

No stained glass or velvet in this church. The floor needed a coat of varnish, the wainscoting needed paint. It was a far cry from the cathedral my parents attended, but I felt a warm spirit here I'd never felt there.

I had the children sing carols for the next half hour. They were slightly off tune but made up for it with volume. By some miracle, everyone was ready at zero hour. I stayed with my choir, ready to slip behind the curtain at the proper moment.

Mary, Maude, Billy, and the other Ruggles children sat on the end chairs, so they could march on stage for Act Two: the Ruggles Family at Home. Cast members

234

waited behind the curtain while Pastor Jenkins, a gaunt, white-haired gentleman, welcomed the folks and opened in prayer. Then Honey told about Carol Byrd's birth on Christmas morning and how her mother found a name by listening to the boys' choir singing at the church next door. On cue, my choir belted out "Carol, Brothers, Carol" and the curtain opened.

Act One passed without a hitch. Dressed all in white with a white quilt and lacy pillows propped behind her, Julie charmed the audience. When Millie's outlandish costume got a belly laugh, she blushed with pleasure. Tubby played jolly Uncle Jack to perfection.

Finally, the Ruggles children swarmed into Julie's bedchamber. Billy hung on the bedpost and swung on the backs of the chairs until Millie gave him a boot as she passed.

When they finished the meal and the children left the table, Julie said, "Oh, wasn't it a lovely. . ." Suddenly her face contorted—shock, realization, then stark fear.

She screamed and scrambled off the bed. Her foot caught in the quilt. She fell headlong into the back of a chair. The chair knocked Billy, and he landed against the Christmas tree, sending it and all the china ornaments crashing to the floor.

Julie's gown flew up to her knees, showing a wide patch of red-striped long johns and bare feet. The children pointed and laughed. Soon most everyone in the audience was laughing, pointing, and laughing again.

In the wings, Honey burst into tears and disappeared through a side door. Still squealing, Julie tried to kick her foot loose from the quilt. Millie ran to her rescue. Afraid she'd been hurt, I rushed to help. A second later, Tubby had the presence of mind to pull the curtain.

"A spider," Julie sobbed in Millie's arms. "It was on my hand." She sniffed, very unladylike. "Oh, I've ruined everything!"

Millie looked to me for help.

"You're not to blame, Julie," I said, touching her arm. "It could have happened to anyone."

"Let's get you home," Millie said. "I'll fetch your coat. You can put it over your gown and sneak out the side door, like Honey did."

"Honey ran away?" Julie pulled back from Millie. Her face full of dread. "She'll never forgive me. Never in a hundred years."

The children scampered down to their parents. Tubby and Bob and the girls slumped in chairs beside the overturned table.

I peeked around the curtain. The last of the folks were heading out the back doors. On a cold, wet night like this, the best place to be was home. I wanted to be there myself. Too bad I had to drive Tubby and Lucy to the train.

We found Honey already in the car when we loaded up a few minutes later. Since Mr. Simmons had his Model T at the church to take his household home, I headed right to Waterbury with Lucy and Tubby. We drove eight miles in silence. Lucy hunkered down into a corner of the backseat. Tubby slouched in front. They didn't offer any conversation during the hour-long wait, either.

At eleven o'clock I hung my dripping coat on the Simmonses' banister and dropped my hat on top of it. They were too wet for the closet. I hesitated, too keyed up to go straight to bed. The library fire looked inviting.

Except for the glow of orange coals, the room was dark, the furniture black lumps in the shadows. My hands stretched toward the heat when I heard a sniffle. I peered through the gloom.

Huddled in a corner of her chair sat Julie. Her tear-smudged face wrenched my heart. She tilted her head. "Who's there?" she whispered. "Mother?"

"It's Jim." I knelt before her. "What's the trouble?"

Fresh tears flowed. "Honey won't speak to me. She's moved in with Alice. I've never known her to get so mad."

My lips tightened.

"If I weren't blind. . ."

"Now, hold on." I pulled her chin up with my forefinger. "Being blind has nothing to do with it. Sighted people are afraid of bugs too. Please don't torment yourself."

She touched my cheek. More than that, she touched my heart. The next moment, she was in my arms. I wanted to comfort her like I'd never wanted anything before. My lips found hers, tenderly, sweetly. I was in another world.

ten

Jim's kiss reached down to the deep recesses of my being. I lost myself in his arms, overwhelmed with his gentleness.

Honey's face slowly took shape and moved to the front of my mind. Trembling, I jerked away.

He immediately turned me loose. "Forgive me." His voice was haggard. "I had no right. I don't know what came over me."

I wanted to tell him it was okay, not to worry, but the words wouldn't come. I tucked my chin down.

He stood close to my knee. "I'd best go upstairs. Can I get you anything?"

An ember popped. The upholstery leather felt smooth beneath my burning cheek. I shook my head, unable to speak. I listened to his footsteps until they disappeared down the upstairs hall—savoring the bittersweet secret that no one in the world must ever know: I was desperately in love with the man my sister intended to marry.

❅

"Wake up, Julie!" Millie said, shaking me. "It's Christmas morning. Everyone's waiting in the parlor. Go and splash your face while I get you something to wear."

I staggered next door to the bathroom. The icy water made my nerves tingle. Had I imagined last night? Dreamed it? No. Something in me had changed forever.

"Is Jim downstairs?" I asked Millie as she slid a scratchy wool dress over my head.

"Everyone's there. Honey's in a chair, tapping her toe. Alice and Bob are sitting next to each other on the hearth, looking like kids on after-school detention. Your parents are on the sofa, and Esther is making hot cider in the kitchen."

"What about Jim?" I said louder. Millie could be so infuriating.

"He's leaning on the mantel shelf, staring into the fire. I don't think he's said two words all morning."

With fumbling fingers, I pulled on a sweater and pushed cold feet into my shoes.

When I sat on the sofa next to Mother, she put her arm around me. "It's snowing, Julie dear. We've got a white Christmas."

Millie sat on the rug at my knee. Her hair brushed my arm whenever she moved.

Dad cleared his throat. "Let's have a word of prayer, thanking God for His special gift that first Christmas morning. His deep voice made the rafters ring. When he was through, he said, "Jim, since you're standing, would you do the honors?"

"With pleasure, Mr. Simmons."

Just hearing his voice made my heart skip. I pinched my lips together, afraid my face would betray the tempest brewing inside me. Would Jim kiss me, then give Honey an engagement ring a few hours later?

As Jim called name after name, Mother whispered what the gifts were. To Alice from Honey: a white feather boa. To Julie from Mother and Dad: a pair of skates.

To Honey from Jim: a painted wooden mouse on skis, three inches tall. "How lovely!" she exclaimed, but I sensed her disappointment. I drew in a slow breath that felt like the first one in days.

To Julie from Jim. . .

His fingers brushed mine as he placed the lumpy package in my hands. Mother untied the string that held the cloth around the gift. Alive with curiosity. . . seeing with my fingertips. . .I felt two tiny people on top of a flat box slightly larger than my hands. The top surface felt like glass, the sides like wood.

"Here, let me." Mother reached for something on the side.

Tinny, plinking music made the box vibrate. The people swirled around in time with "The Skater's Waltz." Enchanted, I ran my hand over the sides, found the stem, and wound it again.

"I found it in a tourist shop the day we went to Stowe," Jim said from somewhere far away.

I looked up. "I'll cherish it." The couple reminded me of my first time back on skates, a crisp breeze in my face and my hands clasped by a certain wonderful gentleman.

Esther's voice broke the spell. "Watch out, everyone! Hot cider coming through."

The rest of the day was a series of exhilarating sensations: a roll-and-coffee breakfast, a rousing round of carols at the piano, a turkey dinner with all the trimmings.

Suddenly time flew like a December wind. On Monday, only two days more, Honey and her friends would drive away. Would I ever see Jim again? Honey's ring hadn't appeared. Hope kindled a tiny fire beneath my left rib.

That night Honey snuffed out the flame.

It was past nine, and exhausted, I'd just climbed into bed, when Honey marched into my room. The music box stood on my bedside table where I could reach it.

"We have to talk," she said, standing over me. Usually when Honey started with those words she meant: I'm going to talk and you'd best listen if you know what's good for you.

I clamped my jaw and waited.

"Why are you chasing Jim? You know he's mine. I brought him here to meet the family because I intend to marry him. Then you get your head filled with juvenile. . ." She paused to take a breath, and I dove in.

"Honey, he's not a puppet. He's a man. All your life you've bossed everyone, including me. If you think you can do the same with Jim Clarke, you're in for a surprise."

"You know him better than I do?"

I tried to keep a lid on my temper. "You only see what you want to see. To you Jim is a rich fellow with a plush future. But that's not what he's really like. He's a sensitive guy who wants to work with poor city children. He may not be a lawyer at all."

She whispered her answer, but her words were

241

intense. "He'll be a lawyer all right."

A moment later, her voice softened. "I feel sorry for you, Julie, shut up here with the social life of a caterpillar. It's no wonder you found one of the fellows attractive. I'm just sorry it had to be Jim."

This was really rich. "You'd rather I liked Tubby. . . or Bob?"

"Not seriously, silly. Just for fun."

My temper flared. "For your information, I didn't chase anyone."

"That's not the way it seemed to the rest of us. I'm sorry to tell you this, but it's embarrassing the way you've been mooning over him—leaning toward him at the dinner table, hanging on his arm. I'm not the only one who noticed. Lucy mentioned it to me before she left."

My face burned. Had I been forward with Jim? I tried to remember, to reexamine my actions. I rubbed my forehead. Everything was jumbled. I couldn't think straight.

Honey put her arms around me. "I feel bad for you. Truly I do." She sounded sorry. "We won't talk about it again, okay?"

I nodded and curled down under the quilt. I heard her turn out the light and close the adjoining door. With trembling fingers, I reached out to touch my music box. My shoulders heaved, and I hid my face in the pillow.

Despite my exhaustion, I hardly slept. Humiliation seared me like a hot poker. What must Jim think of me? Twenty years old and acting like a schoolgirl with her first crush. I'd made a royal fool of myself. How could I be so stupid?

"I'm not dressing," I told Millie the next morning.

Honey and Alice were downstairs getting into coats to go sledding on the hill behind our house. Runaway horses couldn't drag me outdoors with them today.

"Why are you still in bed?" Millie touched my forehead. "Are you sick?"

I pushed her away. "Stop treating me like an invalid. I'm not sick. I'm tired."

She perched on the side of my bed. "What's gotten into you, Julie? Yesterday, you floated on a cloud. This morning you look like you've been up all night eating stewed persimmons."

"I don't want any breakfast. You can bring me a tray for lunch."

She stood. "Suit yourself. I'm going sledding with the gang. If I stay to argue, I'll miss half the fun." She opened the door, said, "See you later," and scurried away.

I pulled the quilt over my ears.

I must have slept because when Honey and Alice burst into their room chattering like two jays and laughing between every sentence, they startled me. I traced the hands on my alarm clock. Eleven-thirty.

I might as well get dressed. No sense staying in bed all day. I felt in the closet for my flannel shirtwaist and corduroy jumper.

"I'm glad to see you're up," Millie said, startling me. "Time to come down for lunch."

"I told you. I'm not going down."

She flopped into the chair. "You really are in a pet, aren't you? Come on, tell Dr. Millie what the problem is."

Praying for courage to do what I must, I turned around for her to fasten my buttons.

"I've got a little job for you, Millie." I swallowed. "Don't try to talk me out of it. Just do as I ask this once . . .please."

"You're serious." She sounded worried.

I reached for the music box. This time I didn't wind it up. "Wait until you catch Jim alone, then give this to him. Tell him I can't accept it."

"Why not? It's a wonderful gift. You'll hurt him if you give it back."

I pushed it into her hands. "Please, Millie! Don't argue." Tears welled up behind my eyelids. "It's best this way."

She hesitated.

I waited for her to scold me. But all she said was, "I'll bring you a lunch tray," and then she went out.

I dug in my drawer for a handkerchief and sank into the chair. If I could hold on through today and tomorrow, Monday they'd all be gone and I could get back to normal.

Normal? Did that exist for me anymore?

"r. Clarke." At Millie's words, I looked up. "Julie asked me to give you this," Millie continued, hurrying across the library rug. She thrust the music box at me like it was full of hot coals.

I stayed in my chair and stared at it. "Why?"

"She says she can't accept it." Millie set the wooden box on the hearth near my hand.

"Where is Julie? I want to talk to her."

"She won't come downstairs." The red-haired girl stepped closer and whispered, "I don't know what's happened, but she's in an awful pet. Looks to me like she cried all night. I can't imagine what's gotten into her."

My first impulse was to bound up the stairs and make Julie tell me what had happened. I let out a slow breath, trying to put the pieces together, and not liking the picture no matter how I turned it.

Millie darted from the room. I hardly noticed.

I picked up the music box and turned it over in my hands, remembering Julie's pleasure when she'd received it yesterday morning. What had changed her attitude?

I went up to my room to hide the music box before

anyone asked questions I didn't want to answer. When I burst in, Bob stood before a mirror with a hairbrush in his hand.

"What's on for the afternoon, old man?" he asked without turning. "I've had all of the great outdoors I can stand for a while. Let's play parlor games after lunch."

I mumbled a noncommittal response and slid the box under the quilt near my pillow.

Bob picked up his sport coat and shrugged into it. "I wonder what's cooking for lunch. I could eat a moose."

I was hungry when I reached the dining room, but Julie's empty chair killed my appetite. I pushed away from the table before the others finished.

"What is it, darling?" Honey turned to me, mild concern in her eyes.

"I think I'll walk to Shegog's. It's nothing important." I forced a smile. "Be back in a while."

The moment I stepped through the door, the wind clawed at my face, pulled at my hat, and sucked away my breath. I pulled a wool muffler about my chin and leaned against a pillar on the porch. Going to the store was an excuse. I wanted to be alone, to sort things out.

Sunbeams glittered on the snow that covered every surface: the trees, my Oldsmobile and Mr. Simmons's Model T, the mill across the road.

Julie couldn't stand to be near me. Did it matter so much?

I tramped through the woods for more than an hour. Sorting through a fellow's priorities is never easy. For me it was sheer torture. All my life I'd craved my father's approval. I'd endured unspeakable agonies trying to

246

please him. The trouble was, I never could. It came down to one question: What did I really want in life?

Two ways lay before me: a gorgeous wife, a top-notch job, fabulous wealth and social standing. Or a life of service, of living with the problems of others, of self-denial. The choice seemed ridiculously easy. So why was I so miserable?

I kept telling myself that Honey was perfect for me. I believed it, too.

Alice, Bob, Honey, and I played Mah-Jongg the rest of the afternoon. I laughed louder than anyone. Why not? I had everything going for me down to the last detail. . .special ordered by my father.

✳

Sunday morning, Honey clung to my arm, smiling close to my face, tempting me. I didn't look at Julie when she came down with Millie and took her father's arm for the walk to church. I sat with Honey in the second pew —two rows ahead of the Simmons family—so I wouldn't have to make a choice about where to keep my eyes. Honey, warm and possessive, was enough for any man.

After the singing, Pastor Jenkins shambled to the pulpit. He looked almost too frail to get through the message. He stood quietly for a moment and took inventory of the congregation. His black eyes rested on me, and suddenly I felt like an eight-year-old on the first day at a new school.

"Open your Bibles to Matthew 6:28," he quavered. " 'Consider the lilies of the field, how they grow; they toil not, neither do they spin: And yet I say unto you that even Solomon in all his glory is not arrayed like one of these.'" He cleared his throat. "Today we're going to have a little lesson on God's economics."

I looked at the shiny elbows on his black coat, at the worn edge on his collar, and I wondered what he could teach me, heir to a man who drove a Rolls and owned three massive homes. But during the next hour that old parson made more sense than anyone I'd heard since Dave Yancy left the university.

I also learned that keeping someone out of your line of sight won't stop you from seeing them. For a solid hour I had to keep pushing aside the image of liquid brown eyes and a sweet, natural smile.

After the service, we left the church. On the steps I paused to shake the old parson's hand and thank him for the message. As we walked away, I turned to Honey. "I have to make a phone call."

She latched onto my arm and smiled into my face. "Mind if I come along?"

Covering her glove with mine, I made myself grin. "Do you have to ask?"

"You've got something on your mind," she said, watching me.

"It's nothing. Honest."

We strolled across the road toward the store, and I glanced at the village people crossing the bridge, the same bridge Julie and I had skated under a few days ago.

"Is Julie ill?" I tried to sound casual. "She looks pale."

Honey tilted her head. "Why are you worried about Julie?"

"She's your sister. Why else?"

She laughed. "I suppose it's the Good Samaritan in you."

I stopped in midstride. "What's that supposed to mean?"

"I was referring to your charity work." She plucked at my sleeve. "It's terribly sweet of you, Jim, to want to help those poor urchins in New York. It shows your soft spot, I suppose."

"Honey, I'm not sure I'll enter law school next fall. I think God wants me to work with my boys full time."

She dismissed my statement with a toss of her head. "Your father would never allow it."

I swallowed hard, feeling as if I stood on the edge of a precipice. I knew what I should do, but did I have the courage to do it?

Shegog's lay just ahead, a thin gray spiral rising from its chimney.

She pressed her lips together as though deciding something. "Before you make your call, I want to tell you how sorry I am for the way Julie has been hounding you. You have to understand she's not used to social settings like—"

"Hounding me?"

"You know. Getting you to play checkers with her, keeping you at the piano."

"Honey, did you speak to Julie about me last night?"

"Darling, I couldn't let her go on like a giddy child. It's embarrassing to her and to the rest of us."

My blood pressure went up ten points. "How could you be so cruel? Julie would be devastated to think she's made a spectacle of herself."

"Exactly why she had to be told." She turned those wide, guileless eyes on me. "Don't you understand?"

Suddenly, I understood much more than Honey imagined. "My phone call can wait," I told her. "Let's walk by the river. We need to talk."

twelve

Julie, what's the matter with you? You aren't ill, so why won't you come to dinner?" Mother asked, hovering over me. "Please, come to the dining room with the rest of us."

"I can't, Mother. I just can't."

"Why not?"

I pressed my lips together. Finally, she got tired of asking and clumped down the stairs. I'd won, but I didn't feel like a winner. Roast beef and mashed potatoes are tasteless when eaten from a tray in a lonely room, even with French apple pie for dessert.

When Millie came for my empty dishes I told her, "My head feels like someone's pounding it with a hammer."

She touched my hair. "Poor dear. Let me get you an icepack. I'll be back in a jiff."

But Mother returned, not Millie. "Here's a spoonful of sleeping powder mixed with sugar," she said, "and a glass of water."

I swallowed, then shivered and gulped the cool liquid. Not that it took away the awful taste. I let my head fall to the pillow, more miserable than I'd been since the accident.

"Julie," Mother sat near me, "has Honey upset you? I want to know before she leaves in the morning."

"Don't blame Honey. She's only tried to help me." My eyelids felt heavy. "I'm the one. . ."

I didn't hear her leave.

❄

"Julie? Can you wake up?" Honey spoke into my ear. "I've got something to tell you." She gently shook me. "Please wake up. We've got to leave soon."

The soft urgency in her voice brought me around. "What is it?" I rubbed my face, fighting off the drugged feeling that held me down. "I'm awake. What is it?"

She hesitated. "I want to apologize." She touched my arm. "Sometimes I get so caught up in things, I forget to think about how everyone else feels. We've been through this before, I know."

I waited for the rest of it. She meant it now, but there would almost certainly be another incident like the pageant. Honey couldn't seem to learn the lesson.

"I didn't mean any harm, Julie," she went on. "You really were a lovely Carol Byrd."

My anger softened. Honey had come home full of energy and expecting a great time. Everything had gone wrong. I felt bad for her.

"I forgive you," I whispered. I hugged her tight, wanting to say more but not knowing how.

She broke away, murmured "Bye," and hurried out.

Who told Honey she'd hurt me? Mother?

I threw back the covers and scooted to the window.

Through the glass I could hear Alice's shrill giggle and Jim's voice calling good-bye. The car chugged to life. It sounded rough, more like Dad's Tin Lizzie than Jim's smooth Olds. I hoped they wouldn't have a breakdown.

Tires crunched over snow and gravel and faded away. Finally, sweet silence told me they had gone. I leaned my forehead against the cool pane. I'd expected to feel relieved. Instead I felt empty.

I turned toward the closet. I had to get to my piano and have a long session with Chopin. Only music could ease my emptiness.

Jim was gone.

I slipped into a housedress, any old one, and touched a brush to my hair.

The cool banister felt comfortingly ordinary under my hand. My slippers made a whisper on the stairs. I heard Millie laughing in the kitchen followed by Esther's booming scold. Mother would be tidying the parlor, taking down all the decorations. The household had returned to normal the moment the gang drove away.

Why couldn't I? I felt like a stranger to myself, half a person where a whole person used to be.

I turned toward the library door, my hand outstretched to find the knob. Inside my sanctuary, I closed the door behind me and leaned against it, smelling the fire in the grate, hearing it crackle, feeling its warmth.

Another smell—a man's cologne, achingly familiar. Did Jim stop by here this morning? His scent lingered behind to torment me.

I tilted my head, straining with everything inside me to "see" both past and present. Something was different, and it was more than just me.

A slow, melodious tinkle shocked me with the rush of a tidal wave. "The Skater's Waltz." My music box.

I gasped. "Who's there? Jim?" Tears welled over before I could stop them.

In an instant, Jim's fingers twined in mine. "It's me," he said.

"You didn't go." I was too astonished to be shy, too much in love to care.

"I couldn't leave you. I finally realized what a short-sighted fool I've been. If a man lives for money and prestige, he's nothing but a shell."

"But Honey—"

"Isn't right for me. I told her so yesterday." He lifted my fingers to his lips. "I won't be going to law school. When I phoned my father I expected him to disown me, but he didn't. For the first time in my life I heard respect in his voice when he said good-bye."

He pulled me closer. "I love you, Julie. You're sweet and sensible. . .and real. Will you marry me?"

"Oh, yes." My hands reached for his face.

He pulled me into his arms and kissed me. My world exploded into a million dazzling lights that swirled and spun in a frenzy of colors. In the middle of it all I saw Jim, the part of him that no one else could see, the part of him that belonged only to me. Sometimes the heart has eyes of its own.

Rosey Dow

Rosey was born in Dover, Delaware, and lived there until college. She minored in English, but despised her creative writing courses. Six months before graduation, she married a preacher boy. Three children later, she impulsively mailed in a coupon for a writer's correspondence course. By the time she finished the course, she had a new hobby. For fourteen years she wrote reams without a single sale. In December 1996, her first book, *Megan's Choice,* appeared in the **Heartsong Presents** line and put her on the 1997 list of ten favorite new authors for **Heartsong**. Since then she's sold several articles and another novel, *Em's Only Chance.* Serving with her husband as church planting missionaries in Grenada, West Indies, she home-schools their seven children and helps edit a monthly newspaper along with other missionary activities.

PAPER ROSES

JoAnn A. Grote

one

Minneapolis, Minnesota, 1893

How can life have gone from perfect to perfectly awful in only two weeks? Vernetta Larson wondered, seating herself at the luxuriously appointed Thanksgiving dinner table. The crystal and china glinting in the light of the gas chandelier seemed to mock her with their reminder of the life of wealth she'd taken for granted for so long.

Her tall, broad-shouldered Swedish father took his usual seat at the head of the table and bowed his head. His voice rumbled out with the same humble gratitude to the Lord as always.

How can he sound so sincere? Vernetta asked herself. *Is he truly thankful, even now?* In all her nineteen years, she'd not found it this difficult to be thankful, and things must seem worse to him.

"Hmph!" Her mother snapped her lace-edged napkin open with a plump, well-manicured hand and laid the napkin across the lap of her ice-blue satin gown. "Thanking God, indeed! We should demand to know why He let this happen instead."

No need to ask what her mother meant by "this." The financial depression, commonly known as the Panic, had finally reached its tentacles into their home. The bank Vernetta's father had started twenty-five years ago had failed two weeks earlier. Hundreds of other banks across the country had failed, but Vernetta hadn't expected her father's bank to fail.

The gray color of her father's face cut her to the quick. He'd looked poorly since the bank collapsed. Must her mother grind salt into his wounds? She bit her bottom lip hard to keep from expressing her thoughts. Her father wouldn't tolerate criticism of her mother, even in his defense.

"Now, Lena," he was saying in the strong Swedish accent that lingered even after twenty-five years in America, "I know you don't mean that. It isn't our Lord's fault that I and the other bank officers invested our depositors' money unwisely."

Her mother's blue eyes snapped. "And how were you to know railroads were a bad investment, I'd like to know, with tracks being laid from here to yon and back again?"

A grin spread across her father's broad face and twinkled in the blue eyes beneath his graying blond hair. "Now that's the woman I married, defending her man against the world."

A delicate flush swept over Mother's round face beneath the heavy, dark hair that was piled in a loose bun. "Anton, honestly!" Her lashes swept her suddenly rosy cheeks.

Father had often told Vernetta she looked like her

mother had at her age. She'd never been able to see the resemblance between herself and the portrait of her mother at eighteen that hung above the parlor fireplace. Vernetta's long hair, which she wore up with a fashionable fringe of curly bangs, was not-quite-brown and not-quite-blond, certainly not the rich brown of her mother's. Her eyes weren't blue like her parents, but a striking, unusual violet. She had the traditional wide Scandinavian face but had a narrow chin instead of the rounded, broader chin of her mother.

Mother was fingering the fluted edge of the bud vase that held a single red rose. Father had given her that rose. There was one by each of their plates. They were beautiful, but Vernetta knew it was hard for her parents, seeing the single roses. For as long as Vernetta could remember, her father had bought two dozen red and white roses for the Thanksgiving table and for the Christmas table also. It was a tradition he'd started the first year he'd made enough money to more than meet the young couple's expenses.

Vernetta smiled at her mother's flustered attitude. *She looks like a young bride, very much in love,* she thought. She couldn't recall ever seeing her mother look that way. It was sweet but cut into her heart with fresh pain.

Would her own face ever fill with love for another that way? Love had walked out of her own life last evening. She pushed down the pain that had filled her chest since she awoke. She'd thought she might receive an engagement ring from Andrew Reed for Christmas. He'd been courting her for six months and had profusely proclaimed his affection for her.

Last night he'd made it clear that he wouldn't be escorting her in the future. He'd actually told her that his parents wouldn't allow him to see a young woman whose father had embarrassed himself by losing his business and his family fortune. *I'm better off without him if his love is based on my father's money and position,* she told herself for the twentieth time since he'd spoken the awful words. The thought helped her hold her head up in pride but didn't help her wounded heart.

She hadn't told her mother of Andrew's decision yet. Mother had been thrilled that a future lawyer, the son of a state senator, was courting her daughter. "The best marriage prospect in the state," she'd said. Vernetta sighed.

The swinging door between the kitchen and formal dining room opened, and a maid entered with a large china soup tureen. Along with her came a welcome drift of warmth from the large cookstove and the smell of wood smoke mixed with the mouth-watering odors of pumpkin pie and roast turkey.

Dora was the only servant left in the household. She wouldn't be here, Vernetta remembered, if she hadn't offered to work for room and board. Jobs were almost impossible to find in these days of high unemployment.

Dora moved smartly as always. The white apron covering her black dress was crisp, as was the small white hat she wore pinned behind the blond braid that circled her head. She set the tureen in the middle of the lace-covered, mahogany table and served the three Larsons.

Vernetta accepted a steaming bowl of rich oyster stew, the usual first course in their Thanksgiving meal. "Thank you, Dora."

The front-door chimes sung through the house, and Dora hurried to answer them. She was back in a minute with a calling card on a small silver tray.

Father took the card and frowned. Vernetta thought his face grew grayer. His broad shoulders drooped beneath his fine jacket. "A newspaper man?" he growled. "Haven't they torn me apart enough? Must they also invade my home and family on Thanksgiving?"

Vernetta's heart felt like it was being squeezed. She pushed back her chair and stood in one smooth motion. "I'll ask him to leave."

"The gentleman said he wishes to speak with you about boarding, Mr. Larson." Dora's quick, softly spoken clarification stopped Vernetta before she reached the door to the hallway. She swung around, staring at her father.

Mother slapped her napkin onto the table beside her plate. "He is no gentleman if he interrupts us on Thanksgiving, Dora."

"Yes, ma'am," Dora murmured, retreating to the kitchen.

Mother leaned forward, glaring at Vernetta's father. "Anton, I told you I won't have my home turned into a boardinghouse!"

Father's huge chest lifted in a sigh. He looked so tired that Vernetta's chest clinched in pain for him. "Lena, I cannot possibly afford to keep this house without some kind of income. I didn't think the ad would be in the newspaper until tomorrow. I apologize for this intrusion." He handed Vernetta the gentleman's calling card. "Please ask him to come back tomorrow."

Hurrying down the walnut-paneled hall, the sound of her footsteps hidden in the depths of the carpet runners, Vernetta could hear her mother's angry voice through the closed door. Her cheeks grew hot. Could the possible boarder hear the tirade?

She set her thin lips firmly and lifted her chin. *No matter how bad things become, I won't allow myself to become bitter like Mother,* she promised herself. She barely knew the woman her mother had become since the bank failure. *Starting tonight, each evening I will find something for which to be thankful, no matter how trivial, and write it down in my diary. I won't allow my soul to become warped.*

The man, who had been seated on the upholstered mahogany chaise near the door, almost leaped to his feet when he saw her, his brown derby in his hands. A few snowflakes still sat on the camel-colored wool coat covering his brown, high-buttoned business suit. His black hair was a tumble of curls he'd obviously tried and failed to repress.

Vernetta found herself responding immediately to his friendly brown eyes and quick smile. Remembering their roles, she suppressed the smile that had come to her lips in answer to his own. She glanced at the card. "Thank you for your interest in our ad, Mr.—"

"Thomas Michael McNally." He bowed from the waist with a flourish of his derby that brought back her smile.

"Yes, so your card states. It is Thanksgiving, Mr. McNally. Could you please return tomorrow?"

"Unfortunately, I can't, Miss Larson. I have to catch a train for an out-of-town assignment in an hour. I won't be back until midnight tomorrow."

Was this true, she wondered, *or was it Irish blarney?* In spite of his Irish last name, there was no hint of an accent. His people must have been in America for a long time.

"One of the men who works in the advertising department at the *Tribune* knows I'm looking for a room," he continued. "He knew from the address this would be a fine place to stay and, that is. . . ." His fingers played with the edge of his derby, and he stumbled over his words.

Vernetta felt blood seep from her face. *He recognized Father's name as the one placing the ad,* she realized. Once it would have been a sign of the station her father had achieved. Now it was a sign of his failure. Mr. McNally's knowledge of her father's business affairs was likely also the reason he knew she was Miss, not Mrs., Larson.

She lifted her chin, folded her hands together at her waist, and watched him. She wasn't about to offer him a way out of his predicament. The newspapers hadn't been kind to her father. *I'd have thought when they reported his bank's failure to the world, they'd have also remembered all he's done for this city through the years.*

Their gazes met. She thought his eyes surprisingly honest—for a newspaperman. He spread his arms slightly and lifted his thick, dark eyebrows. "I didn't want to miss the opportunity to stay in such a fine home. Most board-inghouses aren't anywhere near this nice, though I expect a lady like yourself wouldn't know that firsthand. I realize it's inexcusable, intruding on your family at Thanksgiving, but—"

"But you aren't above offering an excuse, just the same," she ended for him, unable to control her grin at the obvious.

His laugh filled the hall. She decided she quite liked the sound of it and the way his eyes almost shut in a mass of crinkles when he laughed. "You're quite right, Miss Larson. Ungentlemanly behavior, at the very least. I most humbly apologize."

"Let me show you a room."

"That won't be necessary. I'm sure the room will be more than adequate. However, I would prefer the quiet of a room at the back, if you have one, after the noise of the news office."

She told him the rental amount in the most business-like voice she could muster. Her father had decided to charge more than most places, knowing the value of their location.

He nodded without hesitation at the price, as if agreeing it was fair, and she breathed a quiet sigh of relief. With greater confidence, she explained the boarders would be eating in the kitchen and would have the use of the family living room. Father knew Mother wouldn't allow the invasion of their formal dining room and parlor.

Vernetta showed the young man to the living room, which was across the broad hall from the dining room.

The living room was comfortable, with wallpaper striped in shades of mauve and pearl, mauve plush-covered furniture, and a welcoming fireplace. "You may wait here while I ask my father if we might accept you as a boarder, Mr. McNally."

He seemed a pleasant young man. Crossing the hall, she whispered to the Lord, "Perhaps his cheerful spirit would be contagious, Father. Our home could use a little cheer!"

Entering the formal dining room, she avoided looking at her mother, whose disapproval seemed to fill the room. Mother had not been able to change Father's mind about renting.

"I'll trust your judgment," he assured Vernetta. "If you believe him to be a man of high character, rent him a room."

Mother's voice rang in disapproval as Vernetta left the room. Vernetta couldn't remember ever before hearing her mother's voice raised so high in anger. Would nice Mr. McNally hear those derogatory comments about the class of people from whom boarders came and about newspapermen in particular?

Upon entering the family room, Vernetta realized immediately that he could not help but hear. He looked almost as embarrassed as she felt. His brown eyes were filled with sympathy. His dark brows lifted. "Your mother?"

She nodded, trying to swallow her embarrassment. Her fingertips played with her rose-colored gown's silk skirt. "Her manners aren't usually so. . .so unacceptable. It's difficult for her, opening our home to strangers."

"Change is always frightening. We often react with bitterness or anger to the things that frighten us, don't you think?"

His words surprised her as much as the gentleness in his voice. He'd never met her mother, yet in only a moment he'd helped her understand her mother better. She smiled slightly. "Yes, we do."

He cleared his throat. "You, um, haven't said yet whether your father gave his approval."

"Oh! Yes, he did."

Mr. McNally's smile filled his face. "That's grand! I'll move in Saturday, if that's acceptable."

She assured him it was and walked him to the door. Snow was still falling in large, drifting flakes. *A nice start to the holiday season,* she thought.

Mr. McNally shifted his derby in his hands and cleared his throat. "I want you to know, Miss Larson, that you needn't fear I'll invade your family's privacy because I'm a newspaperman. I won't print anything derogatory about your family. I wouldn't print anything about your family at all without your father's approval."

Rather than reassure her, his comments sent chills along her arms while she watched him hurry down the snow-covered walk. She hadn't for a moment considered that danger! Could he be trusted? Or had she betrayed her father's trust in her judgment?

She was still worrying about it when she slipped onto her chair in the dining room.

"You'll have to eat quickly, Vernetta," her mother said. "You won't have much time to prepare for tonight's party. Wait until Andrew sees you in your new green satin with the black velvet trim! He'll likely propose to you on the spot."

"Lena!" Father's protest wasn't loud or even very serious. Vernetta suspected he made it because Mother expected it of him.

Mother waved a hand at him in dismissal. "We all know Andrew is smitten with her. Manners may prohibit our discussing it with others, but why not mention the obvious within the family?" She picked up her crystal goblet. "When is Andrew stopping for you, Vernetta?"

Vernetta's stomach clenched. She took a deep breath, trying to release the tightness. This was the moment she'd dreaded. Facing her mother with the news was almost harder than hearing it from Andrew.

She lifted her head, forced a smile, and looked into her mother's expectant eyes. "Andrew isn't coming, not tonight, not ever again."

two

Mother slowly set the crystal goblet back on the table. "What do you mean, not ever again?"

Vernetta's hands clenched the linen napkin in her lap. The anger and apprehension in her mother's eyes made her want to steal away and pretend everything was as usual between herself and Andrew, but that wouldn't change the facts. Her smile trembled. She tried to keep her voice light. "Andrew has decided he doesn't care to escort me any longer."

"Nonsense! He dotes on you!" Mother snorted and shook her head. "I suppose you said something foolish and hurt his pride. You must be careful of men's pride, you know. Men like to think they are strong, but their pride is their weak point. A wise woman is careful to build it up."

Vernetta caught her bottom lip between her teeth. Mother certainly hadn't been building up Father's pride lately!

"What foolish thing did you do to raise Andrew's ire?" Disgust dripped from her mother's voice.

Anger heated Vernetta's cheeks. "I did nothing

foolish. He. . ." She caught back the revealing truth just in time. She glanced at her father's puzzled expression. It would tear him apart if he knew Andrew was no longer seeing her because her father had lost his fortune. Father would be sure to think her broken heart was his fault. She swallowed hard. "Andrew simply discovered his feelings for me weren't what he thought."

"Nonsense! Of course they are the same." Mother wagged a finger in Vernetta's direction. "I want you to apologize to him at the first opportunity for whatever it is you have done."

Vernetta drew an angry breath. "Mother! I—"

Father threw his napkin down beside his plate. "Lena, that's enough of this. If Andrew has so little sense that he would walk away from our daughter, then he isn't good enough for her."

Tears heated Vernetta's eyes at her father's defense, his love warming her heart.

"We must think of our daughter's future, Mr. Larson," Mother reminded him indignantly. "Her social standing may be hurt irretrievably if she doesn't apologize to Andrew."

"No one worth their salt will think less of Vernetta because that young man is no longer escorting her."

"But—"

Father cut off Mother's comment with a sharp wave of his hand and a scowl. "I'm sure any number of respectable young men will gladly take Andrew's place, if she's willing to allow them to do so."

"Mr. Larson—"

Angry lights darted in his eyes, but his voice didn't

raise a note. "The subject is closed. Let's remember this is a *Thanksgiving* meal."

Vernetta kept her gaze on her plate as she started eating. She was grateful for her father's reprieve. *But I've no doubt Mother will reopen the subject as soon as we're alone.* Her stomach tightened at the thought.

❅

Two days later, Vernetta stood patiently in the mirrored fitting room of the most exclusive shop in a downtown emporium. The woman who was fitting her elegant party gown and the clerk who had waited on her were as familiar as old friends. She had purchased her tailor-made gowns here for years.

In the past, the visits had been times of anticipation. Now the reflection of herself in the satin and lace gown enveloped her in sadness. *I feel like a thief,* she thought, *as though I'm stealing from Father, ordering gowns I know he can't afford.*

She'd argued with her mother over the dresses. "My gowns from last year will be adequate. Surely no one has bothered to remember what I wore last year."

Mother's eyes had flashed. "Do you want to advertise that your father is putting us into the poorhouse? No, your image must defy those awful newspaper tales. Besides, since you've chased away Mr. Reed, you must be especially careful of your appearance if we wish you to attract another worthy suitor."

The look her mother flashed assured Vernetta that Mother believed "we" did indeed wish to attract another "worthy suitor."

Thomas Michael McNally's smiling face, entirely

lacking Andrew's pretentious facade, flashed in her mind. She saw her reflection smile in response to the cheerful Irish eyes that filled her imagination. The regret that flashed through her at the realization that such a man would never be considered a worthy suitor surprised her.

"I think we're done for today, Miss Larson," the clerk said from the floor, where she'd been seated while pinning a piece of the lace insert to the gown's skirt. "What do you think of it?"

Vernetta's gaze swept unenthusiastically over the gown's reflection. "It's lovely."

With the clerk's assistance, she removed the pinned garment and dressed in her simple but elegant gray cashmere suit, which was trimmed with black embroidery. As she entered the main shop, the head clerk hurried over, her face wreathed in smiles. Vernetta responded to the clerk's thanks for her orders even as her mind was elsewhere.

The daring thought blazed through her mind, taking her breath. *Maybe I could find a position here.* A picture of her mother's face, filled with horror at the idea of her daughter being a mere store clerk, came immediately to mind. Vernetta pushed it away. *Mother's fragile pride isn't as important now as Father's money problems.*

"Mrs. Drew," she interrupted the head clerk before she could lose her courage, "I would like to apply for a position here."

Mrs. Drew's straight brows met above her thin nose. Her eyes grew a bit glassy, but she didn't lose her smile. "A position? What type of work are you seeking?"

Vernetta was glad for the years of social training that kept her voice low and pleasant, without a trace of the tremors she felt in her spirit. "Why, I don't know exactly. A sales clerk, perhaps. I do know your line of clothing well after all the years I've purchased here."

Mrs. Drew pressed her lips together and shook her head. "I'm sorry, but we've no positions available. The store's owner is keeping on more employees than the work justifies already." Pity filled her eyes. "It would have been delightful working with you, I'm certain." She spread her hands slightly. "Perhaps when the current financial troubles have passed. . ."

"Of course. Thank you." Vernetta tried to keep her chin up and her walk casually graceful as she left the room, but inside she felt like running out the door in tears, like a small girl.

She pushed through the emporium's heavy front doors onto the sidewalk. Tall buildings on either side of the downtown street tunneled the December wind in shrieking gusts that whipped a pedestrian's clothing. Vernetta's warm, magenta muffler blew over the shoulders of her gray coat. She tucked her chin into the muffler's soft folds.

The cold, stinging wind brought the tears to her eyes she had managed to repress since the conversation with Mrs. Drew. The bustling Christmas shoppers filling the walk were blurred to her. The scent of roasted chestnuts from the nearby street vendor didn't warm the air.

Her long, heavy wool skirt brushed against something. "Excuse me," she murmured, barely glancing in

274

the direction of the child her skirt had touched.

"Flowers, miss?"

"No, thank you, I—" She focused her gaze on the child. The sight stopped the words in her throat.

The girl hunkered inside a worn brown corduroy coat. It was woefully short. From beneath it stuck slender legs encased in once-white woolen stockings with holes in the knees. Attempts had been made to darn the holes, but even the darning was wearing through.

Isn't her skirt even long enough to cover her knees? Vernetta wondered.

The girl held up a homemade satin flower, clutched in a glove as holey as her stockings. With the other hand, she brushed her hair from her face. Wind-whisked, golden-brown waves tangled about her red ears. Snowflakes hung like miniature stars on her lashes.

Vernetta's heart crimped. *The child must be freezing!*

"Flowers, miss?" the girl repeated between chattering teeth.

"What a lovely idea!" Vernetta smiled at her, opening her purse. Her smile died. She had no money with her. She'd forgotten that she'd given her last coins to the maid for the marketing that morning. Her father's financial worries had caused her many disappointments, but none so painful as this. To think she didn't even have a few pennies for a purchase from a flower girl!

The wind tossed the end of her muffler into her face. She brushed it aside impatiently, then noticed the girl's gaze resting on the muffler. Vernetta hesitated only a moment. She pulled the strings of her purse shut and smiled again. "I'm sorry. I haven't any money with

275

me today, but perhaps we can work out a trade."

The girl's brows met in a puzzled frown above huge gray eyes.

"I'd truly love some of your beautiful flowers. Would you accept my muffler in exchange? It's new. This is the first time I've worn it."

The girl stared at the muffler as if unable to believe such good fortune could be hers. "I. . .I don't know."

Clearly the child wasn't accustomed to bartering. Was she afraid her parents wouldn't want her to bring home a scarf instead of money? *But it's worth far more than the pennies her entire supply of flowers would bring,* Vernetta assured herself.

Quickly, she removed it from her neck. Icy air struck her exposed throat. She winced at the sharp pain of it but didn't change her mind. The girl had no hat or muffler. *She must feel like an ice sculpture!* Vernetta thought, holding out the muffler.

The girl reached her worn gloves to touch it. A soft gasp came from her chapped lips when her fingers closed around the luxurious thickness.

Vernetta knelt before her and wrapped the muffler over the girl's head and ears, then around her neck. "How is that?"

"Oh! It's wonderful!" The girl's words were barely a whisper.

Vernetta beamed at her. "I'm glad you like it."

"How many flowers do you want?" the girl asked cautiously.

Vernetta looked over the flowers in the oak basket. Her muffler was worth many more flowers than the basket held, but she couldn't take all of the girl's wares. Silk and satin flowers mixed with crepe-paper roses. Surely the crepe-paper were the least costly to make. The observation decided Vernetta immediately. But how many to request? To ask for too few would belittle the girl's creations. "Let's see, do you think a dozen paper roses would be a fair trade?"

The girl's eyes sparkled. Her mouth spread in a grin above her pointed chin. "Oh, that would be a fine trade, miss." She held out the basket. "Would you like to choose them?"

Vernetta chose a selection of pink, red, and white paper roses.

"You'd best let me wrap them in one of these old newspapers, miss, so's the wind won't wreck them." The girl pulled a newspaper page from the bottom of the basket and deftly rolled the flowers in it. "Here you are, miss."

"Thank you. I'm Miss Vernetta Larson. What is your name?"

The girl looked suddenly shy. Her winter-whisked cheeks couldn't possibly grow redder, so they didn't betray whether she blushed. Her voice was low, and Vernetta leaned forward to catch her words before the wind snatched them away. "Lily, miss. Lily Mills."

"What a pretty name! How old are you, Lily?"

"Eight."

Only eight years old and trying to make her living on a cold Minneapolis street! "I shall enjoy your flowers, Lily. I'll think of you each time I look at them. They've brightened my day."

277

Her own problems did seem lighter as she hurried down the street, the bundle of flowers held close against her coat. *But, Lord, how can You allow poverty to put children into such a position?* her heart cried.

three

Vernetta's troublesome thoughts about the flower girl evaporated when she walked through the walnut and etched-glass door into her home. Round-topped trunks and worn valises, some of tapestry and some of leather, were piled about the large entrance hall. Two tall women with white-gray hair in large buns were giving contradictory directions at the same time to a smiling Thomas Michael McNally.

Vernetta recognized the women as Cora and Cornelia Wibbey, unmarried sisters in their sixties. They'd rented the bedroom at the front of the house, the one with large windows overlooking the front walk.

Mr. McNally's gaze met Vernetta's, and they shared an amused smile over the sisters' vocal disagreement. The shared amusement sent happy warmth through Vernetta's chest. *I was right about him,* she thought, setting her newspaper-wrapped bouquet on the marble-topped hall table. *His cheerful spirit will be good for our home.*

He tucked one valise under an arm, grabbed a valise handle in each hand, and started up the stairs. The sisters followed, holding their skirts out of their way, neither sister missing a syllable of instruction to Mr. McNally, urging him to handle the valises with care and telling him where each was to be placed, though he could not even see the door to their room as yet.

How kind of him to help them carry their things upstairs, she thought. Dora, as the only remaining servant, would be hard-pressed to provide all the service the guests needed. Father was at the bank, and Vernetta could not see her mother waiting on the boarders. She reached for one of the smaller valises, intent on helping.

"There you are!" Mother bustled toward her, the sound of her footsteps hidden in the thick oriental carpet. "I thought you'd never get back from the dressmaker's."

"Is something wrong?"

"Everything is wrong! All these extra people in the house are making me addlepated."

More likely you are making them addlepated, Vernetta thought. She turned toward the hall closet, removing her coat and hiding her smile from her mother. "What have they done?"

Mother's arm swept through the air, indicating the pile of luggage remaining in the entryway. "Look at all this. . .this. . .*rubbish* they are moving into our home! First that newspaperman arrived—"

"Mr. McNally?" Vernetta asked, keeping her tone innocent, trying to establish delicately the fact that "that newspaperman" had a name.

"I think that's his name." Mother made a small dismissing motion with her hand. "Anyway, he came with his paraphernalia right after you left. The women arrived right on his heels, and Captain Rogers arrived before the busman had carried in all the women's luggage. Goodness! The busman was opening and closing the door, letting in the wind and cold, as though we'd nothing better to do than heat all of Minneapolis!"

Vernetta patted her mother's shoulder. "It's over now, dear. Surely all the boarders' belongings have been delivered."

"I should hope so! It took Dora and me all day yesterday to find places to store our personal belongings in order to make the rooms available for the boarders."

As Vernetta remembered it, Dora had been the one to pack the belongings and carry them to the attic. "I haven't met Captain Rogers yet. Is he in his room?"

"Yes. He said he needed a nap." She wiped the back of one hand across her forehead. "*I'm* the one who could use a nap! I do hope he won't be sickly or expect us to nurse him."

"I'm sure he's only tired, Mother. He must be quite elderly. Wasn't he a captain in the Civil War?"

"So he says." She sighed deeply. "I'd best check to see that Dora has everything in hand for luncheon." She swept down the hall in a rustle of skirts and with an air of important haste.

Vernetta reached for the paper roses, shaking her head. Her mother's attitude would be amusing—if it weren't so sad.

From the china closet that filled most of one dining-room wall, Vernetta selected three porcelain vases. She filled them with the roses, then set the cheerful bouquets on a silver tray and carried them up the stairs.

Maybe the flower girl's roses would brighten the boarders' rooms.

✳

After dinner, Vernetta stopped in the kitchen. "Did you remember to serve coffee and dessert to the boarders in the living room, Dora?"

"I'm preparing it, miss, as you asked me to do." Dora indicated the silver tray on the table. Delicate rose-sprinkled china cups and saucers sat beside a matching cream pitcher and sugar bowl. Scalloped sugar cookies rested daintily upon an etched crystal plate. Linen napkins with small pink roses embroidered in the corners lay to one side.

The silver coffee service was on another silver tray. Vernetta knew Dora would be using it to serve after-dinner coffee to her parents in the parlor, as usual. Her mother didn't know Vernetta had instructed Dora to serve the boarders in the living room. She was sure her mother wouldn't approve. "They are boarders, not guests," she had repeatedly informed Vernetta throughout the day.

What did the flower girl have for dinner tonight? Vernetta wondered, gazing at the simple dessert trays. *Did she have something warm and filling after the day spent in the cold Minneapolis wind and snow?*

Dora set the coffee-filled silver teakettle, which matched the coffeepot with which she would serve Vernetta's parents, on the tray for the boarders. Vernetta reached for it and smiled at Dora. "I'll serve the boarders."

Dora's eyes grew large. "Oh, no, miss, you mustn't! Your mother would never approve."

"Nonsense. It is the boarders' first evening in our home. It wouldn't be proper not to welcome them. Besides, Mother and Father are waiting for you in the parlor."

❈

With a brass poker, Thomas pushed at the bottom log in the fire grate. It broke quickly with crackling sounds into charred pieces that glowed a cheerful orange.

The Wibbey sisters were seated on the plush mauve sofa on the other side of the room. Old Captain Rogers was reading the Minneapolis newspaper in the matching stuffed chair.

"Tell us about your war adventures, Captain Rogers," Cornelia was urging in a sugary voice that didn't match her lined, narrow face.

"Maybe the captain doesn't care to discuss the war," Cora reprimanded. "Might be his memories are too gruesome for women's delicate natures. Isn't that so, Captain?" She smiled at him in a manner Thomas thought oozed "understanding female."

Thomas thought he caught a sigh as the captain lowered the paper to show gentlemanly politeness to the women. "Some memories might be, some might not. The war was a long time ago. I prefer to live in the present."

Cornelia straightened her shoulders beneath her crocheted shawl and darted a "see, I was right" look at her sister, who ignored her.

Thomas's gaze dropped to the captain's right leg. There was something wrong with it, something that caused the captain to walk with a cane. Had he injured it in the war? Was that one of the reasons he preferred to live in the present instead of rehashing old war stories with other veterans as so many of the veterans of the War between the States liked to do?

He set the poker back in its brass holder and shifted his shoulders. His brown sack jacket was almost too warm to wear inside this evening, with the fire going. At the last place he'd rented, he would have removed his jacket without a thought while he relaxed after dinner.

A smile tugged at his lips. *Miss Vernetta Larson didn't live at my last boardinghouse. Not that she'd give me a second look.* A woman of Miss Larson's stature wouldn't have anything to do with a mere newspaper reporter. He likely wouldn't even see her this evening. Mrs. Larson had made it clear the boarders were to eat in the kitchen, relax in the living room, and generally stay as far from the Larson family members as possible. He understood Mrs. Larson's feelings, but he didn't like the unworthy way they made him feel.

He glanced up as Vernetta entered. "Let me help you with that." He quickly replaced the poker and hurried across the cabbage rose carpet. "Those cookies look mighty tempting."

"Thank you," she murmured as he took her tray. "You may set it here." She indicated the marble-topped table in front of the couch.

Settling herself in a delicate chair, she reached for the teapot and smiled at the Wibbey sisters. "Do you take cream or sugar in your coffee?"

"Both, please." Cornelia's gentle smile shone through her wrinkles.

Cora's back straightened. "You needn't be serving us, deary. You should be visiting with your family not us boarders."

Thomas could see, however, that Cora was pleased at Miss Larson's service. So was he. He'd thought from the moment he met her that Miss Vernetta Larson was a young woman with a large heart. He liked the way she treated himself and the other boarders as guests. *Especially the others,* he hurriedly assured himself. It gave his heart a warm glow to see Miss Larson welcoming them as friends.

Thomas had just taken his cup from her when the door chimes rang. A couple minutes later, the maid entered. To his surprise, she handed him a small envelope.

He noticed the notepaper's fine quality as he removed the note with Mrs. Jonathan Johanson written in script across the front. Quickly he scanned the contents. His heart sank.

Vernetta's sweet voice cut through his disturbed thoughts. "I hope it's not bad news."

"Nothing irreparable," he assured her, "but it is a problem. I work with a newsboys' Sunday school each week. As part of the program, we supply a lunch for the children. It's an important part of the ministry, as many of the children aren't adequately fed at home, especially during these hard times."

He lifted the note slightly. "The woman who was to supply the lunch tomorrow informs me she is down with the grippe." He tried to smile. "I wonder if any of you has a suggestion as to how I might arrange lunch for a bunch of hungry youngsters on short notice?"

"Why, how thoughtless of the woman!" Cora's eyes flashed. "Surely she would have made arrangements for the food before the last minute. Perhaps she only means that she'll not be able to be there to serve the food. You can surely find a way to transport it from her home to the mission."

He shook his head. "I'm afraid that isn't the case."

Vernetta's face looked troubled. "The children mustn't go without lunch. Dora," she addressed the maid, who was leaning over the tray, "do we have anything we can prepare for the children?"

Dora hesitated. "I could probably find something, miss, if Mrs. Larson would allow it."

Thomas's hopes disintegrated. Mrs. Larson didn't appear the type of woman whose heart would be touched by the children's plight.

Determination fixed itself upon Vernetta's features. "I will speak with Mother about it. Perhaps it would be best if we had a menu in mind when I do so. Mr. McNally, how many children do you expect?"

"There's usually about forty, all together."

He saw the surprise and concern flash across her eyes, but her training didn't allow it to show in her manners, words, or tone. "Dora, what do we have to feed forty hungry youngsters?"

Dora rubbed the palms of her hands over her starched white apron. "We haven't enough meat to serve so many. I could make a hearty stew or soup, though. And maybe doughnuts. Doughnuts are always popular with children and filling too. The cost wouldn't be too great," she assured.

"Thank you, Dora. I'll speak with Mother immediately." Vernetta rose gracefully.

Thomas stood too. "I don't wish to cause trouble. If you think your mother wouldn't approve—"

"Not approve of feeding hungry children? Nonsense."

He wasn't as certain of Vernetta's mother's generosity as he was of hers. "I'll be glad to pay for the food. It's the preparing of it that's beyond my abilities."

Her laughing eyes lit his heart. "I'm sure that can be remedied with Dora's help."

Dora blinked in surprise, then fell in with Vernetta's spirit. "To be certain, miss."

Thomas's cheeks heated as the Wibbey sisters chuckled their approval of Vernetta's plan to educate him in the art of cooking, but he only grinned at Vernetta. "I'll be grateful for the lesson."

It wasn't long before the large, modern kitchen was bustling with activity. The shining black stove with its fancy grillwork poured forth welcome heat. While Dora prepared the doughnut batter and heated oil, Thomas and Vernetta washed and dried the dinner dishes, and the Wibbey sisters browned meat and cut vegetables for the soup.

For Thomas, the most fun was watching the doughnuts plump up crispy brown and fat in the hot oil. The doughnut making had just begun when Mrs. Larson called Dora away to prepare the family's Sunday clothes for church the next day, brushing and pressing outfits and polishing shoes and boots. The remaining ladies and Thomas took turns retrieving the bobbing golden circles, rolling some in powdered sugar.

"Don't you be eating the young ones' dinner!" Cornelia slapped lightly at Thomas's hand when he reached for a cooled doughnut. Her eyes were laughing like those of a grandmother teasing a hungry grandson.

Thomas winked at her. "I'll share it with you. Just one, to make sure they are fit for the newsies." The women laughed at him as he split the doughnut four ways.

"Tell us about the newsboys' club," Vernetta urged.

He glanced at her. Powdered sugar dappled one cheek, flushed red from the heat of the stove, and the tip of her chin. Her eyes sparkled with the fun of cooking with the others. *She looks delectable,* he thought.

"Well," he started, "the club was started by the church I attend. The church men were concerned for the newsboys' welfare and souls. Most of them come from poor homes. Many don't have families, and their entire support comes from selling newspapers."

The women nodded. Sympathy replaced the sparkle in Vernetta's eyes.

"We struck on the idea of starting a Sunday school for the boys. We were afraid they wouldn't attend with the other children. We were right. They wouldn't even come to the church for a class. Then one of the church women, who has a store downtown, offered the use of the store basement. We jumped at the opportunity. It was right in the boys' neighborhood, and they started coming. It didn't take long to find out a lot of them don't get enough to eat, especially in these hard times, so to sweeten the draw, we added the lunch. We also give away books for those who attend regularly."

"What a wonderful ministry," Vernetta said.

The Wibbey sisters murmured their agreement.

"Perhaps. . ." Thomas hesitated. Would Vernetta think him bold or ungentlemanly in his request? Surely she would take it in the manner he offered it. "With the woman who was in charge of the lunch ill, we could use another volunteer tomorrow. Would you care to assist us, Miss Larson?"

"I should be glad to." Vernetta's immediate response and the warmth in her eyes assured him of her sincerity.

He smiled at her across the hot stove, but it was her generous heart that warmed him.

four

Vernetta was glad her father hadn't yet sold all of their horses and carriages. She didn't know how they would have managed if they'd had to transport the soup and doughnuts downtown by streetcar. Though her father gave permission to use the carriage, her mother did not agree to Vernetta's request that Dora be allowed to help at the mission. "She is needed here. Surely you don't expect me to prepare and serve the boarders' Sunday meal?"

In front of the mission storefront, Thomas lifted a large basket and handed it to Vernetta. She could smell the fresh, bready scent of the doughnuts hidden beneath the large oatmeal linen towel. She followed him as he carried the heavy soup kettle.

"Watch your step," he warned. "The snow has mostly been cleared, but there are a few icy patches left."

They went down the steps that were protected from the sidewalk by a cast-iron railing and entered the basement of a millinery shop. Immediately Thomas was surrounded by noisy boys, ranging in age from ten to sixteen.

"Hi, Mr. McNally!"

"Need some help there?"

"Thought ya mighta got lost in a snowdrift! What took ya so long?"

They greeted Thomas with friendly pats on the back or slaps on his shoulders, in the manner men and boys have that is so incomprehensible to women.

Vernetta smiled at the boys, who swarmed between her and Thomas. They came in every size and shape, but their clothes were the same: hip-length coats over vests, cotton shirts, corduroy trousers—all ragged.

One boy, taller than the others and with broader shoulders, bumped his shoulder against Thomas's. "Who's the new lady?" He whisked his hat off politely, but his brown eyes met hers boldly, in a manner to which she wasn't accustomed. Vernetta swallowed a gasp and took a small step backward.

Thomas introduced her. "Miss Vernetta Larson. Miss Larson, this is Erik Johansen, leader of the news boys in this part of the city."

Vernetta could tell he hadn't noticed the boy's ungentlemanly gaze. She nodded cautiously. "How do you do, Erik?"

The boy reached for her basket. "Let me help ya with that, Miss Larson."

Vernetta allowed him to take it from her. "Thank you."

She followed Erik and Thomas into another room. It was small, with wooden barrels and crates piled along the cold walls. An old wood-burning cookstove was already giving off heat. Thomas set the soup on it.

Erik set the basket of doughnuts down on a long, well-worn wooden table, then slid his hat back on.

Thomas slid it off in one smooth move. "You forgot, it stays off while you're inside."

Erik flushed, and Vernetta turned away, glancing over the bare kitchen, not wanting to embarrass the proud lad further. "Will you get a couple of the other boys together and see that the classrooms are set up, Erik?" she heard Thomas ask. Then Erik shuffled out of the room.

Vernetta was glad to discover that there were other women at the mission to help serve the lunch. Thomas introduced her to them, then invited her to join him in looking over the rest of the Sunday school.

Children were milling about everywhere: not only boys, but girls too. They looked like feminine versions of the boys with their tattered, misfitting clothing and dirty faces and hair.

"I thought this was a newsboys' Sunday school," she whispered to Thomas. "What are the girls doing here?"

Thomas turned surprised eyes to her. "Didn't I mention the flower girls? Not long after the school for the newsies started, it was expanded to include the girls."

He shook his head, sadness filling the lines of his face. "They're as bad off as the boys, working the streets with their wares, some of them living on the streets as well."

"Surely not!" Her whisper burned her throat. She looked at the ill-clad, ill-cared-for children, laughing and running about while they waited for class to begin.

He took her elbow and bent toward her to say in a low voice that wouldn't carry to the children, "They have a rough lot in life. We do all we can for them." His touch urged her forward.

The tour didn't take long. Thomas explained how the part of the large basement room that wasn't used for storage for the millinery was divided into classrooms with screens and with blankets hung over wires. Simple oak chairs were set in each classroom. Easels with slates stood at the front of the rooms. A few pictures on construction paper, obviously the work of the children, were pinned to the blanket walls.

All along the tour, boys stopped Thomas. He introduced many of them to Vernetta. She was relieved that most of the boys did not look at her in Erik's insolent manner but was dismayed by the tough way they spoke and acted. *Like men in boys' bodies,* she thought.

Thomas stopped to speak to a boy, and Vernetta walked slowly back toward the public portion of the basement.

"No! Give it back!" a young girl's voice cried out from the middle of a circle of boys. Vernetta stopped, looking to see what was the matter.

A cloth doll appeared in a boy's hand, held above his head. The doll was passed from one high-held hand to another, amid boyish laughter and the girl's repeated pleas.

Vernetta took a step toward them. Before she could reach the circle, someone brushed by her.

Erik reached above the smaller boys with ease and

grabbed the doll. "Quit actin' like slobs! Don'cha have anything better to do than tease girls?"

The younger boys bit their lips and backed away. Erik handed the doll to the girl. "Here ya are, Lily. Don't mind them."

Large, water-drenched gray eyes looked up at him. "Thanks, Erik."

Surprise made Vernetta's heart skip a beat. "Lily!" It was the flower girl from whom she'd bought the paper roses. Vernetta hurried forward.

Erik frowned at her and moved so he half-blocked the girl from Vernetta. "We don't need you. I can look after her."

Vernetta glanced at him in surprise. "I'm sure you can." She smiled and leaned forward. "We met the other day when I bought some of your beautiful flowers, remember?"

Lily only nodded. She leaned against Erik's leg. Her gaze didn't leave Vernetta's. One small hand reached up to clutch the soft muffler about her neck.

Does she think I'll ask her to return it? Vernetta wondered, shocked at the thought. "It's so nice to see you again. Is this your doll? What is her name?"

"Amy." Lily continued her hold on the muffler.

A whistle cut through the air. It was Thomas, calling everyone together for prayer and hymn singing.

"Come on, Lily." Erik started toward the group. Lily, her hand tucked safely in his, hurried along with him.

Thomas stopped beside Vernetta. "The grippe must be taking a lot of victims. We're short on teachers today. Would you mind helping out by teaching one of the

Sunday schools for the flower girls?"

Vernetta agreed and was rewarded by Thomas's huge smile. She was glad to find Lily among her students. By the end of the class, the shy girl even smiled at her and had removed her grip on the muffler.

The sound of the horse's hooves were muffled by the snow and slush on the road as Thomas and Vernetta drove home in the carriage. As they passed through a residential area, the laughter of children danced through the crisp, nose-biting air.

Thomas laughed and pointed to children playing Fox and Geese on a large front yard. "They are so bundled in winter clothing that they run like penguins!"

Vernetta laughed with him. Remembering the children they'd been with earlier, her laughter died. "The newsboys and flower girls should be playing like this—lighthearted, enjoying the snow—not trying to earn a living on cold, dirty sidewalks."

"Yes, they should be able to live like the children they are." Thomas touched the gloved hands in her lap with one of his own. The touch lasted only a moment, but the intimacy of it surprised her. Her gaze darted to his face. His brown-eyed gaze met hers. "I knew you'd be like this—good and kind." His voice was quiet and rich, and the simple compliment seemed very personal.

Vernetta's breath seemed to stop. Her heart hammered in her chest.

Thomas broke their locked gazes to guide the horse as they met another carriage. "Mrs. Pilgrim said she was going to ask you to teach regularly."

Vernetta took a deep breath, trying to regain her

equilibrium. "She did ask, and I agreed. I think it will be fun."

Thomas's grin split his face again. "I'm glad. Mrs. Pilgrim said the girls like you."

"I like them." Two boys in a snowball battle caught her eye. "It seems whenever I'm downtown, there is a newsboy on every corner. It's humbling to realize I wouldn't have been able to tell one from another before today. As though they were as interchangeable as. . .as the marbles with which they play!"

She knew Thomas must hear the shame in her voice, but she didn't know how to hide it. She *was* ashamed she hadn't paid more attention to these brave boys.

"Many of the boys, like Erik, and the flower girls are orphans." Thomas spoke quietly. "Others are runaways or have been abandoned by their parents. Right now with the Panic, more than the normal number of newsies and flower girls live with parents who are out of work."

"And I felt sorry for myself because Father lost his fortune." Her whisper sounded strained, even to her own ears. "We still have so much compared to those children."

"I don't know that we can always measure loss in that manner. Every loss requires healing and adjustment. Your father lost more than money. He acquired his fortune by his dedication to serving people. When the bank failed, he must have believed he'd failed those people. I'm sure believing that is a greater measure of failure to him than losing his fortune."

Vernetta stared at him, gratitude for his insight filling her with wonder. "Yes, that is exactly how he feels."

Neither spoke while Thomas guided the horse across the trolley tracks, the carriage jerking. Then Vernetta said, "The offering this morning surprised me. I would think the children would need the little money they make so badly that they wouldn't have anything to give. Yet every child put something in the plate."

"We encourage tithing. We also encourage saving. Most of the children have started savings accounts because of the Sunday school and add to their accounts regularly, though it might be only a few pennies. We don't force either tithing or savings. We believe the decision is between the children and God and their families, if they have families."

"I'm surprised their parents allow them to give money away during these hard times."

Thomas held the reins loosely. He had a thoughtful look on his wide, handsome face beneath his gray bowler. "I believe tithing and saving are ways of expressing their faith in our God of hope, don't you?" He guided the carriage to the horse stoop in front of Vernetta's home.

She recalled the verse from the fifteenth chapter of Romans that he'd read to the assembled classes that morning: "Now the God of hope fill you with all joy and peace in believing, that you may abound in hope, through the power of the Holy Ghost." She nodded slowly. "Don't you find it difficult to hope when you see the poverty the children live in?"

297

He sat looking out over the snow-covered lawns. "I think it is the work with the children that *gives* me hope." She watched his face as he struggled for the right words. "I know that no one person can solve all the children's problems, but if we each do what is put in front of us—what we are able to do financially, physically, and emotionally—how can things help but get better, even if bit by bit?"

Warmth spread through her chest at his words. "I guess they can't."

His answer to her question reminded her of when he first came to her home to ask about a room. She'd hoped he would become a boarder, for she'd felt they needed his cheerful spirit. *It was his spirit of hope we needed*, she thought. *My family needs that, the way the entire country needs the God of Hope now, in the midst of the Panic of 1893.*

five

Vernetta bit her bottom lip and frowned, bending over the gown she was mending. She'd caught the hem with the heel of her shoe. Sewing had never been her strong suit, and it took all her concentration to keep her stitches even and small. She shifted slightly, so the light from the painted parlor lamp fell more strongly on her work.

She looked up at the quiet rap on the parlor door. Her mother, seated across the room on a delicate upholstered rocker, muttered, "What can those boarders want now," before raising her voice. "Come in."

Cora and Cornelia Wibbey bustled into the room, smiles filling their wrinkled faces. "Mrs. Larson, may we use your kitchen to make cookies?" Cora asked.

"For the men at the Veteran's Home," Cornelia elaborated.

"We'll pay for the ingredients, of course," Cora added in a breathless tone.

Vernetta smiled. The ladies' attitude reminded her of ten-year-old girls who might ask the same favor. She found the manner with which they approached life delightful.

Mother held her needlework in one hand and made a shooing motion with the other. "Yes, yes, of course. But see that you clean up the kitchen after yourselves. Dora hasn't the time."

"Thank you, Mrs. Larson." Cornelia turned to leave.

Cora stood where she was, glancing about the parlor. "What a lovely room, Mrs. Larson! You've created a charming atmosphere. No wonder you spend so much time in here."

"Thank you, Miss Wibbey."

Cornelia grasped her sister's hand. "Come along, Cora. We must get started if we want to get those cookies baked this evening."

The door swung shut behind them silently. Mother gave a deep sigh and returned to her Swedish tatting. "Honestly, the boarders have become such a bother. I told your father they would, but he didn't listen to me. He said if they used the living room and kitchen, they wouldn't be under foot." She dropped both hands into her lap and glared across the room at Vernetta. "As though we could keep from running into them coming and going! The Wibbey sisters are the worst of the lot."

"How do you mean?"

"They are talkative and inquisitive. Why, they act as though they wish to be *friends* with us, and with Dora." Mother pinched her lips together and picked up her needlework again. "They should know their place."

Vernetta concentrated on her stitches, trying to quiet the indignation filling her chest. What was it Thomas had said the day they'd met? Oh, yes. That

300

people often react with bitterness or anger to change and the fears change brings in its wake. "Do you know what Miss Cornelia meant by saying the cookies were for the men at the Veteran's Home? Do they have friends there?"

"Not that I know of. I expect they mean to send the cookies with your father and Captain Rogers. The captain has friends at the home at Minnehaha Park. That young newspaperman has convinced your father to go with the captain to visit some Civil War veterans tomorrow."

"What a wonderful idea! It will be good for Father."

"Hmph! I'm not so sure of that. It would be better if he spent his time among men of his own class."

Vernetta bit back an angry retort.

"I expect the Wibbey sisters aren't baking those cookies for the veterans out of the goodness of their hearts," Mother added. "They've set their caps for the captain, or I'm not Swedish."

Laughter bubbled up inside Vernetta. "Both of them?"

"Of course, both of them." Her mother's eyebrows rose in surprise. "Isn't it obvious?"

"Now that you mention it, I guess it is. It's rather cute, isn't it? But I hope their hearts aren't truly involved. Wouldn't it be awful if one of the sisters won his affection and the other was left alone?"

"They should know better at their age." Mother straightened her shoulders. "Speaking of knowing better, I hope you aren't letting your heart get away from your head."

The smile the Wibbey sisters had brought to Vernetta's lips froze. "What do you mean?"

"You are friendlier than necessary with that young newspaperman. I think it would be better if you gave up the notion of working with the newsboys' Sunday school."

"Why would you object to my working with the children?"

"Don't put words in my mouth, child. I condone mission work, but I don't like you working so closely with that newspaperman. Your pride is bound to be a bit battered after losing Andrew. It would be only natural if you encouraged Mr. McNally's attentions."

"Mother, I have not—"

"I understand why you want to show Andrew that other young men find you attractive. However, a newspaperman will not make a man of Andrew's stature jealous. Such a friendship might chase away not only Andrew but other young men of our social standing."

Taking a deep breath to settle the indignation rising within her, Vernetta set the gown on the sofa beside her and stood. "I'd like to speak with Father. Is he in?"

Mother snorted inelegantly, her gaze still on her fancywork. "I expect you'll find him in the living room with Captain Rogers and that newspaperman. I can't imagine why he neglects our presence to spend time with them!" She looked up. "Now, don't you forget what I said about encouraging Mr. McNally's attentions."

"I won't forget, Mother." Vernetta slipped into the hallway, glad to leave her mother's acid remarks behind.

As her mother predicted, she found her father in the living room talking with Thomas. Captain Rogers was not with them. Yellow flames danced and crackled merrily in the fireplace in front of which the two men sat in wing chairs.

Vernetta was glad for the friendship her father was finding with Thomas and the captain, glad he was going to the Veteran's Home. It would do him good to center his attention on something besides his financial problems.

He still went to the bank daily. It was closed, but there was much to do to pass the bank into receivership. Vernetta knew from what he'd said that the work was depressing. He was no longer receiving an income for the work, either, and because of the time spent at the bank, he had no time to seek employment elsewhere.

"Who would hire a man whose bank has failed anyway?" he'd asked Vernetta one day. The memory sliced at her heart.

"The work you are doing with the newsboys is a good thing, Thomas," Father was saying. "They need young men to learn from, men they can look up to."

Thomas leaned forward, his elbows on his knees, his hands linked loosely. "I love the work, sir. From the first time I heard of the Sunday school, I've wanted to be part of it. I guess working at the newspaper makes the newsboys special to me."

Father wagged an index finger in Thomas's direction. "The time you give to those children is an investment in their lives. It will pay rewards in the future, the same as money that is invested earns interest."

"I hope the investment earns a good interest rate on each and every life." Thomas's voice was lower than usual. Vernetta heard the crack in it and knew he spoke his heart.

"There are no guarantees," Father warned. "We can't make choices for others, even when we can see their own choices are leading them into dangerous and unhappy places. There will be boys in whose lives you won't be able to tell you've made a difference. That will not lessen the importance of the lives your investment will change."

Thomas stared into the dancing flames. Vernetta could hear nothing but the crackle and pop from the fireplace as he considered her father's words. Then Thomas shifted his gaze to Father's face.

"You're right, sir." His voice was still low and quiet. "If I might be so bold, I hope you take your own advice to heart. You should not judge yourself and your career only by the investments that failed. You made many wise investments in the past that benefitted the people you served."

Sudden tears burned Vernetta's eyes and blurred her view of the two men.

Father cleared his throat. Still, his voice sounded thick. "Thank you, my boy."

Thank You for Thomas, she prayed silently. *He has been such a gift to our family.*

She blinked suddenly, staring at Thomas through her tears. No wonder her mother's implications about Thomas and herself had made her so angry. Her mother's perceptions had been far clearer than her own. *I think I am falling in love with him!*

A strange mixture of wonder and dread filled her.

Her mother would be furious if she discovered Vernetta's feelings for Thomas. Likely she would think her daughter had fallen for "that young newspaperman" simply to upset her.

No need to worry about that yet, silly goose. Thomas Michael McNally has shown no signs of falling in love with me!

Sadness touched the edges of wonder that had filled her only moments before, like the brown wilt at the edges of a rose's petals.

six

T he next Sunday Vernetta waited for Thomas in the sleigh after Sunday school. He stood nearby on the sidewalk, talking with Erik. Watching them, she remembered the discussion between her father and Thomas. The memory warmed her more thoroughly than the thick buffalo lap robe Thomas had tucked about her.

A minute later he climbed up beside her and they started home. There had been a snowfall the night before, and the sleigh shushed along smoothly on its runners. The street was filled with others enjoying the sleighing. People greeted each other noisily as sleighs met and passed in the street. Sleigh bells lent melody to the crisp air, which carried the smell of wood smoke from numerous chimneys and stung Vernetta's nose.

"Hey, McNally!" a young man called from a sleigh that drew alongside them. "Looks like you have a good sleigh and horse there. Come to the lake and let's race!" It was common for young people to race their sleighs on roads along the city's lakes.

Thomas laughed and waved him away. "Not with the lady with me!"

Vernetta saw his friend's gaze sweep over her face. "Don't blame you!" he called. He urged his horse on and in a minute left them behind.

Vernetta glanced at Thomas from the corner of her eye. She was learning to cherish this time traveling between the downtown Sunday school and home with Thomas. There were so few times they were alone. She found it easy to confide in Thomas during these times. Perhaps his concentration on driving helped; she knew every expression in her eyes and face were not open to his gaze.

"Every time I'm around the newsboys and flower girls I feel more useless," she confided now. "I've tried to find employment to help with the family finances, but with no success. I don't know how to do anything for which anyone will pay. Even the flower girls have more skills than me!"

"You're too hard on yourself. You forget that many of the children's out-of-work fathers have experience working and still can't find jobs. It's the hard times that are the cause, not your lack of skill."

"Your words are kind, but I'm not sure they are accurate in my case."

"Look at the impression you've had on the flower girls. Surely you don't consider that useless?"

"What do you mean?"

"Haven't you noticed they've begun imitating you? The way you carry yourself, your manner of speech, the way they are trying to be more careful of their appearance?" He flashed a smile at her. "They are imitating a most lovely example, if I may be so bold."

She turned her gaze quickly to the beaver-fur muff that warmed her hands. She couldn't stop her smile at the unexpected compliment. *He finds me attractive!* Her heart swelled with joy.

His attention back on the horse and street, he said, "It was a great idea you had, bringing soft towels and soap for the kids to wash up with before dinner. Good training for them. And the flower girls liked the fragrant soap you brought."

Indeed, the hall had smelled like lavender when the girls were done washing their hands and faces. Vernetta remembered the way Lily had held the lavender-scented soap to her nose and breathed deeply before washing. "Now I'll smell like you, Miss Larson," she'd said in a timid voice.

A greeting called from another sleigh brought her back to the present. She waved and smiled at her friend, but her mind was still on Lily. "Sometimes," she told Thomas, "when I think of Lily, the story of the little match girl comes to mind. I don't want Lily to end up like the match girl. Remember how the match girl lit the matches she was to sell, burning up her only way to make a living, and then died during the cold winter's night?"

His brown eyes went almost black with emotion. His jaw was tight. "That won't happen to Lily."

She met his gaze steadily. "Thanks to you and people like you who started that Sunday school—investing in children, as Father said."

He flicked the reins lightly, his attention apparently back on his driving. She sensed he was uncomfortable with her obvious admiration of his heart's work and changed the subject. "I've been trying to think of something I could do to make money. At the very least I would like to make enough to pay for the—"

She stopped abruptly. She'd almost said she wanted to pay for the holiday gowns her mother insisted she have. Even though she felt her mother was wrong, she had no intention of insulting her to anyone else, even Thomas. "Do you think. . .I might be able to write articles for a newspaper?"

Thomas jerked up straight, almost causing the horse to stop. "A reporter? I'm sure you are a capable writer, but it isn't so easy as it apparently seems to research a news story, write it in the number of words the editor wants, and get it done before the presses roll."

I hurt his feelings! The realization tightened her chest. "I didn't mean to imply that it doesn't take skill to do your work. It's only. . .I'm trying to find something I can do."

"Maybe you could submit some short pieces for the social page." His voice sounded as though he was somewhat mollified by her apology.

His answer was dissatisfying. Small social pieces weren't likely to pay much, but his advice made sense. She decided she would keep her eyes and ears open at the next of the season's many parties.

✶

Thomas looked up over the top of the evening paper as Cora Wibbey's voice drifted into the living room from the hall. "Don't be modest, dear. Everyone will want to see how lovely you look before you leave for the party."

Cora entered the room. Vernetta, her cheeks bright

red, protested quietly but followed along. What else could she do with Cora's hand clamped tightly about hers? Thomas stifled his grin with difficulty, laid aside the paper, and stood up. Captain Rogers rose also, leaning on his cane.

Cora stopped in the middle of the room. "Miss Vernetta is going to a Christmas party. I knew you'd all want to see how pretty she looks."

Cornelia pushed herself from the sofa and hurried across the room. "What a beautiful gown!" Her fingers caught the edge of the material that stood out over the top of the puffed sleeves. "Such a perfect shade of brocaded silk. Petunia it's called, isn't that right?"

"Yes," Vernetta admitted quietly. "Thank you."

Cornelia stood back, admiring the gown. "That deep purple gore of velvet with the lace trim in the middle of the skirt adds so much."

"Turn around," Cora insisted.

Vernetta obediently turned, careful to lift her train.

The captain cleared his throat. "Lovely, my dear. Simply lovely."

Vernetta stepped quickly to his side and pressed a kiss to his cheek.

Cornelia waved a hand toward Thomas. "Well, aren't you going to tell her what you think?"

"Perfect. You are perfect, Miss Larson." The words came out almost a whisper. He was surprised they made it out at all past the painful lump in his throat.

Her unusual violet eyes widened slightly, and his gaze tangled in hers. All he could hear was his heart pounding in his ears.

"I like the paper rose you've pinned in your hair," Cora said.

Vernetta's fingers touched the edge of the white rose, and Thomas's gaze followed. "Lily made it," she told them.

"Perhaps your escort will want you to wear the flowers he brings instead," Cornelia suggested.

Vernetta's smile looked a little tight. "No escort tonight. I'm attending with friends."

Thomas's heart clenched. He pressed his lips together firmly and caught his hands behind his back. He wished he were of her social class. If he were, he could escort her to the party and see that she had real roses to rest in her beautiful hair. The paper rose was a fine example of where her heart lay, but would her friends look down on it?

He watched out the front door's etched-glass window as Vernetta and her friends left, but what he saw was her eyes when he told her she was perfect. *I'm falling in love with her.* The thought caught him by surprise, but he recognized the truth of it immediately. *Forget it, McNally. She's out of your league, even with her father's present financial situation. Besides, she's still nursing a broken heart over Andrew.* Dora had told him all about Andrew, the family's expectation that he and Vernetta would marry, and the breakup. He couldn't imagine any man walking away from Vernetta.

He heard Dora's step in the hall behind him and turned, forcing a grin. "How about going ice-skating with me, Dora? It's a fine evening for it."

"My young man is taking me skating, but you're

welcome to join us."

"I think I will, if you don't mind a third party." Thomas started up the stairs to get his skate blades, wishing Vernetta would be joining them at the pond, her gaze lingering in his mind.

seven

Thomas was in the living room when Vernetta returned from the party. Unable to sleep, he'd taken a volume of Dickens from Mr. Larson's library shelves and settled in a wing chair before a dying fire. His efforts to read had been futile; his mind was filled with Vernetta.

He hurried to the hall when he heard the front door close. He knew there would be no one else to greet her; her parents and Dora had been in bed for hours.

She jumped slightly, startled, when she saw him, but recovered quickly and smiled. "Hello."

"Hello. Let me help you with your cape." She turned her back to him, and he lifted the soft black velvet from her shoulders. The smooth ivory curve of her neck tempted him. What would it feel like to press his lips to her neck? He pushed the thought away. "Did you have a good time?"

"Oh, yes! It was such fun!" Her eyes sparkled up at him in the light from the opal gas lamps on the walnut walls. "When my friends asked about the paper rose in my hair, I put on my best surprised face and said, 'Why, paper roses are all the rage for Christmas this year,

313

haven't you heard?' " Her laugh rang out.

Thomas grinned. "How did your friends respond to that?"

"Skeptical at first. Then I explained that during the financial troubles, using paper roses was a way to decorate themselves and their homes, be fashionable, be thrifty, and be charitable all at the same time." She laughed again. "I was so convincing that a girl who is hosting a party next week asked my assistance in buying the flowers she will need to decorate. I can't wait to place the order when I see the flower girls at Sunday school!"

"They'll be thrilled. Perhaps you should write a newspaper article about this current rage for paper roses. That would ensure your friends that you are telling the truth! Of course, you wouldn't want to use your real name for the byline."

She clapped her hands. "What a wonderful idea! Do you think your editor would print it?"

"I'll try to convince him to use it." It was fun acting the conspirators. "I was telling Dora tonight at the skating pond that—"

"You and Dora went ice-skating?"

"Yes, I—" Something in her eyes made him lose his train of thought. Why was she looking at him that way?

"I love ice-skating." Her voice was quiet, and the light had left her eyes. "It was a beautiful night for it. If you'll excuse me, I'll retire. I'm awfully tired."

"Of course." He watched her climb the stairs. What had he said to take the life out of her that way?

❄

Vernetta slipped into bed. She piled the pillows

between her and the ornately carved headboard, then leaned back against them and picked up her journal. She pulled the pale pink satin comforter over her knees and opened the journal. It was her usual bedtime ritual. Normally she began writing as soon as she opened the book. She should have had a lot to write about tonight, after the Christmas party, but the only thing in her mind was a picture of Dora and Thomas skating together.

"Likely Mother was very happy to see them go off for an evening together," she whispered. Her heart burned at the thought of Dora and Thomas skating hand in hand, laughing together in the moonlight, enjoying hot cider and popcorn, standing around the fire that was always kept going for the evening skaters.

Every night she made it a practice to record one thing for which she was grateful. Usually she couldn't stop at one! Tonight, she couldn't remember anything for which to be thankful.

"Lately, Father," she spoke quietly into the softly lit room, "it seemed life was beginning to turn around. Working with the flower girls has been so rewarding. The boarders have brought in a little money and also added cheer and fun to our house. Thomas has befriended Father. And. . ." Her voice dropped to a whisper, and her throat ached. "I thought Thomas was beginning to care for me."

She drew her knees up to her chest and hugged them, letting the pain wash over her. Finally she swallowed hard and took a deep breath. Things no longer seemed to be improving. Tonight the difficult things

315

seemed harder than ever to bear: Her parents were still dealing with the pain of the bank failure, the newsboys and flower girls lived in poverty's gray depths from which there appeared little hope of escape, the entire country remained in the middle of financial chaos.

"On top of everything else, I'm falling in love with a man whose romantic interests lie not with me, but with my maid!" A tiny smile tugged at the edge of her lip and caught the hot, salty tear that rolled over her cheek. She couldn't help seeing the irony in her situation. Never in her wildest imaginations had she ever thought she would be jealous of her maid!

With a sigh, she put out the light in the lamp beside her bed, too preoccupied to notice the pretty roses painted on the china shade. She slid down between the sheets and pulled the comforter about her shoulders.

"I'm trying to trust You, God," she whispered into the shadows, "but I don't understand how You can allow so many hard things." Guilt wrapped around her fears and questions like a fog. If her faith and that of other Christians in the country were strong enough, wouldn't it have meant an end to the hard times?

❈

The next morning, Vernetta spent hours at the delicate writing desk beside the window in her bedroom, working on the article Thomas had recommended that she write. When he came home for lunch, she handed it to him. Fear swamped her as she watched him read the short article. *What if he thinks I'm a terrible writer?* She wanted to snatch back the paper over which she'd labored so diligently.

316

He looked up from the page with a grin. "This is great! I'll show it to the editor this afternoon."

All afternoon, she tried to find things to occupy her mind and stop worrying what the editor would think, but she was unsuccessful. When the hour neared for Thomas to return home, she pretended to do needle-work in a chair by the parlor window. She dropped the needlework and hurried to the front door when she saw him coming up the walk. If it was bad news, she didn't want to hear it in front of others.

Thomas laughed when he walked in the front door and found her standing just inside. From the sympathetic twinkle in his eyes, she guessed that he could read the hope and dread that filled her as she waited for his report.

He rested a hand on her shoulder. "The editor liked your article. It will be in the Sunday paper."

Vernetta rose to her toes and clapped both hands over her mouth. Excitement and pleasure coursed through her. She slid her fingers down just enough to ask, "Oh, Thomas, truly? This isn't Irish blarney?"

She saw his expression soften and the laughter in his brown eyes quieted to a tender glimmer. Even his voice softened. "No, my lo. . . No, lass. No blarney." His hand moved from her shoulder to touch her cheek. The touch warmed her in spite of the cold that lingered on his fingers from the outdoors. Her breath caught in her throat and her emotions tumbled about in her chest in wild and wonderful confusion.

He dropped his hand and began unbuttoning his coat. Was he as flustered as she by his touch? she wondered.

Thomas opened the door to the hall closet. "The

editor said if you wish to write other articles for the society and home pages, he'll be glad to consider them."

Joy flooded her. She clapped her hands lightly. "It seems too good to be true!"

"I almost forgot the best part!" Thomas reached into his coat pocket, withdrew some coins, and held them out to her. "Your pay."

The coins tinkled as they fell into her palm. Dismay mingled with awe. It wasn't very much money, but it was something. No matter how little it was, she knew God was answering her prayer in providing a way in which she could contribute, however slightly, to the family income.

She knew her eyes were shining when she looked up at him. "My father has given me an allowance to spend upon myself for years, but this is the first money I've ever earned."

"You earned it well. It was a good article."

She felt wrapped in the smile that shone in his eyes, and she was glad that he was the person who was sharing this special moment with her.

❈

At the next Sunday school, Vernetta placed orders with the flower girls for flowers for some of her friends. The girls beamed with delight at the size of the orders. They assured Vernetta they would have no trouble making enough flowers to meet her friends' requests.

Thomas's eyes glowed as he caught Vernetta's gaze. "I knew God had a special purpose in your work with the flower girls. All the volunteers here are special, but you've touched the children's lives in so many ways in which they've not been touched before."

A warm glow enwrapped her heart at his words. She was growing to love the children and her work with them. She didn't need Thomas's approval, or anyone else's approval, to be happy that she was here. It wasn't his approval of her that touched her so. Rather, his words only added to her belief in his goodness and to her growing love for him.

Vernetta had convinced the other volunteers at the Sunday school to put on a Christmas pageant with the children. Some of the volunteers had been reluctant at first. "The children's parents and families will never come," said the woman who had been working with the mission the longest.

"It's important to do it anyway," Vernetta insisted. "Recreating the Christmas story will make it more real to the children."

To Vernetta's utter amazement, Thomas convinced her mother to play the piano for the Christmas program. "I still can't believe you talked her into this," she whispered to Thomas as Mother played "Silent Night" at the first practice. "However did you do it?"

He shrugged. "I told her the children seldom heard music played by someone of her talent and that by playing she would be giving a great gift to the children." He smiled down at her. "I didn't tell her what a gift the children's appreciation would be to her."

Vernetta watched the children singing the well-known hymn. Most of them, she was sure, noticed no difference between her mother's playing and that of the woman who usually played for the hymn singing, but

Lily was entranced by the playing. In spite of the song leader's attempts to move Lily back with the other singers, the little girl stood beside Vernetta's mother, her fingers curled over the wood in front of the keys. Her gaze followed the woman's long, lean fingers with something akin to hunger. The sight caught at Vernetta's heart.

"You were right," Vernetta whispered. "Mother is a gift to the children."

The Christmas play practice went better than Vernetta had dared hope. The volunteers appeared to have forgotten their misgivings and put all their energy into teaching the children their parts and places.

When Thomas, Vernetta, and her mother were walking out to the carriage afterward, Thomas shook his head. "Looks pretty hopeless to me. The children couldn't seem to remember when to do anything or where to do it."

The two women laughed. "Practices for children's Christmas pageants are always like that," Vernetta's mother told him. "They will do beautifully the night of the play."

Vernetta's and Thomas's laughing gazes met over her mother's head as he helped the older woman into the carriage's backseat. It certainly appeared Mother was well on the way to being won over by the children!

Vernetta missed the usual comfortable visit with Thomas on the way home while she sat in the backseat with her mother.

When he helped her out of the carriage in front of their home, Vernetta said, "Mrs. Pilgrim is one of the leading society women in this part of the city. Do you think the editor would like an article on her work with the flower girls' Sunday school?"

"I think that's a wonderful idea!" Thomas agreed heartily.

Mother frowned. "An article? What do you mean, Vernetta?"

Vernetta's face burned. She'd forgotten she hadn't told her mother about the article on the paper roses, which was to come out that day. She'd been afraid her mother would disapprove of her daughter being a "newspaperman." Thomas, whose hand still lingered on her arm after helping her from the carriage, gave her arm a slight, encouraging squeeze before removing it. In halting words, Vernetta told her mother about the paper flowers article.

Mother's lips pursed. She straightened her shoulders beneath her fur-trimmed cape. "Well, if you are going to write articles, they may as well be about worthy causes and not the unsavory topics newspapermen are apt to call news."

Vernetta stared at her in surprise. She heard Thomas cough to cover a chuckle and fought to control her own grin.

"I think you have a good idea," Mother continued. "Showing Mrs. Pilgrim's involvement with the mission might encourage other women to give more of their time to needy causes."

Still dumbstruck, Vernetta followed her mother up the walk. They'd only gone a few feet when the front door flung open. Dora raced across the porch and down the walk. "Thank the Lord you're home! It's Mr. Larson! He has great pains in his chest. The doctor says it's his heart!"

eight

Vernetta's own heart felt as though it would burst from fear and pain. She and her mother hurried to her father's bedroom, not stopping to remove their coats. The doctor intercepted them at the door and ushered them back into the wide upstairs hall, shutting the door behind them. He held his finger warningly to his lips.

Mother clutched the doctor's hands, her gaze searching his face. "How bad is it, Dr. Brown?" she whispered. "Will I. . ." Her voice broke. "Will I lose Anton?"

"Heart situations are always difficult to predict, Mrs. Larson. For the moment, he seems to be improving. His heart rate is decreasing, and the pain is easing. He will have to remain in bed for a few days and take things easy once he's up and about again." He held up a finger in a warning manner. "Mind, he's not to do any work."

It was the sympathy in his eyes rather than his words that cut through Vernetta's chest. She knew the doctor couldn't guarantee her father's heart wouldn't yet take his life.

"May I see him?" Mother asked with tears in her eyes.

Dr. Brown patted her hands. "For a couple minutes. Then you must let him rest."

But Mother refused to leave his room. She pulled a chair close to his bed and told the doctor, "I won't disturb him, I promise. I'll just sit right here, where he can see me when he wakes up, and so I'll be here if. . . if he needs anything."

At her mother's orders, Vernetta arranged for a nurse, recommended by Dr. Brown, to stay with them and care for Father. Vernetta didn't dare bring up the subject of how they would pay the nurse. She was relieved when Mother brought it up herself. "We'll ask her to take part of her payment in room and board. Have Dora prepare a room for her. For the rest of the fee. . ." Mother paused and sighed deeply. "Perhaps I can sell some of my jewelry or some of our artwork. Anton must have a nurse, in case. . ."

Vernetta knew the meaning of the words her mother did not speak: "In case your father has another episode with his heart." A nurse would recognize the symptoms before she or her mother and would know the best thing to do for him until the doctor arrived. *Thank the Lord for the telephone,* she thought. *We'll be able to reach the doctor quickly.*

❄

Later that evening, Thomas had a few moments alone with Vernetta in the living room while Mrs. Larson was introducing the nurse to Mr. Larson. He listened as she explained her mother's decision.

"I'm so relieved she's willing to part with her prized personal possessions," she said. "When the bank collapsed, Mother revolted at the suggestion of selling anything."

Thomas stood in front of the parlor fireplace, one elbow resting on the mantel. His chest seemed too small for the sympathy he felt as he looked down at the young woman sitting in the nearby wing chair. If only he could spare her the pain of fearing for her father's life!

"When our loved ones face serious illness, we often find our values change, or perhaps more accurately, we become more clear about them," he said gently.

"Yes, I suppose that's true. I hope Father won't need to pay the cost of a stronger lesson for us." A tear lingered at the edge of one of her beautiful eyes, catching the light from the table lamp beside her.

The sight crushed him. Thomas wished he could put his arms about her, draw her to his chest, and comfort her. But all he could do was lift a prayer for her and her father.

Dora bustled into the room. "I may be speaking beyond my station, miss, but I was thinking—" She paused, then rushed on. "I was thinking that it's time to begin the Christmas baking. The missus always likes lots of baked goods about for guests who drop in. The stove is still warm from dinner, so it wouldn't take much to heat it back up. Baking cookies always makes me feel better. I thought it might cheer you up a bit to help. It won't change your father's awful sickness, but—"

"What a thoughtful idea," Vernetta interrupted her, rising. "It will be nice to have something to keep my mind from despondent thoughts."

Thomas watched the women leave the room together. Dora's offer had been unconventional and perhaps, as she had said, beyond her station, but it had been offered with love. He was glad Vernetta had accepted it as such. He didn't imagine many women would accept such an offer from their maid with the grace with which Vernetta had accepted Dora's offer.

There was no longer any doubt in his mind that he loved Vernetta, but as wonderful as he believed her to be, he couldn't believe she would ever agree to marry a man of modest means such as himself.

❄

As the days passed, Father obeyed the doctor's orders and kept to his bed, but Vernetta was worried. *Has he lost his will to live?* she wondered.

Whenever she spent time with him, he spoke of the bank failure. "I don't mind so much for myself that I lost my money," he repeated again and again, "but I hate that I've lost Lena's respect and that I've failed the depositors' trust, lost the life savings of so many."

It did not matter how many times she and her mother assured him that he was not a failure and that he hadn't lost their love and respect. He would not be convinced.

After one such session, Vernetta joined her mother in the parlor. Mother was pacing back and forth, wringing her hands. When she saw Vernetta, she burst out, "How could I have been such a fool? When. . .how did I allow my values to become so. . .so misplaced? When did money and other people's opinions become more important to me than my husband?"

Vernetta reached out to her impulsively, but her mother kept pacing. "Mother, I know those things have never been more important to you than Father."

Her mother nodded furiously in disagreement. "Oh, yes, I'm afraid they were." She stopped in front of Vernetta. "Why didn't I let him know as soon as the bank failed that I was willing to make whatever financial and social sacrifices necessary to help him get back on his feet financially? Why didn't I let him know I love and admire him and will continue to do so even if he *never* regains his former status? It's what I would have done as a young bride."

Vernetta took her mother's hands. "It's not too late to tell him now."

Mother's shoulders slumped. "I have told him. I asked his forgiveness. It's too late. All he can see is how he thinks he's failed me. Failed me! I'm the one who has failed him."

Vernetta squeezed her mother's fingers. "You haven't failed." Yet inside, she felt her mother's despair and understood it.

❄

Thomas passed the store windows, filled with Christmas displays and enticing gifts and decorated with pine roping and brightly painted Christmas tree decorations. It was snowing, so the sidewalks were white and hard to maneuver.

He stopped in front of an especially interesting display of a village of small houses in winter, but he barely noticed them. *I wish I could make Christmas a happier time for Vernetta,* he thought. Things had been hard enough for her before Mr. Larson's heart had frightened them all so. *With her added fear for her father's health, both physical and mental—* Thomas shook his head.

A pretty silver vanity set caught his eye. He'd like to give Vernetta a Christmas gift, something beautiful like this set. Of course, it was inappropriate for their friendship, and even if it weren't, she likely had a fine vanity set. Until recently, her father had always given her everything she needed and, Thomas suspected, everything material that she desired. It was a wonder she had grown up so sweet and unspoiled.

No, the vanity table set was definitely out. Besides, hadn't the article in the *Tribune* delineating popular Christmas gifts said that it was considered an outrage if a man, even a relative, gave a woman something as personal as manicure sets or toilet articles?

He stopped to say hello to Lily, who was selling her wares in front of a photographer's studio. He spoke with her for a few minutes, then left with a paper rose tucked in the lapel of his coat. He tried to push aside the familiar aching in his chest at the sight of a child working on the cold streets. There were too many of them. A man couldn't walk a block without passing more than one. Maybe one day such things would not be allowed. Progress with child labor laws was slow, but Minnesota had passed a law recently that would cut the number of hours children could work for merchants. The law didn't apply to children who sold their own wares on the streets, though.

When he'd crossed the street, Thomas turned and

looked back at Lily. In her dark coat and muffler, she was silhouetted against the photographer's window. A grin slid across his face. "Ah, yes," he said aloud. "That will be the perfect gift for Vernetta."

After dinner, Thomas visited with Mr. Larson. As usual, the older man was deep in self-pity, mourning in his Swedish accent that he'd lost his depositors' money. Thomas gathered up his courage, took a deep breath, and said, "Perhaps there's something you can do for the people who were hurt by the bank failure."

Mr. Larson grunted in surprise. "What could I possibly do? I've lost my fortune, too, you know."

"Only your financial fortune. You haven't lost your hard-earned knowledge and wisdom."

Mr. Larson waved a hand in impatience. "Knowledge and wisdom! I'm a man whose bank failed! People don't pay for knowledge that leads to failure."

Thomas leaned forward, elbows on his knees. He hadn't thought the idea through before he mentioned it, but now he knew it was sound. "You could write a book and maybe speak about bank failures. Put in writing why your bank and others failed. Interview banking friends whose banks didn't fail and ask what they believe they are doing right. That would help other bankers and the depositors who put their faith in them."

For a moment, he thought he saw a glimmer of excitement in Mr. Larson's eyes. Then the man slumped even deeper into his pillows. "I was a banker, not a writer."

Thomas grinned. "I'm a writer. I'll be glad to edit your work and help you find a publisher."

Mr. Larson stared at him for a long moment. Then a smile began to tug at one corner of his mouth. His eyes began to glimmer again. *"Uff da!* You are a persistent man, Thomas McNally. Maybe—only maybe, mind you—your idea will work."

He rubbed a large hand across his chin. "There are some friends who might even allow a failure an interview." He listed a few powerful men whose names Thomas knew the public would certainly respect. By the time Mr. Larson was through, Thomas could see the man was excited about the idea.

Mr. Larson sat up, no longer leaning against the bed pillows. "If this works out, if I make money from this, maybe one day I can pay back my depositors." His voice was thick with emotion and brought a lump to Thomas's throat. "It might take the rest of my life," he continued, "but I can try. When the Panic subsides and the real estate market is better, perhaps I can sell this house and move to a smaller place. That would give me more money to use to pay the depositors." He smiled and met Thomas's gaze. "I think Mrs. Larson will support me in this, now."

Thomas swallowed hard. "I'm sure you're right, sir. She's a fine, strong woman."

Mr. Larson grinned. "She is, isn't she? She's had a lot to put up with, too, with me for a husband."

Thomas laughed and rose. "Truer words were never spoken. I've stayed longer than I should have. The nurse will accuse me of overtiring you."

"Tell the nurse to bring me writing paper, pen, and ink," Mr. Larson ordered. "I have work to do!"

"I'll tell her, but I don't expect she'll bring them before morning."

When Thomas stepped into the hall, he was surprised to see Vernetta standing to one side of the doorway. It was obvious she had no intention of entering the room, so he closed the door.

Vernetta grasped his hands. Her eyes shown with joy. "Thank you, Thomas!"

"For what?" He tightened his fingers about hers, enjoying the rare intimate touch.

"I overheard your discussion with Father. I was going to visit him, but when I heard you two talking, I hesitated in the hallway. I heard you suggest to him that he write a book about the banks. I know he can do it."

"Of course, he can," Thomas assured her, still reveling in her touch, in the glory in her eyes.

"I was afraid he'd lost his will to live. If I was right, you've given it back to him. You've helped everyone in our family regain hope."

"Me?"

"Yes, you. You introduced Mother and me to the flower girls and newsboys, giving us a reason to think of someone beyond ourselves. You've helped me get newspaper articles published, to bring a little more money. Most important, you've given Father a reason to live, a way to make something good come out of the worst experience of his life."

Thomas shifted his shoulders uncomfortably. "I hardly think I did all that."

Her laugh sounded like music to him. "Oh yes, you

did. The Bible tells us we may entertain angels unaware, but I must admit"—she glanced up at him coquettishly from beneath her lashes—"I never thought an angel would come to us with a name like Thomas Michael McNally."

Thomas laughed. The idea was absurd! "I'm no angel. I'm a man, and I'll thank you to remember it, Vernetta Larson."

Vernetta shook her head. "To me, you will never be a mere man." She squeezed his fingers quickly and started toward the stairway.

Thomas watched her, his heart pounding, wanting to believe her comments meant she would welcome him as a suitor. "Don't be foolish, McNally," he admonished himself in a harsh whisper. "She may consider you an angel, but women don't often fall in love with angels."

nine

The evening of the Christmas program, the basement mission Sunday school was alive with
activity. The reporters at the *Tribune* had taken
up a fund to contribute a Christmas tree for the pageant.
It was so large that the trunk had to be cut off so the tree
didn't hit the ceiling.

"The children will love it!" Vernetta cried. "How
wonderful of your reporter friends to provide it."

"You're one of my reporter friends now." Thomas
stood beside her, admiring the tree.

A reporter! She hadn't thought of the title in relation
to herself. A thrill ran along her arms at the thought.
"You didn't ask me to contribute to the tree fund."

"I thought you were contributing enough with your
time." He shook his head. "Afraid the reporters' dona-
tion didn't include decorations."

"I have the perfect decorations." She turned toward
the kitchen, where Cora and Cornelia were busy
unloading baskets. "Miss Cora, Miss Cornelia, please
come here."

Thomas watched their approach, puzzled.

"What would you think of decorating the tree with

your mittens?" Vernetta asked them.

Cora clapped her hands in delight. "A mitten tree! What a wonderful idea!"

Thomas crossed his arms over his chest and leaned forward. "Mittens?"

Cora's soft, wrinkled face lit up. "We wanted to do something for the children. . ."

"So we asked our knitting group to help us make mittens," Cornelia finished.

"They have enough to give each child a pair." Vernetta smiled at Thomas, but he looked blurry through her tears. The Wibbey sisters had told her of their project only that morning, and their generosity warmed her heart.

The Wibbeys, Mother, Vernetta, and Thomas hung the mittens on the tree. They covered the tree so thoroughly that the branches were almost hidden. Then Vernetta and Thomas attached small beeswax candles in tin holders to the edges of the branches, where the flames wouldn't catch the branches above on fire.

"We'd best give out the mittens before lighting the tree," Thomas said, setting a large pail of water beside the tree in case of fire.

When they were done, Captain Rogers set a small wooden fence around the bottom of the tree. He laid moss within the fence and then placed wooden animals he'd carved and Mother's nativity. Vernetta, Lena, Thomas, the Wibbeys, and the other volunteers raved over the captain's work. Thomas grinned at Vernetta. "I see this has become a family affair."

Her heart leaped at his words: a family affair. What a wonderful thought, that he and she would be part of the same family. She tried to shush her thoughts. Didn't he and Dora have a special relationship? It would serve her well not to forget.

"It's too bad Dora couldn't be here with us," she said carefully, "but she did help us bake cookies for the lunch."

Thomas leaned close. "Don't tell your mother, but I think Dora is planning to spend the evening at the skating rink with her beau."

Vernetta felt her jaw drop. "Her. . .her beau?"

Thomas nodded. "Didn't she tell you about him?"

Vernetta could only shake her head.

"He's a nice chap, recently arrived from Sweden. Dora's head over heels for him."

"You. . .know him?"

"They let me join them ice-skating a few times." He turned as the door opened and a bunch of newsies came in noisily.

I thought he *had taken Dora skating!* Vernetta's heart leaped with joy. *Thomas doesn't love Dora!* With an effort, she turned her attention to the newsies.

Their arms were filled with pine roping and wreaths, and their faces were filled with grins. "What do ya think?" Erik asked, stopping in front of Thomas and Vernetta and lifting his laden arms. "We went ta parks and down along the river and gathered the pine ta make these ropes and wreaths ta decorate the mission."

"They are beautiful!" Vernetta assured him. She and Erik had grown to know and respect each other

335

since she began working at the mission.

"Great job, boys," Thomas chimed in.

"Wow!" Erik started toward the Christmas tree, almost forgetting his usual swagger. "Check out this, newsies!"

The boys flocked around it, loud in their praise of the tree's size and beauty.

Soon the boys were stringing the rope along the top of the piano, the top of the picture that hung over the piano, and from the corners of the room to the light that hung from the middle of the ceiling.

They were barely done when the flower girls arrived in a group. Lily was clutching a bouquet of tissue-paper roses so huge that it hid her drab, ill-fitting coat. Lily's gaze quickly searched the room, then lit up when she saw Vernetta. The girl hurried over, followed by the others. Bright, expectant smiles filled the girls' too-thin faces.

Lily held out the bouquet. "These are for you, Miss Larson." Her voice was almost as soft as real rose petals.

"*All* of these?" Vernetta struggled to stop the laughter that filled her throat. It was such a huge bouquet! Surely Lily's family couldn't afford to give away so many flowers. *I'll have to find a way to give them back and still spare Lily's feelings,* she thought. The roses crackled when she gathered them in her arms.

"They're from all of us," Lily told her. "We each made one, just for you."

Tears sprang to Vernetta's eyes. She couldn't dash them away with her arms filled with roses. Her gaze swept the faces turned toward her as trustingly as flowers turn toward the sun. Every face held a smile, but Vernetta recognized a trace of fear, as well, and realized the girls were afraid she wouldn't value their gift.

She dropped her gaze to the flowers. A tear fell upon a tissue petal, leaving a wrinkle as a permanent memory. Vernetta lifted the bouquet to her face. It seemed she could almost smell the fragrance of roses. *It isn't the roses,* a voice in her heart said, *it's the fragrance of love.*

Vernetta swallowed hard. She smiled shakily and tasted a tear on the edge of her lips. "It's a magnificent gift. The most beautiful gift I've ever received."

She shifted the roses clumsily to one arm, which was barely able to contain them. Then she knelt and held out her free arm. Lily slipped into it. Vernetta's heart swelled until her chest hurt when Lily's arms tightened about her neck. One after another, each girl received a hug and thank you.

As the last girl slid her arms around Vernetta's neck, Vernetta glanced up. Thomas leaned against the wall, his arms crossed over his chest, his Irish smile not as jolly as usual. Was it tears she saw glistening in his eyes as he watched her and the flower girls? Or were they only a reflection of her own tears?

Lily touched a delicate, red-and-white tissue-paper rose. "This is the one I made."

"It's the prettiest one of all," Vernetta whispered in her ear. Gently, she pulled it out of the bouquet. While Lily held the other flowers, Vernetta fastened Lily's rose to her gown with the dainty silver bar pin she was wearing. Lily's huge smile showed her pleasure.

Vernetta heard a man greeting Thomas loudly and looked up to see who was behind the unfamiliar voice. A man was setting down a tripod and a large camera.

Thomas introduced the man to Vernetta. "I've asked him to take pictures of the children tonight. Why don't we begin with one of you with the flower girls?"

"Oh, I would like that!" How nice it would be to have a picture of the girls she was growing to love.

The children's program went well. More of their parents and families showed up than the volunteers had dared hope, and the children outdid themselves in their efforts to impress them. They succeeded.

Standing to one side in the crowded basement, Vernetta watched the children's happy, proud faces and the proud, loving faces of their families. Children's voices rang with the music of "O Little Town of Bethlehem": "The hopes and fears of all the years, are met in thee tonight."

Her heart skipped a beat. She tensed, suddenly alert to the words of the beloved hymn. Hope meeting fear. Hope in the form of God's Son, Jesus Christ, meeting humanity's fears.

I didn't understand! she thought. *I thought hope meant the elimination of fear, the elimination of the evils that cause fear, or at least knowing the answers to eliminating fears and evils.* For the first time, she saw they existed together, that hope was God's presence in the midst of fears, His promise that the fears wouldn't win in the end. She relaxed against the wall. A serenity she'd never known filled her chest.

After the program, Cora and Cornelia distributed the mittens to the children and other volunteers handed out small bags of peanuts supplied by the church. At first, Erik and some of his followers hung back, telling Thomas they weren't charity cases and didn't need the mittens.

Vernetta held her breath, her arms clutched tightly over her chest, watching Thomas anxiously. What would he say? Many of the children had chapped, raw hands from going without mittens or gloves.

Thomas listened attentively to the boys, nodding, his hands in his trouser pockets. "It's your decision," he finally said quietly. "Many of the women who made these have no families of their own to give gifts to, no children of their own to love. I don't think knitting these mittens was an act of pity but an act of love." He shrugged. "Of course, I may be mistaken. You must each do what you feel in your own hearts is right."

Erik shifted his feet uncomfortably. The other boys watched him. Vernetta knew whatever Erik decided for himself, he decided for them all.

After what seemed many minutes to Vernetta, Erik lifted his chin. "Guess it would be rude not ta take the mittens when the old women worked so hard on 'em."

Vernetta let out a soft sigh of relief.

When the boys started forward to accept their gifts, Thomas sidled over to Vernetta. He nodded toward the piano. "See that?"

Vernetta's mother was still seated on the piano stool, one arm about Lily's shoulders. Lily leaned against her, looking as comfortable as though they'd known each

339

other all of Lily's short life. Vernetta's heart contracted in a sweet pain at the sight. She pulled a lace-edged handkerchief from the wrist of her gown and dabbed at her eyes. "Everything seems to bring tears to my eyes tonight," she told Thomas in a jerky voice.

He smiled down at her. "Christmas is a time for miracles of the heart."

"Yes," she agreed, wondering at and thrilling to this man's sensitivity, as she had so often since he'd come into her home and life.

Lap robes and happy memories of the evening kept everyone warm on the way home. The Wibbey sisters chatted merrily about the program and mitten tree. Mother revealed that she'd decided to offer free piano lessons to any of the flower girls who wished them. "Little Lily wants *so* to learn to play, and surely others will want to learn, don't you think?"

Shocked and delighted, Vernetta could only nod.

"Will there be any objection to my using the hall and the piano?" Mother asked Thomas.

He assured her that he would arrange it, and she settled back contentedly against the thick leather carriage seat.

Vernetta was the last to be helped from the carriage by Thomas. "Would you like to go walking after I've put away the carriage and looked after the horse?" he asked, with her gloved hands clasped in his.

"That sounds lovely."

The home was filled with the smell of pine from the fir tree that stood in the bay window in the parlor and the pine roping that decorated the tops of the doorways in the broad hallway. With Dora's help, she found some vases and filled them with her treasure of paper roses while waiting for Thomas, her heart racing with anticipation.

Was it wishful thinking, or had his glances and touches been more intimate than usual tonight? She tried to quiet her heart. Perhaps it was only the knowledge that he was not in love with Dora that encouraged her to believe he was romantically interested in her.

It was snowing when they went out. Large, soft flakes drifted lightly down, making a gentle hissing sound as they slid through the bare trees. Mellow light from the gas streetlights spread blue shadows on the snow-covered yards, walks, and street.

A rabbit peeked out at them from beneath the spreading branches of a fir tree. They laughed together at it, and in their shared laughter, Thomas slipped his arm about her waist and drew her close to his side.

Vernetta almost stopped breathing. It was so special, walking together that way. She heard him clear his throat.

"I hope the pictures the photographer took tonight turn out well," he said.

"I'm so glad you thought of having photographs taken."

"I'm glad you feel that way, because. . ." He hesitated.

She looked up at him, curious, waiting. Her cheek brushed the wool of his coat, and her awareness of his nearness cleared everything but Thomas from her mind.

He cleared his throat again and looked away from her gaze. "I hired him to take a picture of you with the flower girls. I hope you won't think it presumptuous of me, but. . .I. . .the picture is my Christmas gift to you."

Vernetta stopped, and Thomas stopped, too. His arm slipped from her waist. He stared at her, his brown eyes unusually anxious. *Surely he cannot think I find his gift unwelcome!* She held out both hands. "It is the loveliest gift you could have given me. How is it that you know my heart so well, Thomas Michael McNally?"

He took her hands. "I have a suspicion about that."

She wasn't certain she was ready to hear his suspicion! She gently pulled her hands from his and began walking again, her heart beating like a child's Christmas drum. She changed the subject and told him about her revelation during the Christmas program, her new view of hope.

"Since Father's bank failed, there have been many times I was afraid hope was as unreal as the flower girls' paper roses, but I tried to cling to hope, to God's promises, anyway." She stopped beneath a streetlight, snowflakes falling softly about them, and looked into the face that had become so dear to her. "You helped me do that. In many ways, it's due to you that I've discovered the God of Hope is real."

"I can't believe I'm responsible. I saw the strength and courage in you the first day I came to your home. You accused me once of being an angel. I warned you then that I am only a man." He rested his hands on her shoulders. "Dora told me about Andrew."

She blinked. It took her a moment to realize he was speaking of the man she'd thought only weeks ago that she would marry.

"I realize it may take a long time for your heart to heal from losing him," Thomas was saying, "but I give you fair warning that my hope is for your love, and I don't intend to give up hoping until I win it."

The suddenness of his declaration took her breath. Then happiness swept over her like a winter wind sweeps down a hillside, filling her with joy and delight and amazement. "I haven't thought of Andrew in weeks."

She saw hope flash in his eyes. Dropping her gaze in shyness, she made herself continue. It was forward and inappropriate to express her feelings this way, she knew, but it was so important that he understand. "Andrew can't measure up to the man you are, Thomas Michael McNally."

His fingers tightened on her shoulders. "Are you sure of that, Vernetta?" His voice was husky.

"Completely," she whispered. "I could never love Andrew after knowing you."

He pulled her into his embrace with a deep sigh. "Oh, Vernetta!"

She leaned against his chest. She'd never experienced the contentment that filled her now, the knowing that this was the place she was meant to be for the rest of her life.

She felt his lips touch her hair, the edge of her eyebrow, the corner of her lips. His breath was warm against her ear as he whispered, "And if I should ask if there's any hope I will win your heart, Vernetta?"

She slid her arms around his neck. "It is already yours, my love."

His arms tightened in a bear hug. Then he released her just enough to bend his head to hers and claim her lips. Vernetta melted into his embrace as simply and naturally as the snowflakes melted against their cheeks.

JoAnn A. Grote

JoAnn is quite fond of her native state of Minnesota and has used it for the setting in eight of her nine **Heartsong Presents** books. Not long ago, she moved back to Minnesota after several years of living in North Carolina and is enjoying being near family again. The Montevideo area and the many rivers, including the Mississippi, often play a major part in her stories. She also draws from the Swedish heritage of her family and locale. After some time spent in moving, helping out family members, and writing full-time on children's books (11 books in the **American Adventure** series), JoAnn is getting back into the romance writing mode. She dedicated two years to full-time writing, but recently she returned to the tax office as an accountant. JoAnn's own life was strongly affected by the novels she read when younger. Such authors as Grace Livingston Hill and Emilie Loring encouraged her to believe in God and develop high standards and ideals.

A Letter to Our Readers

Dear Readers:

In order that we might better contribute to your reading enjoyment, we would appreciate your taking a few minutes to respond to the following questions. When completed, please return to the following: Managing Editor, Barbour Publishing, Inc., P.O. Box 719, Uhrichsville, OH 44683.

1. Did you enjoy reading *Fireside Christmas*?
   ❑ Very much, I would like to see more books like this.
   ❑ Moderately—I would have enjoyed it more if _____
   _____
   _____

2. What influenced your decision to purchase this book? (Check those that apply)
   ❑ Cover   ❑ Back cover copy   ❑ Title   ❑ Price
   ❑ Friends   ❑ Publicity   ❑ Other _____

3. Which story was your favorite?
   ❑ *Navided de los Sueños*   ❑ *Dreams*
   ❑ *Eyes of the Heart*   ❑ *Paper Roses*

4. Please check your age range:
   ❑ Under 18   ❑ 18–24   ❑ 25–34
   ❑ 35–45   ❑ 46–55   ❑ Over 55 _____

5. How many hours per week do you read? _____

Name _____

Occupation _____

Address _____

City _____ State _____ Zip _____

Hearts♥ng Presents
Love Stories Are Rated G!

That's for godly, gratifying, and of course, great! If you love a thrilling love story, but don't appreciate the sordidness of some popular paperback romances, **Heartsong Presents** is for you. In fact, **Heartsong Presents** is the only inspirational romance book club, the only one featuring love stories where Christian faith is the primary ingredient in a marriage relationship.

Sign up today to receive your first set of four, never before published Christian romances. Send no money now; you will receive a bill with the first shipment. You may cancel at any time without obligation, and if you aren't completely satisfied with any selection, you may return the books for an immediate refund!

Imagine. . .four new romances every four weeks—two historical, two contemporary—with men and women like you who long to meet the one God has chosen as the love of their lives. . .all for the low price of $9.97 postpaid.

To join, simply complete the coupon below and mail to the address provided. **Heartsong Presents** romances are rated G for another reason: They'll arrive Godspeed!

YES! Sign me up for Hearts♥ng!

NEW MEMBERSHIPS WILL BE SHIPPED IMMEDIATELY!
Send no money now. We'll bill you only $9.97 postpaid with your first shipment of four books. Or for faster action, call toll free 1-800-847-8270.

NAME _____

ADDRESS _____

CITY _____ STATE _____ ZIP _____

MAIL TO: HEARTSONG PRESENTS, P.O. Box 719, Uhrichsville, Ohio 44683

YES1-99